PATTERNS OF REALISM

PATTERNS
OF
REALISM

Roy Armes

South Brunswick and New York: A. S. Barnes and Company
London: The Tantivy Press

791.43 0945
£36132

208084121

20005867 C

©1971 by Roy Armes
Library of Congress Catalogue Card Number: 70-146745

A. S. Barnes and Co., Inc.
Cranbury, New Jersey 08512

The Tantivy Press
108 New Bond Street
London W1Y OQX, England

ISBN 0-498-07788-8 (U.S.A.)

SBN 900730-048 (U.K.)

Printed in the United States of America

Contents

Part Four
EVALUATION

Part Five
DOCUMENTATION

There is no mistaking the positive, materialistic quality possessed by the Italians in common with their Latin ancestors. This, after all is said, constitutes the true note of their art and literature. Realism, preferring the tangible and concrete to the visionary and abstract, the defined to the indefinite, the sensuous to the ideal, determines the character of their genius in all its manifestations. . . . When we complain that the Italians are deficient in the highest tragic imagination, that their feeling for nature lacks romance, or that none but their rarest works of art attain sublimity, we are but insisting on the realistic bias which inclined them to things tangible, palpable, experienced, compassable by the senses.

JOHN ADDINGTON SYMONDS

To Annie

Acknowledgements

I SHOULD LIKE to thank Miss Savina Rauber for her help in checking the translations from the Italian and the following persons and organisations for their help with the illustrations: Mr. Jerry Bauer and Secker and Warburg Ltd., Mr. Robin Bean, Miss Frances Mullen Clark, Collins Ltd., Contemporary Films Ltd., Mr. Peter Cowie, Giulio Einaudi Editore, M. Jean A. Gili, the Italian Institute, Mr. Roger Manvell, the National Film Archive, Peter Owen Ltd., Mr. Emerico Papp, Unitalia Film, Mr. Fred Zentner of the Cinema Bookshop.

In addition thanks are extended to the following authors, publishers and agents who gave permission to quote from copyright works: Basic Books Inc. (George A. Huaco's *The Sociology of Film Art*); Ernest Benn Ltd. (Muriel Grindrod's *Italy*); Calder and Boyars Ltd. (Nathalie Sarraute's *The Age of Suspicion*); Jonathan Cape Ltd. and Alfred A. Knopf Inc. (James Cain's *The Postman Always Rings Twice*); Collins Ltd. (Norman Lewis's *The Honoured Society* and Giuseppe Tomasi di Lampedusa's *The Leopard*); Dennis Dobson Ltd. and Oxford University Press (Siegfried Kracauer's *Nature of Film*); Grove Press Inc. (*Cahiers du Cinéma* in English); Hamish Hamilton Ltd. (Luigi Barzini's *The Italians*); Michael Joseph Ltd. and Longanesi & C. (Luigi Bartolini's *Bicycle Thieves*); Peter Owen Ltd. (Cesare Pavese's *This Business of Living*); Penguin Books Ltd. and Giulio Einaudi Editore (Italo Calvino's *A Preface* from *Italian Writing Today*); Laurence Pollinger Ltd. and the publishers, Cassell & Co. Ltd. and Victor Gollancz Ltd. (Carlo Levi's *Christ Stopped at Eboli* and *Words Are Stones*); Princeton University Press (Erich Auerbach's *Mimesis: The Representation of Reality in Western Literature*); Redman Books Ltd. (Curzio Malaparte's *Kaputt* and *The Skin*); Routledge and Kegan Paul Ltd. and Alfred A. Knopf Inc. (Arnold Hauser's *The Social History of Art*); Martin Secker and Warburg Ltd. (Alberto Moravia's *Two Women* and *A Ghost at Noon*); Editions Seghers (Giuseppe Ferrara's *Luchino Visconti*, Pierre Leprohon's *Vittorio De Sica*, Mario Verdone's *Roberto Rossellini*); Mr. Luchino Visconti and *Bianco e nero* (the script of *La terra trema*); Mr. Cesare Zavattini (the script of *Umberto D*); also Dr. Francis Koval, and the editors of *La Revue du Cinéma (Image et Son)*, *Cahiers du Cinéma*, *Films and Filming*, *Sight and Sound*. Finally I am very grateful to the staff of the British Film Institute library and information department for their help with all my inquiries.

Note: the superior numbers in the text refer to the references in the Bibliography, to be found at the end of the book.

PATTERNS OF REALISM

Part One

THE PROBLEM OF REALISM

What is more real in our universe than a man's life, and how can we hope to preserve it better than in a realistic film?

ALBERT CAMUS

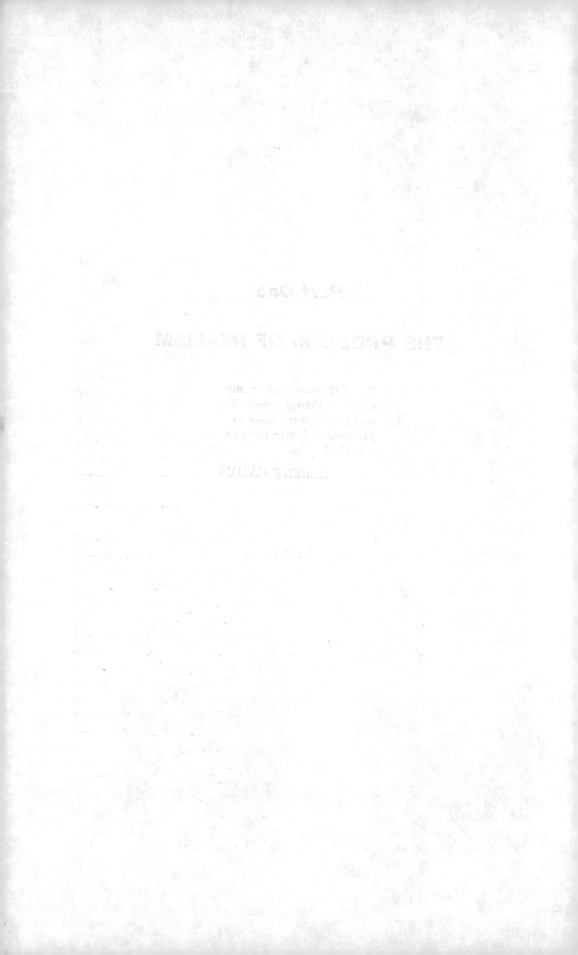

1. Realism and the Cinema

THE PROBLEM of how best to represent reality in art is as old as Western literature itself. In its broadest sense realism is an attitude of mind, a desire to adhere strictly to the truth, a recognition that man is a social animal and a conviction that he is inseparable from his position in society. This may be regarded as the great tradition of Western art, unchallenged until the abstractionism of our own century, and Erich Auerbach, whose *Mimesis—The Representation of Reality in Western Literature* deals with realism in this sense, is able to draw his examples from a whole wealth of significant writers between Homer and Virginia Woolf. But as Ernst Fischer[57] has pointed out such realism of *attitude* is to be distinguished from realism of *method*, which is a specific historical development having its origins in the work of such men as Fielding in literature and Courbet in painting. Realism in this sense has dominated the arts for the last two hundred years, to such an extent in fact that the assumption is often made, particularly by writers on the cinema, that it is the only valid approach. It is important therefore to remember that, fruitful as the method of realism may be, it remains only one of the possible means of expression, of itself confers no particular value on a work of art and in no way constitutes a guarantee of truth.

The rise of realism in the modern sense as a major force in literature is intimately bound up with the growth of the novel in the Eighteenth century, in the course of which a new view of man's relationship with the world around him evolved, thereby necessitating the creation of a new form of literature that would reflect this by dealing with named and individualised characters in a specific, detailed setting. The effects of this change are still with us today, even if its original economic, social and philosophical causes—the growth in wealth and importance of the middle classes and such new notions as individualism and originality—can be ignored. Writers such as Defoe, Richardson and Fielding in England broke with the ancient doctrine of levels of representation (whereby realism was deemed suitable only for comedy) and dealt seriously with the lives of ordinary individuals. They began the process of fitting these individuals into a coherent and convincing setting—Richardson dating precisely all the letters of *Pamela* and Fielding making the adventures of Tom Jones consistent with the political events of the alleged year of that novel's action—but it is not until the beginning of the Nineteenth century and the emergence of such novelists as Stendhal and Balzac in France that the depiction of the social setting takes on a predominant role.

1830 may be regarded as the year in which realism crystalised into

the form we know today. Arnold Hauser, in his *Social History of Art* refers
to the heroes of Stendhal and Balzac as "our first intellectual contemporaries"[67] and Erich Auerbach explicitly links Stendhal's *Le Rouge et le Noir*
with modern realism in film and novel: "In so far as the serious realism
of modern times cannot represent man otherwise than as embedded in a
total reality, political, social and economic, which is concrete and constantly
evolving—as is the case today in any novel or film—Stendhal is its founder."[6]
The relevance of this particular tradition of realism to our own century
becomes clear if we consider it in the light of Auerbach's two-fold definition:
on the one hand, "the serious treatment of everyday reality, the rise of more
extensive and socially inferior human groups to the position of subject
matter for problematic—existential representation," and, on the other, "the
embedding of random persons and events in the general course of contemporary history, the fluid historical background."[6] It was to this Nineteenth
century bourgeois tradition and its principal Italian representative, Giovanni
Verga, in particular, that the young writers and would-be film-makers of
Fascist Italy looked for inspiration in the crucial years of the early Forties
and it would be difficult to overestimate its importance to the neo-realist
movement as a whole and the director Luchino Visconti in particular.

The Nineteenth-century realist tradition is often referred to as *critical
realism,* for all the great realists have been to some extent at odds with the
society in which they have lived. It is as if the desire to break with accepted
artistic conventions brings with it the need to break social taboos as well.
In the mid-Nineteenth century the element of protest is a subjective one,
reminding us that realism and romanticism have a common origin and are
in many ways contrasting facets of the same phenomenon (one thinks of
the inextricable mingling of the two approaches in such writers as Balzac
or Hugo). Towards the end of the century, however, the *naturalism* of
Emile Zola represents both a change of focus and a sharpening of the criticism. The objectives and aspirations of the working classes are now seen
for the first time as distinct from those of the bourgeoisie, which by this
time constitutes in effect the new ruling class. Aiming at an objective,
scientifically detached view of the social conflict, naturalism propounds the
doctrine of the omnipotence of milieu in shaping—and indeed often in
crushing—the individual. The theoretical basis of neo-realism as elaborated
by Cesare Zavattini is very close to the ideas of Zola in that an overriding
sympathy for the poor is manifested but no solutions are offered to the
problems raised.

The *socialist realism* of our own century differs from naturalism in that
it offers a way out of this apparent impasse. Where Zola sees society as
static, the Marxist with his dialectical view of historical development can
see it as evolving towards a goal for which he can fight; the establishment
of a socialist society. Whatever its moral justifications, the taking of a rigid
stand on contemporary issues is not without its dangers artistically and
propaganda of any kind has a tendency to become the enemy of art, as is
borne out most clearly by the doctrinaire imposition of a demand for "posi-

tive" literature such as occurred in the Soviet Union under the cultural dictatorship of Zhadanov. Nevertheless the principles of socialist realism— the adoption of the view-point of the working class and the belief in the intrinsic superiority of the socialist state (whatever its imperfections) over the capitalist system—have exercised an enormous influence on the Italian postwar cinema, for a number of key figures are Marxists, including Visconti, De Santis, Lizzani and Antonioni. But the simple equation: "neo- realism equals social cinema equals Marxist approach," which is employed by, among others, Raymond Borde and André Bouissy in their study *Le Néo- réalisme Italien—une Expérience de Cinéma Social* is in effect an over- simplification of a complex issue.

A contemporary development of realism in which the cinema has played a predominant role is the *documentary* in which factual accuracy takes precedence over formal patterns and an impersonal message is often substituted for an artistic vision. The reporting of events in a detached manner has, of course, a long history, but it has been given fresh impetus by the film's unequalled ability to present a detailed and apparently objec- tive account of actual happenings. One of the key figures of neo-realism, Roberto Rossellini, served his apprenticeship in this form of cinema, and the documentary principles enunciated by John Grierson in the Thirties— location shooting, ordinary people in place of trained actors and a degree of improvisation in word and gesture—find their echo in postwar Italy.

Clearly there is no single approach to reality that qualifies as the true realism—critical realism, naturalism, socialist realism, documentary all offer a possible and valid approach for the artist. If, however, we need a single touch-stone by which any would-be realist may be judged, we cannot do better than consider the definition offered by Georg Lukács: "A great realist such as Balzac, if the intrinsic artistic development of situations and characters he has created comes into conflict with his most cherished prejudices or even his most sacred convictions will, without an instant's hesitation, set aside these his own prejudices and convictions and describe what he really sees, not what he would prefer to see. This ruthlessness towards their own subjective world-picture is the hall-mark of all great realists."[93]

Theories of film aesthetics have traditionally been built on the assump- tion that the cinema is a realistic medium and that its essence lies in its closeness to real life. Perhaps the most forceful statement of this line of approach is to be found in Siegfried Kracauer's *Theory of Film: The Re- demption of Physical Reality* which, though not published until 1960, ex- presses a view that pays little heed to any developments in the cinema since the Forties, having been conceived too early to take into account the stylistic advances of Antonioni and Resnais, Godard and the post *Dolce Vita* Fellini. The author has no difficulty in assembling an impressive array of achievements in the kind of realistic cinema he advocates: classics like *Potemkin* and *Greed*, silent comedy, Westerns and gangster films, along with the works of the neo-realists and directors like Renoir (*La Grande*

Illusion), Buñuel (*Los Olvidados*), Tati (*Les Vacances de Monsieur Hulot*) and Satyajit Ray (*Pather Panchali*). Though Kracauer's contention that "all of them rely largely on the suggestive power of the raw material brought before the camera" is questionable, the importance of the realistic vein in the cinema is clearly brought out simply by this enumeration. Since *Theory of Film* has been described by Ernest Callenbach as "the bible of neo-realism," it is appropriate to give its theories close consideration.

Kracauer starts out from the premise that film is an extension of black-and-white photography and denies the film any possibility other than that of recording reality. Films, he tells us, "come into their own when they record and reveal physical reality . . . And since any medium is partial to the things it is uniquely equipped to render, the cinema is conceivably animated by a desire to picture transient material life, life at its most ephemeral. Streets, crowds, involuntary gestures and other fleeting impressions are its very meat." He finds it significant that the contemporaries of the pioneer Louis Lumière praised his films for showing "the ripple of the leaves stirred by the wind," and overlooks the equally significant fact that the vogue for Lumière films of this kind lasted only a couple of years (in this sense Lumière was correct to consider his cinematograph to be an invention without a future, a fad that would pass). For Kracauer the true film artist is "a man who sets out to tell a story but, in shooting it, is so overwhelmed by his innate desire to cover all of physical reality . . . that he ventures ever deeper into the jungle of material phenomena."[83] The film is uniquely equipped to capture what Kracauer calls "the flow of life" and the ideal form of film structure is an episodic one which allows this to be both suggested and represented.

The relevance of this to the Italian postwar cinema is self-evident. The particular years 1945 to 1951 are indeed important because the Italian film-makers, by taking their cameras out into the streets and forgetting the dead rules of conventional film-making, did come face to face with reality again. This confrontation provoked a series of films which will stand comparison with those produced at any time and in any country during a comparable number of years, and the effect on world cinema was enormous. But it is no part of our purpose here to argue—as Kracauer often does —that the neo-realist ideal is the only valid one, to pretend that this approach did not leave many questions unanswered, or to suppose that the qualities of *Paisà* or *Umberto D* in any way invalidate the fantasy of Jean Cocteau's *Orphée*, the operatic stylisation of Sergei Eisenstein's *Ivan the Terrible* or the hermeticism of Alain Resnais's *L'Année Dernière à Marienbad*. Indeed the most cursory study of the Italian cinema makes it clear that most of the successful Italian film-makers moved away from true neo-realism and yet produced works of outstanding interest and importance, while Vittorio De Sica, who as late as 1956 still remained loyal to the neo-realist aesthetic, merely witnessed the exhaustion of his creative powers.

We must also part company with the Kracauer who hedges when it comes to stating whether or not the film is an art form: "The concept of art does not, and cannot, cover truly 'cinematic' films—films, that is, which incorporate aspects of physical reality with a view to making us experience them. And yet it is they, not the films reminiscent of traditional art works, which are valid aesthetically. If film is an art at all it certainly should not be confused with the established arts."[83] This defensive, distrustful attitude echoes strangely the words with which Paul Valéry contested the right of the novel to claim the status of art: "While the poetic universe is essentially closed and complex in itself, being the pure system of the aspirations and accidents of language, the universe of the novel, even of the fantastic novel, is tied to the real world."[19] In both cases the critic is hampered by too rigid an adherence to theory. Realism in the film, as in the novel, does mean a closer connection with reality than is the case in most other art forms, but this merely means we must broaden our conception of art, for if Tolstoy, Stendhal and George Eliot are not artists, what are they? And if the films of Tati and Renoir are not works of art, how then can we describe them? There is no room for equivocation here: the film is an art form and deserves to be judged by the same criteria as the other arts. Nor, with respect to the cinema, are the difficulties so great as Kracauer imagines. He forgets that in art any formal or methodological advance in realism is no more than a matter of changed conventions and his equation of film and photography, by leading him to ignore the crucial distinction between temporal arts and purely spatial ones established by the great German critic Lessing as long ago as 1766, causes him to minimise the dimension of time in the film. Existing in time, telling a story and employing human actors, the feature film raises the same problems of plot, characterisation and rhythm as a novel or play.

Still more striking is the lack, in *Theory of Film*, of any consideration of the role of the creative artist in shaping the raw material presented to him by life. We are simply told that the film artist "has traits of an imaginative reader, or an explorer prompted (or prodded) by insatiable curiosity" and that "his creativity manifests itself in letting nature in and penetrating it." Kracauer quotes approvingly Arnold Hauser's statement that "the film is the only art that takes over considerable pieces of reality unaltered,"[67] and appears to think that the ideal film director is faceless, opinionless and virtually "transparent." One might imagine from his definitions that films by Renoir and Buñuel, Tati and Ray are interchangeable. He talks constantly of "film gravitating towards the expanses of outer reality" or "the medium's declared preference for nature in the raw," but never about the feelings or intuitions of individualised film-makers. It is not surprising therefore that even such a key realist film-maker as Luchino Visconti finds no mention in *Theory of Film*, for at times Kracauer equates artistry with falsity and contends that newsreels, scientific or educational films and artless documentaries are more tenable propositions from an aesthetic point of view than "films which for all their artistry pay little attention to the given outer world."[83]

These are not notions that the present study is designed to reflect.

Acceptance of the fact that the film, like the novel, is characterised by a lack of formal purity and that its stylistic conventions tend to be extremely loose is not to be taken as implying a denial of the crucial role of the artist in shaping his material and thereby influencing the degree of interconnection between art work and external reality. Like most realist movements in the arts, neo-realism was an attempt to get closer to reality by refusing old and outmoded conventions which inevitably falsify our picture of it. But since reality itself is not static and human understanding constantly widens as new discoveries are made and old ones are revived, the movement represents only one stage in the evolution of the cinema, not the end and limitation of its development. Each great realist director evolved his own pattern of realism and used it to interpret a chosen facet of reality, and though collectively the important films of the neo-realists reflect the whole variety of Italian life, always the hand of the director is apparent, shaping the inchoate mass of material into an appropriate and satisfying form. Before we proceed to an examination of these stylistic approaches, however, we must look at neo-realism in the light of Italian life, culture and history.

2. The Italian Context

THE REALISTIC INCLINATION of the Italian genius has a long history, dating back at least to the Fourteenth or Fifteenth centuries when the Renaissance was born in Italy. The tendencies of this movement, as John Addington Symonds tells us, "were worldly: its ideal of human life left no room for a pure and ardent intuition into spiritual truth." The painting and sculpture produced in Italy in those years were the perfect reflection of an age "which had begun by humanising the legends of the church, diverted the attention of its students from the legend to the work of beauty and, lastly, severing itself from the religious tradition, became the exponent of the majesty and splendour of the human body."[130] The age of the baroque, when Italy again occupied a foremost place in European culture, shared with the Renaissance this denial of the transcendental. In Italian literature the same impulse finds expression in the *novella* or short story which has remained a characteristically Italian form of writing from Boccaccio to Verga, from D'Annunzio down to Pavese and Moravia. The *novella* is essentially the recounting of some remarkable or memorable incident—the term itself means simply "a piece of news"—and whether it is historical or contemporary in setting, its form has the bite of real life; it is, ostensibly at least, undoctored, vivid and concise. This literary tradition is of considerable relevance to the Italian realist cinema in which there is a marked tendency, clearest perhaps in the case of Rossellini, for the narrative to disintegrate into a series of tiny episodes. Its inherent difficulties, which are again relevant to the realist cinema, derive from the fact that it requires enormous power on the part of the artist if the trivial subject-matter is to be given any real weight and import or is to get beyond the merely anecdotal so as to achieve a unified vision of man in society.

The prevalence of short story over novel, in Italy as in Germany, is a reflection of wider issues: until quite recent times any sort of coherent social view has been impossible because of the political disunity of the country. Traditionally the realities of Italian life have been grim: poverty, injustice, foreign invasion and conquest, most evident in the case of Sicily but to be found to a greater or lesser degree throughout the peninsula. As a result poets have consistently been driven to turn their backs on a society they can only consider corrupt and to seek refuge in the pursuit of pure style. Analogous to this hermetic art in which the need for the communication of human experience is minimised is the Italian taste for virtuosity in artistic performance and for spectacle in art and architecture. The elaborate, convoluted and awe-inspiring products of the Italian baroque are, among other things, monuments to the virtuosity of their architects and builders. Luigi Barzini, a precise observer of his nation's foibles, has aptly summed up this attitude: "The Italians," he writes, "are tempted to applaud more those performances which stray dangerously farthest from reality, those which make do with the scantiest of materials, those which do not even pretend to imitate existing models and still manage to be effective, convincing, stirring or entertaining."[10]

This double focus finds full expression in the Italian cinema which, since its very beginning, has hovered between extravagance and realism, on the one hand the abundance of elaborately fabricated spectacular films and the feats of pure *mise en scène* practised by directors like Vittorio Cottafavi, on the other sober studies of poverty and social problems. Both tendencies were well established by the outbreak of the First World War, and if the neo-realists could look back to Nino Martoglio's *Sperduti nel buio* of 1914, the historical epic likewise has a most impressive ancestor in Giovanni Pastrone's *Cabiria*, made the same year. This alternation is still to be found in the period after the Second World War: 1948, which on an artistic level is the year of De Sica's *Bicycle Thieves*, was dominated, from a box-office point of view, by Blasetti's monumental story of ancient Rome, *Fabiola*. Only rarely—with Rossellini's *Rome Open City* for instance—has the realistic mode found popular favour, for the masses in Italy like those elsewhere prefer escapist extravaganzas to serious discussions of their own all-too-pressing problems. A similar dichotomy to that of the cinema as a whole can often be observed within the directors themselves who may exhibit simultaneously qualities which, on the surface, are mutually exclusive. In a situation where the aristocratic Visconti devotes six months of his life to filming starving Sicilian fishermen, the Neopolitan matinée idol De Sica makes austere films about the Roman proletariat and the Marxist Pasolini directs a serious and deeply-felt version of *The Gospel According to St. Matthew,* the concept of sincerity is not one that can be given a simple definition.

This complexity on the part of the great realists is a clear indication that the realism of Italian art, on the surface so straight-forward, may in fact be a highly ambiguous phenomenon. Luigi Barzini has no doubts that the Italians are by nature a realistic people: "This intense preoccupation with solid, measurable, sensible reality is readily perceived by anyone having even a superficial acquaintance with Italian life . . . It can be confirmed simply by overhearing the conversation at the next table . . . The emphasis is always on the solid, the down-to-earth, the material, with a wealth of precise and substantial details."[10] Such a view is certainly borne out by the postwar scene in both literature and cinema which abound in artists absorbed in and devoted to recording the minutiae of the life going on around them. This life is vigorous and animated, carried on in the streets by an extrovert and uninhibited people relying more on gestures and facial expressions than on words. It offers a wealth of raw material for the artist, for in Italy, as Luigi Mistrorigo has pointed out, "the drama of existence is never, or rarely, hidden in the depths of consciousness or the subconscious, but rather inscribed on the surface of life itself."[103]

If film realism were indeed, as Kracauer and some other theorists would have us believe, no more than a matter of recording what is there, then a camera planted on any Italian street corner would automatically produce a great work of realist art. But in fact, as Barzini is quick to point out, this is not only life lived in the open, it is also life turned into an entertainment, a show with its effects "skilfully, if not always consciously, contrived and graduated to convey certain messages to, and arouse particular emotions in, the bystanders."[10] For this reason the realist film-maker must have the qualities of an artist able to select and probe, disentangle the real from the feigned, order the over-abundant material, in a word be able to give it formal expression. The decline of neo-realism as a movement coincides with the rise of what has been aptly termed "rosy realism," films made cheaply, on location and with unknown players which merely dress up a little more the already dramatised surface of Italian life and are just as much pure entertainment as any glossy and expensive adaptation of a Broadway stage-hit. The very advantages given to the realist film-maker in Italy by the vivid, animated life around him carry with them enormous dangers, and from *Vivere in pace* onwards the true realist cinema has always run side by side with films that flirt with reality and gloss over its problems. The great works of the Italian postwar cinema are those which avoid this pitfall and fully reflect the often confused state of Italy after the bitter struggle that marked the end of Fascism.

This movement in Italy, like National Socialism in Germany, was the product of one man and the reflection of one personality, but Benito Mussolini's success is to be attributed less to the single-minded pursuit of a set of political objectives fixed from the beginning than to demagogic

genius aided by the fact of his sharing, in a magnified form, so many of
the qualities and defects of his fellow-countrymen. Despite flashes of
political genius Mussolini remained what he had been to begin with, a
brilliant journalist who, it has aptly been said, "governed Italy as if he
were running a personal newspaper single-handed . . . ignoring the supreme
responsibility of political power as extraneous to the business."[34] The basic
realities were buried under a welter of slogans and falsified by a propaganda
machine which Mussolini, its creator, himself ended by believing. The
dictator put on a good show—he brought economic stability to the country,
reconciled church and state, acquired an empire of sorts, built roads and
hospitals, drained marshes and increased film production from seven films
in 1930 to one hundred and nineteen in 1942. His public, the Italian people,
loved him. But in the end he destroyed everything he had created and
plunged his country into the squalor of civil war and humiliation of foreign
occupation, so that the question had to be raised, whether his programme
had been anything more than a mere "transformism" which left the real
problems untouched. In a speech in January 1943 Mussolini, in whom
beneath the political bombast there still lurked a journalist capable of
great insight, showed that he could sense the answer history would make.
"The problem is a serious one for us," he said. "We must ask ourselves
whether twenty years of the Fascist regime have changed things only on
the surface, leaving them much the same underneath. We shall see in the
course of 1943."[34]

Fascism had a stifling effect on Italian cultural life, gradually alienating
all artists and writers of integrity. Even a man like Alberto Moravia, who
had a middle-class background and was not particularly concerned with
politics, was eventually driven into opposition. Of his own case he wrote:
"I think this development is inevitable in any totalitarian state, at any
rate for the intellectuals. The choice is between becoming a paid adulator
or being driven day by day into complete silence and finally to prison. All
the rest is idle chatter and sophism."[35] Such literature as existed became
infested with rhetoric and like the Fascist cinema completely lost touch
with reality. Writing of the cinema in the years 1938-43, Carlo Lizzani
found it impossible "even to think that at that period, when the world
was plagued by such misfortunes, one was able to see born and multiply
films as non-existent, as empty, as lacking in the slightest contact with the
national reality as our standard films of those years were."[91] It is hardly
surprising, therefore, that after the war writers and directors should seek
a return to realism, for, as Paul West has aptly noted, "between the arrival
of D'Annunzio and the end of Mussolini, the Italians had their fill of the
flamboyant."[145] If, in the prewar years, the Italian cinema had reflected
the mood of the country in its escapism (there were comparatively few
overtly Fascist propaganda films made), it also seemed to sense the change
of atmosphere in the early Forties. It was in 1942 that the opposition
parties in Italy came to life again and that same year the films heralding
the renaissance were made: Alessandro Blasetti's *Quattro passi fra le nuvole,*

Roberto Rossellini's *Un pilota ritorna* and *L'uomo della croce* (his first documentary, *La nave bianca,* had appeared the previous year), Vittorio De Sica's *I bambini ci guardano* and, most notable of all, Luchino Visconti's *Ossessione.*

After the Liberation writers and film-makers were faced by many problems but the ultimate goal seemed clear to all: to recapture the lost links with reality. It was, strangely enough, a man who had spent years making official documentaries, Roberto Rossellini, who was the first to achieve this and his film *Rome Open City* was a national, as well as inter-national success. The difficulty facing the whole postwar generation was summed up by the novelist Cesare Pavese in an entry in his diary on March 5, 1948: "Fundamentally, humanistic intelligence—the fine arts and letters—did not suffer under Fascism; they managed to follow their own bent cynically accepting the game as it was. Where Fascism exercised vigilance was in preventing intercourse between the intelligentsia and the people, keeping the people uninformed. Now the problem is to shed the privileges we enjoy at the moment—servitude—and not to 'approach the people' but to *be* the people, to live by a culture that has its roots in the people."[113] The literature which adopted this approach in the years that followed the fall of Mussolini has been largely overshadowed for foreigners by the film movement with which it shares the title of "neo-realism" and Mary McCarthy's dictum that "the Italian novel is a branch of the Italian film"[145] reflects a widely held opinion outside Italy. In fact, however, the Italian postwar literary scene contains a number of writers of quite considerable stature and a neo-realist movement that embraces such figures as Cesare Pavese, Elio Vittorini and Vasco Pratolini is not to be underestimated. The strength of the realist tendency becomes even clearer if we append to these three names those of the documentarist Carlo Levi, celebrated for his investigations into the problems of the *Mezzogiorno,* and a novelist of even greater repute, Alberto Moravia, whose work—like that of Visconti in the cinema—lies only partially within the neo-realist orbit.

The developments of the two groups, writers and film-makers, follow an almost identical pattern. Luigi Mistrorigo, who attempts a definition of literary neo-realism, tells us that "it is officially born immediately after the war (1945), but its origins are to be found earlier, for some in 1941 when Cesare Pavese published *Paesi tuoi,* a little before, a little after, according to others. Be that as it may, the movement became famous after 1945, reached its height around 1950 and declined about 1952."[103] In terms of content, too, the similarity is striking: though the product of intellectuals, the literature of neo-realism is born out of contact with immediate reality which is presented as directly as possible, often through narrators who are depicted as ordinary men leading perfectly ordinary banal lives. Again, as in the cinema, neo-realism in literature is an act of revolt against the rhetoric of the Fascist era and yet a continuation of an older literary tradition, the *verismo* of Verga; it dies as a uniform movement in the early Fifties, yet the influence it exerts over younger writers continues up to the present. Despite this unity of interest and approach, however, literature and cinema show little positive interaction. The case of Alberto Moravia is highly significant in this connection. Though he was both a scriptwriter and the film critic of *L'espresso* it would be difficult to point to any definite cinematic influences on his style or, conversely, to pick out important films which in any real way reflect his literary ideas and achievements. Equally, by the time Carlo Lizzani came to adapt Pratolini's novel *Cronache di poveri amanti* in 1953 or Michelangelo Antonioni found inspiration for *Le amiche* in Pavese's *Tra donne sole* in 1955, cinematic neo-realism had already ceased to be a truly potent force.

The neo-realist movement in the cinema, which was born out of the collapse of Fascism and the bitter months of partisan fighting and which sought to identify itself with the people, was closely bound up with political developments in postwar Italy. The film-makers were not men who had lived remote from social pressures, for neo-realism, like Fascism itself oddly enough, is largely a product of journalists. George Huaco in his *The Sociology of Film Art* lists five out of nine important neo-realist directors as writers or journalists—Zampa, Vergano, De Santis, Lizzani and Germi— and one might add Lattuada, who worked in journalism in the years 1933– 1937, and note that, among the scriptwriters who contributed most to the movement, Zavattini and Fellini had both followed this same profession. The films these men made in the early postwar years were characterised by an extremely close identification with contemporary issues. Rossellini began *Rome Open City* immediately the Germans had left and, as Huaco points out, *Bicycle Thieves* was made in 1948 when unemployment reached a peak figure, while Lattuada's *The Mill on the Po*, though nominally set in the mid-Nineteenth century, reflects the agricultural disorders of 1949 when "the agricultural workers in almost all of Italy went on strike for several weeks," and when, in the South, "this strike was accompanied by peasant occupation of the large landed estates."[75]

The political climate of postwar Italy was of particular importance to the cinema since neo-realism was initially a product of the spirit of resistance fostered by the partisan movement. The parties most active in the partisan Committee of National Liberation (CNL) were those of the left: the Communists, the Socialists and the Action Party (which was formed specifically to reflect partisan values). To begin with the partisans exercised considerable influence and the first postwar administration—a coalition of the six parties represented in the CNL—was led by Ferruccio Parri, leader of the Action Party and commander of the resistance forces. But this administration was short-lived, Parri was replaced by the Christian Democrat Alcide De Gasperi in November 1945 and the Action Party virtually eliminated in the elections of 1946 (when it gained only 1.5% of the votes). Almost the only monuments to the partisan ideals were the two films financed by the A.N.P.I., the ex-partisan organisation, Vergano's *Il sole sorge ancora* and De Santis's *Caccia tragica*. The fate of the remaining parties of the left was sealed in January 1947 when the Socialist Party led by Pietro Nenni was torn in two when Giuseppe Saragat broke away to form the Italian Social Democratic Party, taking fifty of the one hundred and fifteen Socialist deputies with him. This disunity was swiftly exploited by De Gasperi who, in May of that year, formed a new government coalition excluding both Nenni's Socialists and the Communists led by Palmiro Togliatti. These two parties, denied a share in the government after three years of participation, presented a joint list to electors at the 1948 election, but De Gasperi's manoeuvring was vindicated when his own Christian Democratic party achieved an absolute majority.

Not surprisingly this new, firmly based government of the centre showed itself increasingly hostile to the depiction of social injustice in Italy. The film production crisis of 1949 led to the passing of the "Andreotti Law" which established wide government control over the financing and censorship of films including a right to ban the export of any Italian film which Andreotti judged "might give an erroneous view of the true nature of our country." The effect of this on neo-realist films, which needed foreign distribution if they were to recoup even their modest costs, was potentially disastrous and Andreotti's campaign against De Sica's *Umberto D* was a clear indication that the government intended these provisions to be strictly interpreted. In the early Fifties, before the absolute majority of the Christian Democrat party was broken, the cinema of social protest had been effectively stifled and in any case circumstances were changing: in an increasingly affluent society the issues were no longer as clear-cut and the artists themselves were developing away from a need to deal exclusively with social problems.

Part Two

THE ORIGINS OF NEO-REALISM

Neo-realism is the product of a cultural and democratic reaction to the standstill of the spirit during the Fascist period.

PIER PAOLO PASOLINI

1. The Cinema Under Fascism

THE EARLY YEARS of Fascism in Italy saw the cinema there at its lowest ebb, and the advent of sound in 1930—in the shape of Gennaro Righelli's *La canzone dell'amore*—occurred at a time when no more than a handful of films were being made each year. Production did, however, rise to over thirty in the next few years, and indeed 1932/3 witnessed a brief flourishing during Emilio Cecchi's short spell as artistic director of the Cines company. Cecchi, a distinguished literary figure and father of Visconti's future scriptwriter Suso Cecchi d'Amico, brought Walter Ruttmann to Italy to direct *Acciaio* from a story by Luigi Pirandello and encouraged the two leading Italian directors of the Thirties, Mario Camerini and Alessandro Blasetti, to produce some of their best work. Blasetti's *1860* (1933), a non-rhetorical look at Garibaldi's achievements, shot on location with non-professional actors, is often cited as a forerunner of neo-realism, and Carlo Lizzani is not alone in finding that "it marks the summit of the Italian cinema during the Fascist era,"[91] but its commercial failure discouraged the director from pursuing further this line of approach. Camerini's *Gli uomini, che mascalzoni* (1932) also occupies a place in the history of the Italian cinema, being the film in which Vittorio De Sica first achieved wide popularity as an actor. This romantic comedy about a chauffeur and a shop assistant who meet and fall in love, then quarrel and try to make each other jealous, ends predictably in reconciliation but keeps the attention thanks to the freshness and lightness of touch it displays. The comic elements and mishaps are deftly handled and the acting is polished and assured within the film's rather narrow range, so that the shyness of the lovers at the end is genuinely touching. It is also set against the authentic backgrounds of city streets and the Milan fair, and this has caused certain critics to see it too as a forerunner of neo-realism. In fact, this is to underestimate the director's degree of stylisation in treatment and the script's undoubted theatrical contrivance, and in so far as the film is a precursor, it is of the "white telephone" films of the later Fascist era and the "rosy realism" of the Fifties, though it is on a far higher level than the typical products of either of these two periods. Aspirations towards realism in these early years of the Thirties remained largely on the theoretical level and no films made at this time met the demands of Leo Longanesi who wrote in an article published in 1933: "We must make films as simple and bare as possible in their direction, films without artifice, shot without scripts, and as far as possible taken from life. It is truth which is lacking in our films. We must move out into the highways, take our cameras into the streets, into the yards, barracks and railway stations. It would be

31

enough to go out into the street, to stop at any point and observe what is happening for half-an-hour, with attentive eyes and without a preconceived style, to make a film which would be both an Italian film and a 'true' one."[137]

Longanesi's words are prophetic, but his kind of cinema did not come into being until well over ten years later. In the Thirties the realist impulse virtually died out in Italy, after the Fascist government, which as early as 1925 had set up the Instituto L.U.C.E. to produce documentaries and newsreels, extended its surveillance to the feature film by setting up the Direzione generale della cinematografia in 1934 and organising the construction of the huge Cinecittà studios which were opened in 1937. The initial result—a rise in production from thirty-five films in 1934 to over eighty by 1939—was augmented by further measures. In 1938 the state imposed strict control of the import and dubbing of foreign films through the organisation known as E.N.A.I.P.E. and built up its own distribution chain, E.N.I.C. These actions, combined with the cutting off of American films on the outbreak of war, led to the creation of a highly protected and flourishing film industry in Italy. In this hot-house atmosphere production reached the unprecedented level of one hundred and nineteen films in 1942, before military defeat brought the first cold blast of reality. The characteristic features of the standard films of this period were artistic mediocrity and a startling separation from reality. The innumerable spectaculars, filmed operas and "white telephone" comedies (so called because of their setting in a studio-contrived social irreality), made by stolid craftsmen like Mario Mattoli, Carmine Gallone, Arturo Bragaglia and Guido Brignone, are now happily only names in the production lists of the Thirties, but one can capture something of the flavour of the period through a film like Max Ophuls's *La Signora di tutti* (1934).

The very choice of Ophuls by the producer Angelo Rizzoli, who with this film inaugurated his newly formed Novella company, is significant. When in 1932 Emilio Cecchi had sought to add tone to his productions by importing directorial talent from abroad, the man he chose was a documentarist, Ruttmann. Two years later it was to the German *émigré* Ophuls, the decorative director *par excellence* and a man more interested in patterns of style than in the social relevance of his content, that the Italian cinema turned—the contrast is indicative of a changing mood in the industry. *La signora di tutti* is, as its director has said, "a little too passionate for non-Italian tastes"[14] in its rhetorical account of a film star's rise and fall. The whole film is an enormous melodrama with incongruous stylistic echoes of the more bizarre silent film dramas, redolent with the atmosphere of the heyday of the Italian *diva*, as its heroine, played by Isa Miranda, brings death and destruction in true *femme fatale* style to all those around her and finally—of course—to herself. The absurdities of the plot, the heavy ugliness of the settings and the theatrical grimacings of the hero (Memo Benassi) did not prevent the film from winning an award at the Venice Biennale and achieving "a certain commercial success."[14] *La signora di tutti* gives a clear indication of the contemporary taste to which established Italian directors all too frequently acquiesced. Mario Camerini, directing six further comedies starring Vittorio De Sica after *Gli uomini, che mascalzoni*, remained content to exploit his minor vein of petit-bourgeois humour and made no attempt to widen his range or deepen his approach. The more eclectic Alessandro Blasetti moved erratically from one genre to another during the first decade of sound, but by the late Thirties had settled on a type of spectacle whose culminating example is *La corona di ferro* (1940). This mythological fable has a timid anti-war theme embodied in the ponderous symbolism of an iron crown sent to the pontiff in Rome by the Byzantine emperor, which pauses on its way to witness the punishment of the evil. It is a confused tale that begins with usurping brothers, babies exchanged in their cradles and a witch's prophecies apparently successfully opposed. Its core is constituted by the love of a Tarzan-like hero (Massimo Girotti) for two women, a beautiful princess and a glamorous, boyish bandit-leader, and its ending is the miraculous imposition of universal concord—a conclusion which seems more than a trifle optimistic for a film made in Europe in 1940. The *décor* is lavishly constructed and the set-piece battles are efficiently handled but *La corona di ferro* bears witness to a suffocating society unable to face an increasingly grim reality.

By one of those strange contradictions in which the Italian cinema abounds, the few actual Fascist propaganda feature films are distinctly unrhetorical. Indeed no less a man than Roberto Rossellini served his apprenticeship working on films of this kind, including two produced by Vittorio Mussolini, the dictator's son. Typical of this type of production are the war films of Augusto Genina, such as *Squadrone bianco* (1936), about the war in Africa, and *L'assedio dell'Alcazar* (1939). The latter dealt with a remarkable incident in the Spanish Civil War, the defence of the fortress of Alcazar in Toledo by a group of Spanish nationalist troops against overwhelming odds. The heroism of the defenders is of course stressed and a love interest introduced through the "redemption" of a frivolous girl who falls in love with one of the officers (played by Fosco Giachetti, the ubiquitous "Fascist-leader" type of the period), but the general impression left by the film is of fairness to both sides and as much regard for human life as is ever displayed in commercial war films. It would be wrong, however, to seek the origins of neo-realism in the works of such veterans as Genina, Blasetti or Camerini for it was not they but the new generation that emerged in the cinema during the war years that created the move to realism. The isolated works of realist intent or impact produced by such men are reminders that the Italian realist tradition of art was not wholly submerged amid the welter of Fascist rhetoric and escapism, but they in no way determine the subsequent development of the realist cinema.

Fascist interest in the cinema did have some positive artistic effects as well as purely commercial ones. The year 1935 saw the founding of the Italian film school, the Centro sperimentale della cinematografia, under the direction of an anti-Fascist, Luigi Chiarini. In the same year came the first publication of the magazine *Cinema* under the nominal editorship of Vittorio Mussolini and Luciano De Feo, while two years later the Centro sperimentale began its own magazine, *Bianco e nero*. It was around the school and the two magazines that the new forces in the cinema gathered. At the former, an excellent practical and theoretical training was given, with the critical writings of Eisenstein, Pudovkin and Balasz forming a part of the course, along with examples of Italian cinematic realism, such as the now re-discovered and re-evaluated *Sperduti nel buio* of 1914. Among lecturers at the school were Umberto Barbaro, who published translations of a number of key critical works on the cinema, Francesco Pasinetti, author of a *History of the Cinema* that appeared in 1938, and the director Alessandro Blasetti, while pupils included Rossellini, Zampa, Emmer, Germi, De Santis and Antonioni, all to become directors of note. Around the magazine *Cinema* gathered a group of leftist-minded young critics including Puccini, De Santis, Visconti, Lizzani, Antonioni and Pietrangeli, while in Milan, Lattuada, Luigi Comencini and Mario Ferreri together founded the first Italian film archive. Thus by the end of the Thirties a vast pool of trained, enthusiastic talent was available to meet the needs of an everexpanding, if depressingly conformist and mediocre, cinema industry.

Before the Fascist state, and with it the highly protected film industry, began to crumble in 1943 under the impact of Allied invasion, the more forceful of this new generation had already made a personal mark. As in France (where a similar renewal was taking place at the same time with the *débuts* of men like Henri-Georges Clouzot, Jacques Becker and Robert Bresson), the initial assignments offered to the young film-makers were usually routine ones as assistant directors or co-scriptwriters. So it was that in the late Thirties Mario Soldati, who had been working in the cinema since 1931 (his second script had been that of *Gli uomini, che mascalzoni*) and Aldo Vergano, who had been associated with Blasetti's first film, *Sole*, in 1928, were joined by many other future directors, and fairly commonplace productions began to carry in their scripting credits names such as Luigi Zampa, Renato Castellani and Roberto Rossellini (beginning in 1938) or Pietro Germi and Federico Fellini (from 1939). The same period saw two important scriptwriters, Cesare Zavattini and Sergio Amidei, making their names, and the directing *débuts* of Vergano (1938) and Fernando Maria Poggioli (1936). But it was in the years 1940-42, during which some three hundred films were made, that the new talent was best able to assert itself. These years are marked by the initial experiences as scriptwriters of Giuseppe De Santis, Alberto Lattuada and Michelangelo Antonioni, as well as by a whole succession of directing *débuts*. In 1940 Vittorio De Sica and Gianni Franciolini made first features, Francesco De Robertis his first documentary and Soldati his first solo film after three collaborations. In 1941 the ranks were reinforced by the appearance of Zampa, Rossellini and Castellani as directors, while Luciano Emmer began making his short

Two faces of the Italian cinema:

Top: Nino Martoglio's SPERDUTI NEL BUIO (1914) and bottom: Giovanni Pastrone's CABIRIA (1914)

Two encounters:

Above: Aldo Fabrizi and Anna Magnani in Roberto Rossellini's ROME OPEN CITY (1945)

Left: Michèle Morgan and Henri Vidal in Alessandro Blasetti's FABIOLA (1948)

The combination of seeming opposites:

Pier Paolo Pasolini's Marxist Christ (Enrique Irazoqui) in THE GOSPEL ACCORDING TO SAINT MATTHEW (1964)

The Key figures
of literary neo-realism:
Right: Cesare Pavese
Below left: Elio Vittorini
Below right: Vasco Pratolini

Wartime escapism:

Top: Massimo Girotti in Alessandro Blasetti's LA CORONA DI FERRO (1940)

Bottom: The official Fascist cinema:

Augusto Genina's L'ASSEDIO DELL'ALCAZAR (1939)

Macario, the comedian as whose gagman Federico Fellini began his film career (top left)

Leading directors of the thirties:
Mario Camerini (top right)
Alessandro Blasetti (bottom left)
Mario Soldati, the founder of calligraphism (bottom right)

The key work of calligraphism:

Renato Castellani's UN COLPO DI PISTOLA (1941) with Assia Noris and Massimo Serato

The postwar continuation of calligraphism:

Above: Sarah Churchill and Vittorio Gassmann in Mario Soldati's DANIELE CORTIS (1947)
Left: Aldo Fabrizi in Alberto Lattuada's IL DELITTO DI GIOVANNI EPISCOPO (1947)

documentaries on art. 1942 brought first films by Lattuada, Luchino Visconti and the director of the Centro sperimentale, Luigi Chiarini.

Among this selection of names one finds several men whose contribution to the postwar renaissance was, for one reason or another, marginal: Poggioli died in 1945, Soldati and Franciolini drifted into purely commercial undertakings, De Robertis continued with documentary-style films peripheral to the mainstream of feature production, and Chiarini returned to film theory and administration. But with the single exception of Carlo Lizzani who, as the youngest member of the group, was only twenty years old in 1942, one finds here all the directors who after 1945 were associated with neo-realism, as well as those who, in the Fifties, pioneered a more introspective kind of film-making. It must be noted, however, that much of their work in the years 1940-42 is mediocre and in this respect it is hardly surprising that a correspondent writing in *L'Ecran Français* in 1945 should have complained that "no sensational revelation is to be seen, either among the scriptwriters and directors or among the actors . . . As can be seen, the most important problem from the artistic point of view is that of the renewal of the ranks."[45] There were certain shared experiences that served to knit these men together—many had, for instance, worked as assistants to Blasetti or Camerini—and several films served as focal points, most notably Visconti's *Ossessione*. Yet the divergencies remained wide and, faced with the diversity these men displayed, few in the early Forties would have predicted that they could conceivably be welded together to form a coherent and unified movement. With regard to age, for example, Vittorio De Sica, thirty-nine in 1942, was nineteen years older than Lizzani. As far as the approach to the medium was concerned, the intellectuals of the magazine *Cinema* studied the Nineteenth-century novelist Verga, but Fellini was content to act as gagman to the comedian Macario. In terms of political or religious attitude, the contradictions were even greater between the Catholic De Sica and the committed, totally convinced Fascist De Robertis, between the Marxists Visconti and De Santis and Roberto Rossellini, whose film *L'uomo della croce* was a work of anti-Communist propaganda. To complicate the matter still further, one of the ways in which the new generation did show comparative unanimity and real originality in the early Forties was in pursuing a course quite contrary to true realism, namely an absorption in the resolution of purely formal problems.

2. Calligraphism or the Pursuit of Style

CALLIGRAPHISM, to use the term invented by Giuseppe De Santis to characterise the formalistic preoccupations and retreat into the past displayed by so many of his contemporaries, can fairly be regarded as one of the two predominant trends of the Italian cinema in the years 1940-42. A move away from contemporary settings can be detected in many of the works of the veteran directors at this time, for while Blasetti was making three costume pictures—*Un' avventura di Salvator Rosa, La corona di ferro* and *La cena delle beffe*—Camerini was busy adapting Thomas Hardy in *Una romantica avventura* and Alessandro Manzoni in *I promessi sposi*. But the real father of the new trend is the writer-turned-director Mario Soldati who made an enormous impact with his sixth film, *Piccolo mondo antico,* based on a novel by Antonio Fogazzaro (1842-1911). This film is, however, merely the best known of a whole series of adaptations from late Nineteenth century and early Twentieth century novels. Soldati himself tried to repeat his success with *Malombra,* taken from the same novelist, and at about the same time Fernando Maria Poggioli made *Addio giovinezza* from a pre-1914 play, adapted *Il marchese di Rocca-verdina* by Luigi Capuana (1938-1915) as *Gelosia* and then took a novel by Emilio De Marchi as the subject for *Il cappello da prete*. Newcomers making their first films followed the same line of approach: Luigi Chiarini turned to Matilde Serao (1856-1927) to make *Via delle cinque lune,* Renato Castellani made *Un colpo di pistola* from a story by Pushkin and Alberto Lattuada's *début* was with *Giacomo l'idealista,* a further adaptation from Emilio De Marchi (1851-1901). It is hardly surprising that these works show a marked family resemblance, since the directors in question often worked as writers on each other's films. Castellani, for example, was one of the scenarists of the three Blasetti films and Camerini's *Una romantica avventura* as well as of *Malombra,* while Soldati responded by collaborating on *Un colpo di pistola* and Lattuada by co-scripting *Piccolo mondo antico* and a Poggioli film.

This withdrawal from immediate reality on the part of Italian film-makers is less surprising if one considers it strictly within the context of its period. In France, under the Occupation, there was a similar drawing away from everyday life, typified by Marcel Carné's two masterly films, *Les Visiteurs du Soir* and *Les Enfants du Paradis*. In Italy the Fascists had already been in power for some twenty years by this time and, faced with the pressures of this regime and a fairly rigorous if erratic system of censorship, artists and writers had resorted to the customary Italian expedient for times of oppression: they had turned away from contact with the contemporary in favour of the pursuit of pure style. In this they had been encouraged by the dominating cultural figure of the age, Benedetto Croce, whose idealist philosophy had, in Luigi Mistrorigo's words, "turned the attention of young intellectuals and artists towards the liberal society of the end of the Nineteenth century."[103] If the preoccupation with fine writing produced little of lasting merit in the novel, it did lead directly to the creation of a form of verse—typified by the poetry of Giuseppe Ungaretti and Eugenio Montale—which put Italy back in the main stream of the European *avant-garde* movement. As Sergio Pacifici has pointed out, the term hermeticism (*ermetismo*) has come to describe less a school than simply "a special kind of poetry written by a small nucleus of artists. Hermeticism, indeed, became a particular way to combat the rhetoric and propaganda of Fascism, a manner of preserving the dignity, and honesty and integrity to which every artist clings. The calligraphism of Soldati, Lattuada and Castellani in the cinema is thus no isolated artistic aberration, but corresponds—albeit on a fairly modest artistic level—to the general cultural atmosphere of the Fascist period.

Mario Soldati's *Piccolo mondo antico* (1940) which set the pattern in the cinema is, typically, a story of unhappy love set against a mid-Nineteenth century background. It takes place in Turin and around the Italian lakes and the "little world" of the title is that part of Lombardy still under Austrian dominion in 1850. The lives of Franco and Luisa are largely conditioned by their social circumstances—they suffer poverty because of the pride that prevents him from opposing his tyrannical aunt, the *marchesa,* in the matter of his inheritance—but they are also affected by the great political events of the day on the fringes of which they live. Franco is both an ardent lover who is secretly married at night to avoid his family's displeasure and a patriot who distributes anti-Austrian propaganda. When his marriage begins to break down, he goes off to Turin to work on a newspaper and concern himself with contemporary issues. His wife Luisa, already deeply troubled by the difficulties of their relationship, has her life shattered by the death of their young daughter Ombretta, drowned while she is out begging the *marchesa* for money. Luisa retreats to the brink of madness, centering her existence exclusively on the child's grave, and a first attempt at reconciliation staged by Franco ends in failure. But later when he passes through Isola Bella with his fellow volunteers on the way to the war, Luisa visits him and they are reunited. As he leaves for the front next day, the child she carries in her womb is a symbol of new life for them both.

Remote from all sense of actuality, *Piccolo mondo antico* is a stylish film, visually very refined and elegant, benefiting from its fidelity to Fogazzaro's novel, which provided some neatly drawn minor characters (most notably the *marchesa,* played by Ada Dondini) and a splendid role for the young Alida Valli. There are a number of very good sequences—outstanding among which is the death of Ombretta—but the film's main excellence lies in the accuracy of its period reconstruction and its use of natural settings. This quality was widely recognised at the time and De Santis, whose articles in *Cinema* provide an invaluable commentary on calligraphism from the realist standpoint, wrote of it: "For the first time in our cinema we have seen a landscape where the air is no longer rarified, which is no longer greedily intent on the picturesque, but one which responds finally to the humanity of the characters, and is as much a decorative element as an indication of their feelings."[31]

Soldati's second adaptation of a Fogazzaro novel, *Malombra,* made in 1942, showed how fragile was the concern displayed in *Piccolo mondo antico* with fitting the characters into the landscape and the events into the

social context. The director used identical elements—the same period setting, costumes, lakeside scenery and even supporting players—but the new
work proved to be an unrestrained piece of theatrical rhetoric. The difference lies partly in the tone of the original novel, but even more in the choice
of the leading actress. Like the earlier film, *Malombra* is built round a
single performance, and here Isa Miranda brings all her fire and tempes-
tuousness to the role of Marina, the spoilt heiress who develops an obsession
with the fate of an unhappy ancestor and allows it to warp her whole life.
The stress in *Malombra* has shifted to the irrational and the decorative and
the film culminates in a finale of splendidly grand-guignolesque absurdity.
On a windswept terrace overlooking the lake a group of black-garbed
figures assemble by candlelight to participate in a formal dinner that ends
abruptly when Marina shoots her hapless lover. Needless to say, *Malombra*
was attacked in *Cinema* by the young theorists of realism, who were equally
perturbed by the first films of the two young directors Renato Castellani
and Alberto Lattuada. Both these men had trained as architects so it is not
surprising that their early films show a marked concern with formal and
decorative qualities. Lattuada, adapting a novel by De Marchi in *Giacomo
l'idealista* (1942) took a subject typically remote from actuality, the film
being, in his own words, "the story of a dreamer who lives outside reality
and gets out of his depth when faced with the mysteries of life."[131] Though
it reflects the director's characteristic preoccupation with the theme of solitude, *Giacomo l'idealista* is also very much a product of its period, and was
attacked as such by De Santis: "Once more the Italian cinema lends itself
to a deplorable regression by a useless 'pretextism' deriving from Nineteenth
century sources. Once more we must denounce this marriage between
cinema and literature as totally arid and sterile, frigid and uninteresting."[31]

Castellani's first film, *Un colpo di pistola* (1941), is a key work of the
period. The director has said that the subject pleased him so much that his
scenario was completed in two nights, but the finished script signed by
four writers represents an elaborate trivialisation of Pushkin's original and,
like many films on which Castellani worked, it has considerable structural
defects. Pushkin's story, *The Shot*, one of the *Tales of the late Ivan Petro-
vitch Belkin* published in 1831, consists of two distinct but complementary
halves. Firstly the narrator hears the account of a duel interrupted because
one of the participants seems only too willing to die and then, five years
later, he learns of the sequel. Within its brief span of a dozen or so pages
The Shot achieves a total artistic unity, gaining as a story of rivalry from
its double focus of narration and the suspense this generates. In the form
Pushkin gives it, *The Shot* is a work of total simplicity without a super-
fluous word or the slightest touch of the merely picturesque, and at the
same time it deals with a social phenomenon of vital interest to its author,
who was in fact to die in a duel some six years after its publication.

The advantages of Pushkin's tight framework of narration are largely
dissipated in the adaptation contrived by Castellani and his co-scriptwriters, Bonfantini, Pavolini and Soldati. The hero's relentless quest for

revenge is lost in the film, which opens with his attempted suicide and makes him seek out his rival in a spirit of reconciliation that is only later turned to hatred. Graver still is the complication of the plot by the inclusion of a banal love story which provides a starring part for Assia Noris, an actress more at home in Camerini's comedies than Pushkin's Nineteenth century world. In *Un colpo di pistola* the two men become rivals for the love of the beautiful Masha who is engaged to one while loving the other, and there is a significant move away from a conflict motivated by a social code of honour to a personal plot based on lovers' misunderstandings and tribulations. This love story is padded out with such conventional novelettish devices as misunderstood conversations, undelivered letters and meetings missed quite by chance, and furnished with a particularly false happy ending.

In this respect at least the film is less a work of true formalism than one of mere empty patterns of elaboration and contrivance, and it is hard to disagree with the inevitable strictures of De Santis, who described it as "a pretentious and dated arabesque, drowned in parasols, Brandenburgs and lace ribbons."[31] Yet *Un colpo di pistola* does have considerable incidental qualities that anticipate the later Castellani. Visually it is most exciting, directed with a care and attention to striking detail akin to that displayed, more recently, by Alexandre Astruc in *Une Vie*, his adaptation of a Maupassant novel. The decorative element of uniforms and ball-room dresses is an integral part of the film, and justifiably so since Pushkin himself wrote that the action of his story took place in dreary provincial towns where the officers "had nothing to look at but each other's uniforms." Fortunately little attempt has been made to recreate the Russian landscape of the original for the occasional attempts at local colour provide the film with some of its weaker moments (the re-union of hero and heroine in church before the final duel for instance). To compensate for this lack there are many outdoor shots that come splendidly alive—the opening ice-skating scene, the first duel at dawn with the mist still hanging in the trees, the picnic interrupted by a sudden shower—showing clearly that for all the limitations of this first feature, Castellani has nonetheless avoided the traps of the studio-bound Hollywood style movie.

While it is revealing to contrast the achievements of the calligraphists with the realistically inclined articles published by De Santis and others in *Cinema*, one must avoid the temptation of over-emphasising the polarity of the Italian cinema of the Forties. In fact calligraphism and neo-realism do have much in common at this early stage, as the ease with which Castellani and Lattuada moved from one to the other should show. The realists too looked back to Nineteenth century literature for inspiration, taking Verga as their model, and it was only the censor who prevented Visconti from beginning his career with an adaptation of Verga's *L'amante di Gramigna*. The rediscovery of landscape is also something shared by the two tendencies, and in this respect at least *Piccolo mondo antico* and *Ossessione* were both moving in the same direction. True realism in the

full meaning of the word was, as we shall see, virtually impossible to achieve
in the last years of Fascism and at least the retreat into formalism allowed
men like Lattuada and Castellani to use their talents without putting them
to the service of the regime.

The careers of these men also take on a new light if one views them
through their own eyes and in this connection Castellani's account of his
progress in his first three films is of interest: "The passage from one film
to the other had its logical explanation. Setting out from an essentially
abstract world (the Russian atmosphere, the literary tone with a certain
Byronesque flavour), I felt the need to deepen the nature of my characters,
make them more real, more 'flesh and blood,' as in *Zaza;* when I had realised
this ambition, it seemed natural to continue in the same direction, and I
wanted to shoot a film starting out from reality, reconstructing hardly anything in the studio, and the result was *La donna della montagna.*"[131] To
regard calligraphism solely as a dead end, an anti-realism, would be false
and Carlo Lizzani, who, as a professed Marxist, can hardly be accused of
excessive indulgence towards formalism, offers a fairer evaluation when
he writes: "The least harm that could come to a group of directors who had
decided on the path of propriety and dignity of form was meeting Fogazzaro, De Marchi, Capuana, Palazzeschi etc."[91]

3. The Quest for Realism

A LONGSIDE THE MORE BRILLIANT and striking works of the
calligraphists, films groping tentatively towards realism, despite the
later prestige conferred on them by the link with neo-realism, tend to look
rather pale and unexciting. Yet attempts at creating more authentic films
were being made throughout the years 1940-42 by men coming from a
wide range of backgrounds—literature, the music hall, Fascist documentary
and the conventional commercial cinema—and it is these often muted efforts
that in fact proved fertile. It is significant that none of the three recognised
great directors of neo-realism—Rossellini, De Sica and Visconti—was
tempted by the calligraphist experiment, though all were active at the
time. The paths of realism were not easy under a regime which lived on
slogans and evasions, but there were certain Italian traditions which seemed
to offer the possibility of renewal. One of these was regional comedy—
typified by the Neapolitan dialect theatre of Eduardo De Filippo—and
Roberto Rossellini has made high claims for a number of rather insignificant popular films in this vein directed by Mario Mattoli and Mario
Bonnard, maintaining that he sees the birth of neo-realism "finally and above
all in certain minor films like *Avanti c'e posto, L'ultima carrozzella* and
Campo dei Fiori where the neo-realist formula, if you like to call it that,
was in the process of forming through the free creations of actors, particu-

larly Anna Magnani and Aldo Fabrizi. Who could deny that these actors were the first to incarnate neo-realism?"[15]

This statement raises several important issues, though it is less provocative if one bears in mind that when Rossellini talks of the birth of neo-realism, he in fact means the birth of his own personal style. His reference to actors is a useful reminder that the common assumption that neo-realism uses exclusively non-professional actors is by no means true. Magnani and Fabrizi made key contributions to the success of *Rome Open City* and in general, thanks to their early work in the music hall, they were able to give a new tone to Italian film acting in the Forties (much as Raimu, Arletty and Fernandel, whose origins were similar, had changed the face of the French cinema some ten years before). But it is wrong to imply— as Rossellini seems to do here—that neo-realism is in some way a product of actors. The movement made use of players unaffected by theatrical rhetoric just as it employed backgrounds devoid of glamour, but it remains essentially the creation of writers and directors. Between the films of 1942 and the first masterpieces of neo-realism there is also another connection which Rossellini does not mention, though he no doubt had it mind, namely the presence among the scriptwriters of Federico Fellini, who was a close associate of Fabrizi in the Forties and subsequently worked on *Rome Open City, Paisà* and other early Rossellini films. But even if Fellini can fairly claim to have "already surpassed the rubbish of white telephones and sugary situations customary at the time"[128] in these films, it must still be admitted that they lacked the authority and weight of impact necessary if they were to exercise any real influence on later film production in Italy.

A second and perhaps more vital source of neo-realism was the documentary tradition with which Rossellini was very closely connected, and which the Fascists had fostered by nationalising the L.U.C.E. organisation (which produced newsreels and shorts) as early as 1925. There had been some interesting short films produced by Cines while Emilio Cecchi was in charge there, and the documentary influence was also quite strong in the "official" films of Goffredo Alessandrini and Augusto Genina. Rossellini's first professional scriptwriting assignment was on Alessandrini's *Luciano Serra pilota* (1938), and after this collaboration with the Fascist party's principal propagandist in the feature film, he moved to the Navy Ministry to direct *La nave bianca* in 1941 under the supervision of Francesco De Robertis, a talented documentarist who was, however, totally committed to Fascism. Rossellini continued in the same vein with *Un pilota ritorna* (1942) and *L'uomo della croce* (1942), before beginning a feature film, *Desiderio,* which he failed to complete. Since Rossellini sees an unbroken continuity in his own work and has gone so far as to say: "In *La nave bianca* I had the same moral position as in *Rome Open City,*"[21] it is worthwhile examining this first film in some detail though it is by no means a masterpiece. But to put it into context we must first look at the career of its instigator, Francesco De Robertis.

Born in 1902, and thus a year younger than De Sica but four years older

than Rossellini or Visconti, De Robertis was head of the film section of
the naval ministry when he made his first documentary, *Mine in vista*, in
1940. Though a regular officer in the Italian navy, he had already dabbled
in the theatre before turning to film-making. His first feature, *Uomini sul
fondo*, had an enormous impact on critics of all persuasions, particularly
in view of the fact that, having been conceived before the outbreak of war,
it lacked the militaristic propaganda that marked the director's subsequent
documentaries. De Robertis characterised his ambitions with this film in
an article in *Cinema:* "*Uomini sul fondo* was for me a didactic film. Shortly
before the war, three submarines—one French, one English, one German—
sank at about the same time, and it became apparent that in the matter
of rescue work our navy led the field. We thought that this should be
brought to the attention of the public at large by a film which would expose
this fact with the greatest possible clarity in dramatic form. *Uomini sul
fondo* is therefore limited to the story of a rescue."[31] Using non-professional
actors, authentic settings wherever possible and a photographic style akin
to that of newsreels, De Robertis anticipated many aspects of neo-realism,
but there is still a considerable gulf between *Uomini sul fondo* and, say,
Rome Open City. For one thing De Robertis had absolutely no interest
in improvisation for, as Mario Verdone tells us, he "defined the material
to be filmed minutely in advance, he arrived on the set with his plans and
his sketches, with the shots already drawn and measured and the camera-
movements calculated."[137] Similarly he was purely a documentarist, hostile
—as we shall see from his comments on *La nave bianca*—to any real narrative
development. He was also content to use types rather than realistically
drawn individuals and admitted that in *Uomini sul fondo* psychology "has
little place in the story and is touched upon only in its relationship with the
dramatic situation: the fate of the men linked to that of the ship." With
regard to De Robertis's later films one is also faced with the problem of
ideology, for his commitment to Fascism was such that after the fall and
reinstatement of Mussolini in 1943 he went North to the Lake of Garda
to supervise the organisation of the film industry of the Salò Republic (a
task Vittorio De Sica had declined). De Robertis himself wrote that *Uomini
del cielo*, his third feature, was designed to show how "fighting exercised
a beneficial effect on the minds of those who have not withdrawn from the
supreme experience which life destines fatally to each man,"[15] and such
a message is of course totally irreconcilable with the humanism of postwar
neo-realism.

La nave bianca, which Rossellini made under the supervision of De
Robertis, is a work that hovers between documentary and fiction. Like
much of the director's work it is episodic in form and falls into two distinct
halves. The connecting link between the two is provided by a somewhat
contrived romance between a sailor and his schoolteacher penfriend. Sepa-
rated when his ship is ordered out to battle on the day they were to meet,
they are brought together on board the hospital ship after he has been
wounded and she has become a voluntary nurse. This muted love story is

handled with a gentle humour (most apparent in the hero's vain prepara-
tions for a meeting with the girl) and ends with them united after various
misunderstandings. The embryonic narrative development is handled very
plainly and straightforwardly (there is only one flashback which occurs
when the girl remembers her teaching days) but the characters remain the
stock types of the documentary *genre* and, despite the authenticity of the
players and settings, they never acquire the depth of real rounded and
individualised human beings. De Robertis, who wrote the original script
of the film, had harsh words to say about this aspect of it. For him the basis
of *La nave bianca* was "the ideological conception of a parallelism between
spirit and matter, between the men wounded in the battle and the equally
wounded ship" and the addition of what he called "the false and banal story
of a pure love between a young nurse and a wounded hero"[15] destroyed
the ethical and stylistic purity of the film. But clearly it is Rossellini who is
moving in the right direction—towards the more complex idea of realism
possible in a work of fiction—even if the initial steps he takes here are
comparatively feeble.

By far the most exciting aspects of the film are the documentary ones.
The Navy Ministry had originally commissioned a purely documentary
work and it was only after fifteen thousand metres of film had been shot
that it was decided to incorporate a story that would show how well men
wounded in battle were cared for. The treatment of war in the film's first
section is very uneven. Some sequences, such as the opening shot of the
ship's guns rotating threateningly to show us the might of the Italian fleet
in port and the repeated images of officers silhouetted against the sky and
guns belching out smoke, are mere visual rhetoric and as such find a verbal
echo in the captain's speech to his crew after the victorious end to the
battle. More successful artistically are the revealing shots of men and machines that convey the enormous technical paraphernalia of modern war.
One of the major themes of the film, in Rossellini's eyes, is "the pitiless
cruelty of machines with regard to men: the unheroic aspect of a man
who lives inside a warship, who acts while remaining almost in darkness,
amidst measuring instruments, goniometers, wheels and cranks. An apparently unheroic, unlyrical aspect, but one which is in fact heroic to a frightening degree."[115] *La nave bianca* is at its best in the depiction of this mechanical hell, inhuman though clearly the product of human skill, as when the
onset of battle is not shown directly but felt through its impact on the
men in the bowels of the ship. The scenes of destruction when the ship is
hit and the ensuing rescue operations are very well handled too, and some
of the material has a most authentic, newsreel look about it.

The second half of the film, that dealing with the hospital ship, the
"white ship" of the title, has a distinctive visual tone thanks to the predominance of white in the paintwork, the uniforms, the hospital beds and
the bandages of the wounded. In contrast with the first part of the film
this section presents a reassuring picture: a wounded Italian is made to see
again, unity and fellowship are achieved through shared religion and enter-

tainment and the lovers are reunited. There is some tension as the wounded
sailors await the return of their ship, overdue on a mission, but generally
the tone is idyllic. The film ends with a close-up of a red cross and basically
with its optimism and happy ending *La nave bianca* shows an acceptance
of the world as it is for Italy in 1941. The musical score of the film, the first
of many provided for the director by his brother Renzo Rossellini, contrib-
utes greatly to this effect, and often music takes the place of dialogue, so
that we are given feeling in place of cold explanation. In the first half of
the film each of the elements, the personal story and the martial one, has
its own musical theme and the two are interwoven as hero and ship suffer
the same fate. The second half is dominated by a new and peaceful melody
though the two earlier themes reappear as the film reaches its triumphant
conclusion.

La nave bianca is an interesting first work, uneven in tone (there are
some very contrived scenes, such as the ship's departure for battle when
Rossellini cross-cuts between the ship and the unduly noble faces of watch-
ers on the quay) and full of conflicting elements. In it patriotism and
rhetoric exist alongside a fascination with machines and many fine instances
of a documentarist's precise insight and desire simply to record. In terms
of pure technique the film anticipates neo-realism in numerous ways and
Rossellini himself, as we have seen, is not aware of any contradiction
between it and *Rome Open City*. But if the ideas which it presents are
examined a gulf is immediately apparent, for the works of neo-realism,
whatever the precise political allegiance of their makers, are films that
probe and attack, while *La nave bianca* is designed simply to reassure. The
Marxist members of the neo-realist group see a total ideological incompatibility between the documentaries of De Robertis and Rossellini and
their own works, and would share Georges Sadoul's extremely severe evaluation of this form of cinema: "The errors of this tendency, which is sometimes called in literature *photographic naturalism,* were found to surpass
by far the errors of calligraphic formalism. . . . The formula of real settings,
real details, real characters resulted in lies infinitely more serious than the
obvious errors of delirious decoration in the studio."[124] If this is an unduly
harsh judgement to pass in retrospect on men trying to present the truth
as they saw it, it does nonetheless serve as a reminder that the documentary,
for all its surface objectivity, is far more politically committed than the
fictional feature film which of necessity deals with human ambiguity.

In the fictional film one approach that did offer the possibility of a
renewal of realism was the middle-class comedy of the type perfected in
the Thirties by Mario Camerini. If the latter's *Gli uomini, che mascalzoni*
may be said to have set the pattern in 1932, it was Alessandro Blasetti who
gave the *genre* a fresh impetus ten years later when, after a succession of
period films, he made *Quattro passi fra le nuvole.* Just as many of Camerini's
films are the fruit of close collaboration between the director, his writer
(frequently Mario Soldati) and his star (Vittorio De Sica), so Blasetti's
film owes much to Cesare Zavattini's script, Alessandro Cicognini's music

and Gino Cervi's performance in the leading role. *Quattro passi fra le nuvole* deals with twenty-four hours in the life of Paolo, a commercial traveller, and ends, as it begins, with the dull routine of his domestic life in a cramped flat with a nagging wife. But the day we see is one on which his ordered existence is turned into chaos when he loses his train ticket and is forced out into the open air and thrown together with a pretty girl, Maria. She is on her way home to tell her parents that she is pregnant and persuades Paolo to pose as the child's father and in this way make easier the painful announcement she has to make. But once at the farm Paolo cannot escape and much against his will he has to spend the night there. His stay does, however, have beneficial results for before he leaves he succeeds in reconciling Maria and her family.

Quattro passi fra le nuvole is a fascinating and amusing minor film which, though in general romanticising life, does contain a genuine core of truth in its portrayal of human relationships. The opening sequences of the film are much better than the very contrived later ones in which it degenerates into a kind of "who sleeps where?" farce, and among its neatest touches are its portrayal of everyday domestic horror and the scenes in the train (where Paolo conducts a feud with the ticket collector) and on the bus (when the passengers celebrate the birth of the driver's first son). For much of the time the film sustains its good-humoured tone and gives a fresh picture of ordinary people and a typical Italian landscape. Zavattini has said that this film was the one in which his own impulses towards realism first found expression, adding: "No doubt the fact of inclining affectionately towards people, this humanity which is perhaps a little over-developed and pathetic but nevertheless sincere, all this no doubt already belongs to the new world [of realism]. The film was still full of gags but the characters were no longer caricatures and the story unfolded, so to speak, under the roof of a house without my feeling the need to change the topography of the house or the relationships of the characters among themselves."[131] *Quattro passi fra le nuvole* anticipates the less important side of neo-realism, the comedies skirting the real issues of life in which Renato Castellani and Luigi Zampa excelled in the postwar years. Indeed in many ways this film is nearer to the mood of *E Primavera* and *Two Pennyworth of Hope* than are any of Castellani's own calligraphic experiments in the early Forties. Zavattini gave a fair assessment of its qualities and defects when he spoke of the characters in all his early films, who, he said, "swerved" at a given moment: "Like a horse that normally has a regular trot and suddenly shies, my characters would swerve, to become perhaps more amusing, but all the same less real."[131] This is precisely the feeling one has with *Quattro passi fra le nuvole*: the truth of the people involved is most skilfully established and then sacrificed to the exigencies of a farcical plot.

The quality of Blasetti's film is immediately apparent if one compares it to any of Vittorio De Sica's early films. De Sica had reached maturity as an actor in the field of light comedy and he was firmly established as a popular star when he became a director in 1940. His first four films were all light comedies built around the performances of actors and indeed *Rose scarlatte* and *Maddalena zero in condotta,* both made in 1940, were adaptations of stage successes. Looking back on his career in 1955, De Sica claimed that from the beginning of his directorial career he "had realised the possibilities there were in taking the camera outside the studios, in the open air, wherever one would be able to capture the way people really live,"[55] but this is hardly apparent in his work before 1942. *Teresa Venerdì,* his third film, is a fair example of his work at this early period. In it De Sica appeared as a hard-up doctor who for some time has had as his mistress a flamboyant variety singer, Lolleta (Anna Magnani in a small but striking role). To raise money he gets a job as medical superintendent at a convent school and tries to sell his house, and thanks to these two actions complicates his life still further by acquiring both a new admirer (Teresa Venerdì, one of the pupils at the school) and an unwanted *fiancée* (Lili, a spoilt millionaire's daughter). The rest of the film, built on a theatrical pattern of contrived situations and confrontations (though it was in fact adapted from a novel), records the various mishaps and confusions that ensue before the doctor is united with Teresa. *Teresa Venerdì* pokes gentle fun at the regimentation of school life, at the music hall, and at the pretentions of the rich (Lili composing a poem and wondering if she can accept a rhyme suggested by a mere servant). De Sica's own performance shows all his polish and talent as a light comedy actor, Adriana Benedetti (the Maria of *Quattro passi*) makes a touching young heroine, and there are plenty of good gags and comic situations, but the film as a whole never adds up to more than an entertaining piece of commercial film-making. Indeed, apart from the skill revealed in the handling of the children, *Teresa Venerdì* gives very little hint of the qualities later to be so manifest in De Sica's work.

The first film in which Vittorio De Sica's talent is really visible to any marked degree is his fifth film, *I bambini ci guardano* (1942) which was, significantly enough, the first he made with Cesare Zavattini (whom he had first met in Verona in 1935 and who subsequently became his inseparable collaborator) and the first in which he did not appear as an actor. *I bambini ci guardano* was not an original script but an adaptation of a novel called *Prico* by Cesare Giulio Viola. Though the screenplay is credited to half-a-dozen writers it is Zavattini's hand that is most apparent. He described the film as "the most important stage in the evolution of my career as a film-maker and even of my career as a human being,"[131] and for all its evident limitations it is a key work for the appreciation of the period. The plot is basically that of a typical woman's magazine story: a beautiful married woman falls in love and commits adultery. Discovered and forgiven by her husband, she cannot prevent herself from going off with her lover again, thereby driving the husband to suicide and losing the love of her young son. The film's originality lies, as the title suggests, in the presentation of this plot material through the eyes and emotions of the young boy trapped within a conflict of loyalties. This double focus of the film—part cliché, part novelty—is typical of it as a whole. The authors have tried sincerely (and successfully) to give a personal and realistic account of a child's experience, but this has not prevented them from producing at the same time a thoroughly professional piece of film-making. While the story-line squeezes every ounce of emotion from the predicament of the child, great efforts have been made to make the background interesting in its own right by the inclusion of a great deal of often comic detail: the visit to the corset shop run by the wife's sister, the shots of high society on the beach, the fumbling efforts of a hotel conjuror, the grim tyranny of the grandmother's house. In a similarly unexciting way the musical score by Renzo Rossellini—who wrote music for four of De Sica's first five films as well as composing for his brother Roberto—is used simply to underline the climaxes of the story.

While willing in this way to compromise with popular taste, Zavattini, who worked longer on the script of this film than on any of his previous works, felt it imperative to "keep to the essential points and observe the greatest possible sobriety."[131] The film's photographic style reflects this perfectly with its clean, unobtrusive compositions which concentrate on presenting the characters in their environment. The only discordant note is furnished by the occasional attempts at an expressionistic style provoked by a desire to heighten the impact, as in the sequence of Prico's dream when he is returning from his grandmother's house. In a similar way the sets are generally simple and realistic, and good if slightly self-conscious use is made of exteriors, but at the very end De Sica uses vast empty and ornate sets for the orphanage in an attempt to accentuate visually the tragedy already clearly visible in the child's eyes. This kind of over-emphasis is immediately and jarringly apparent if one approaches the film with a knowledge of De Sica's later work, but in the context of the cinema of its time, *I bambini ci guardano* is a work of considerable restraint. This, however, does not prevent it from cutting deeply if narrowly. The director concentrates on the child Prico, whose wide-eyed vulnerability is calculated to wring tears from the stoniest hearts, and coaxes a fine performance from the young Luciano de Ambrosis. Indeed it is hard to think of more sensitive handling of a young player before François Truffaut's *Les Quatre Cents Coups* made over fifteen years later. In both films it is a scene of interrogation that is perhaps the most striking: in *I bambini* the sequence in which the father questions Prico about his mother's behaviour, and in Truffaut's film the young hero's interview with a psychiatrist. Zavattini indicated the importance of the film in his own, and in De Sica's career, when he said: "Through the character of the child who was the protagonist of the film . . . we felt for the first time a human being, whereas all my previous characters had been inclined to be puppets."[131]

True as the portrayal of the central figure of the child is, the authors of *I bambini ci guardano* have not wholly succeeded in raising the film to the level of a comment on society as a whole. Zavattini has said that he and De Sica "had understood that the characters were placed in a certain atmosphere, a certain reality, and that the war was always present,"[131] but this is something they proved unable to convey adequately, for the finished film is not rooted in any particular moment of time and its social significance is limited. One of the main reasons for this is, paradoxically, what gives the film its impact: the decision to tell the story through the child's eyes. Seen in this way the adult problems seem oversimplified, the wife does not emerge as a character in her own right and husband gains our sympathy without letting us understand his motives for suicide. This use of a child as a kind of touchstone of truth is very characteristic of the De Sica-Zavattini team throughout their collaboration and it is interesting to note that in *Ossessione*, which was made in the same year as *I bambini ci guardano*, Luchino Visconti adopted a similar approach by including a scene in which the hero Gino asks a young child whether she thinks he is guilty. But in general whereas Visconti looks at passion directly, De Sica in *I bambini* views it only obliquely. As a result De Sica creates a greater and more spontaneous involvement (through Prico) but at the expense of a broader picture of society and social problems. *I bambini ci guardano* had a considerable impact on contemporary critics and film-makers, and Carlo Lizzani has made clear that it seemed at the time "a call addressed to the conscience, a testimony to truth, a film in which Fascism, its rhetoric, its achievements and its false morality were ignored."[91] But seen in the context of the subsequent work of De Sica and Zavattini it represents only the first step towards realism, a muted promise to be fulfilled only six years later with the achievement of *Bicycle Thieves*.

4. Outside Influences

THE WORK OF ROSSELLINI AND DE SICA in the early Forties is very much in the main stream of the Italian cinema. Their films, deriving from existing traditions, were not censored or banned and though De Sica was never in any way engaged on propaganda for the Fascist party, he was very highly regarded by Pavolini, the minister in charge of film affairs, who invited him to Venice to run the film industry of the Salò Republic when this was set up by Mussolini and the Germans. The films we have considered, *La nave bianca* and *I bambini ci guardano*, are interesting indications of the latent qualities of their directors but in no way decisive works, for Rossellini and De Sica, like most other directors at the time, show the effects of working under a Fascist regime. Donald Heiney, pointing out the extent to which the literature of this period is characterised by escapism, evasions and the lure of pure "style," has gone so far as to assert that "even when they were writing illegally, the Italian writers had the air of treading on eggs, it was the spirit of the times."[69] It is hardly surprising therefore that film-makers, who worked for a mass audience and so were far more susceptible to outside pressures, should be forced into compromise. Virtually all the future creators of neo-realism tried working under Fascism and found their attempts at a realistic portrayal of life frustrated, but in the long run the effect of this was a positive one: instead of being corrupted by Fascism, they were all driven from it or hardened in their opposition to it. Ultimately though, current trends and possibilities in the cinema could not give real inspiration and increasingly in the Thirties and Forties film-makers, like other artists and intellectuals in Italy, sought new models both from abroad and from Italy's own past. It is these fresh shaping influences that we must now turn to consider.

The writers and directors who created neo-realism had all had a thorough grounding in the cinema, most had been employed professionally in some capacity or other before working independently, many had attended the Centro sperimentale, and several had worked as film critics for *Cinema* and *Bianco e nero*, so it is not surprising that the influence of other schools of film-making should be detectable in their work. We know that the films and books of Eisenstein and Pudovkin were studied at the film school, and the Soviet cinema is often quoted as one of the prime influences on this generation, but specific borrowings or allusions are hard to pin down, even among the Marxists of the Italian cinema. Visconti, who did not attend the Centro sperimentale but got to know the works of Soviet film-makers in Paris at the time of his collaboration with Renoir, feels that the films of Ekk, Pudovkin and Eisenstein which he saw then "probably" influenced him.[52] But De Santis, a graduate of the Centro and a close associate of Visconti in the Forties, has denied any specific Soviet influence: "It is possible that at times I rediscovered the tone of the Soviet cinema but this is no doubt because I had the same things to say. In any case I did not consciously undergo this influence."[32] On the evidence available it is hard to dispute George Huaco's contention that "the influence of Soviet expressive-realist films and theoretical writings seems to have been largely inspirational. There is some continuity between the Soviet use of non-professional actors in major roles. But the decisive features of the Soviet expressive-realist film style are not borrowed by neo-realism."[75]

One undeniable filmic influence was that of the French cinema which, as Michelangelo Antonioni has said, was "perhaps the most important one in the world"[32] in the Thirties, for as film critics and journalists the neo-realist directors could hardly be unaware of such men as Jean Renoir and Marcel Carné, who were at the height of their international reputation during this time. The link with France is symbolised by the very term neo-realism itself. There is no single origin of this word any more than there is a single source of the movement it came to designate, despite the fact that Luchino Visconti has maintained that it was coined simply to describe his own first feature: "As far as the term neo-realism is concerned, it was born thanks to the correspondence I exchanged with my editor, Mario Serandrei, who was then in Rome and is still my editor today. He saw the first film-stock developed, the rushes, of *Ossessione* and wrote me a long letter saying, among other things: 'This type of cinema which I am

seeing for the first time etc. . . . I would call it neo-realist.' And from that
the word neo-realism was born, it was really born from *Ossessione*."[52]
Despite this authoritative assertion the first appearance of the word in
print was not in any of the reviews of *Ossessione* but in an article about
the *French* Thirties cinema published by Umberto Barbaro in 1943: "One
can say with a great deal of truth and accuracy of the films of the French
neo-realism that they were a cry of alarm."[48] Before the Italian realist
movement had come into being Guido Aristarco had also used the term in
the same sense, when he wrote, in 1945, that "in France, neo-realism
(Renoir, Carné, Duvivier) did not arise because it was wanted and advocated by critics, but because there were poets with precise aspirations."[48]

The connection between neo-realism and the French cinema is more
apparent still if we consider the major Italian directors individually. Visconti has said that he "underwent the influence of French realism, that
is to say of a certain kind of cinema, Renoir, Duvivier, Carné, etc."[52] More
specifically his debt is to Jean Renoir, for whom he worked as third assistant
(alongside Jacques Becker and Henri Cartier-Bresson) and costume designer on *Une Partie de Campagne* and whom he was also to assist on the
making of *La Tosca*, the film Renoir had to abandon in 1940 on the outbreak
of war. Of the French director, Visconti has said: "Renoir exercised an
enormous influence on me. You always learn from someone, you never invent
anything. You invent, yes, perhaps, but you are terribly influenced, especially when you are making your first work . . . Renoir taught me the way
to work with actors."[21] In a similar way, Antonioni, who served as Marcel
Carné's assistant on *Les Visiteurs du Soir*, has said that for him "watching
Carné work . . . was an infinitely precious lesson,"[29] and elsewhere he has
spoken more generally of the prestige of Carné and the French cinema in
the eyes of young Italian film-makers: "Marcel Carné represented for us at
the time . . . a sort of phenomenon, a man who had broken the barriers
in the name of a true freedom. He represented a new content, certain
aspirations to rebellion, a polemical fervour. And naturally that filled us with
enthusiasm. The truth is we needed something to fill us with enthusiasm."[32]
The admiration of Vittorio De Sica for the work of René Clair, whom he
regards as one of his two masters (the other being Chaplin), is well-known,
but perhaps more surprising is the enthusiasm for Carné shown by Roberto
Rossellini who in 1948 said that he considered him, together with Clouzot,
as the greatest European director.

If further confirmation of the esteem that this generation had for the
French is needed, we have only to consider the tributes of three other
directors. Looking back on his own origins, Federico Fellini said: "If any
cinematic influence can be ascribed to me, as having served me indirectly
on my work for the screen up to *Rome Open City* and *Paisà*, it is undoubtedly the influence of the French cinema which besides, around 1940, had
its impact on just about everyone."[128] Corroboration of this has been given
by Alberto Lattuada: "People have always talked of Italian neo-realism,
but they have never expressed sufficiently the debt we owe to Renoir,

Left: Eduardo De Filippo: the master of dialect comedy

Wartime documentary:
Below, top: Francesco De Robertis's UOMINI SUL FONDO *(1941)*

Fictional realism:
Below, bottom: Gino Cervi and Adriana Benetti in Alessandro Blasetti's QUATTRO PASSI FRA LE NUVOLE *(1942)*

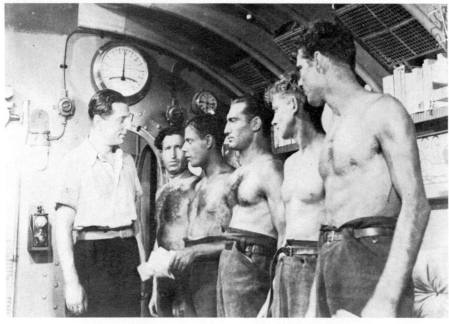

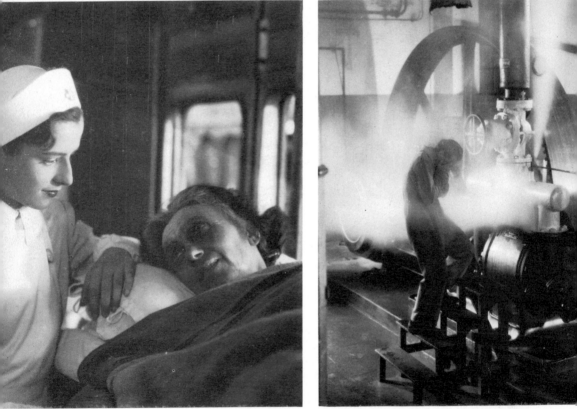

Vittorio De Sica with Adriana Benetti in his own TERESA VENERDI (1941)
(top)

De Sica and Zavattini's least known film:
LA PORTA DEL CIELO (1944) (bottom left and right)

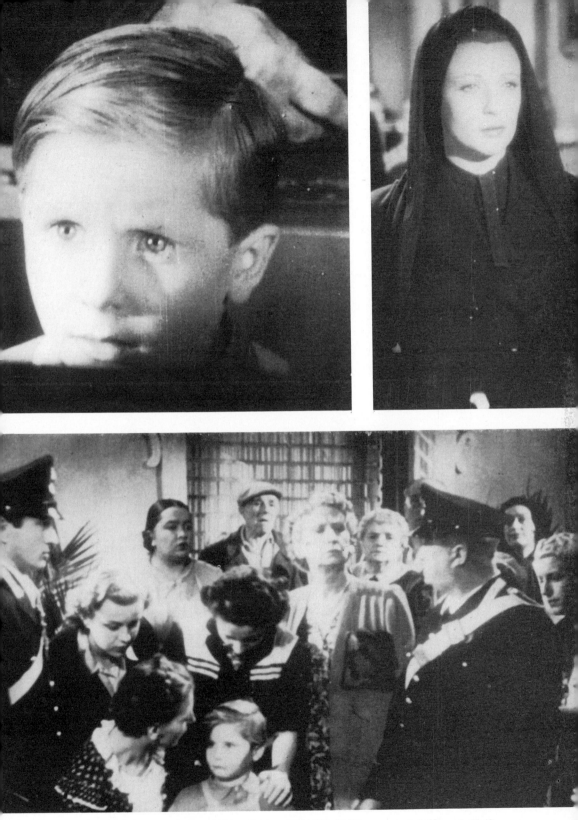

Vittorio De Sica's I BAMBINI CI GUARDANO, *a crucial film of 1942.*
Top left: Luciano De Ambrosis as the boy
Top right: Isa Pola as the mother
Bottom: The boy surrounded by the hotel guests

Luchino Visconti's
OSSESSIONE (1942), a study
of unglamorous passion.
Clara Calamai and Massimo
Girotti as the lovers.

OSSESSIONE

Above: Clara Calamai in her kitchen

Left: Juan De Landa as the husband at the singing contest

OSSESSIONE: *The reward of guilty passion*

Italo Calvino

Alberto Moravia

*Literary witnesses of the war
and the end of Fascism*

Curzio Malaparte

Right: Roberto Rossellini

Roberto Rossellini's later style:
Below, top: Ingrid Bergman (with Alexander
Knox) in EUROPA 51 (1952)
Below, bottom: Vittorio De Sica in
IL GENERALE DELLA ROVERE (1959), a
return to the war

Feyder, Vigo, etc. . . . We have often forgotten the lesson we received from the French prewar film-makers."[77] Lattuada, who provoked a scandal by showing Renoir's *La Marseillaise* at the Milan Triennale in 1940, has stressed that Renoir, Carné and Duvivier were seen in Italy "as instruments of the revolution: they were on the index." Hence, for the young, they were "terribly exciting, just like Feyder and Vigo."[33]

Giuseppe De Santis has revealed that Jean Renoir was the idol of his youth, and added: "Renoir was not the only one who had an influence in Italy, there was Feyder, Clair (who particularly influenced Zavattini and De Sica), L'Herbier, even, and Carné, Yves Allégret . . . and *Pension Mimosas*, there is one of the fathers of the Italian cinema."[32] The connection between France and Italy is a very real one but it should be kept in perspective, for the gulf between pre-1939 France and post-1945 Italy is wide and mere imitation of Thirties styles would have produced no more than a dull and negative Italian equivalent of the postwar French *film noir*. The importance is clearly two-fold. Firstly, there are the individual debts to specific French directors (like Visconti's to Renoir) for contacts that allowed the Italians to discover potentialities within themselves which were suffocated in the atmosphere of the Fascist film-making industry. And secondly, there is the communication, on a more general level, of the complexities of cinematic style and an appreciation of the artistic possibilities of stylisation, both of which were later to provide a vital counterbalance to the purely documentary impulse to record the surface of war-torn Italy. It is important to remember these early French influences when we come to consider the actual achievements of neo-realism and not to pretend, as Siegfried Kracauer does, that the neo-realists were intent solely on recording directly what was there before their eyes.

While the cinematic interests and training of the neo-realist generation have been much discussed, far less attention has been given to their literary connections. Journalism of some kind had been practised by virtually all of them, many were ex-film critics, almost all worked as scriptwriters for other directors before making their own *débuts,* and all figure as co-authors of their own films. Mario Soldati is well-known as a novelist, but De Santis, Lattuada and Antonioni also wrote and published short stories and sketches alongside their journalistic articles. Professional writers too, like Zavattini and Amidei, were to play a key part in the new movement, so it is fair to assume that its practitioners were affected by the literary climate of the time. We have already seen the connection between the escapist pursuit of pure style in the cinema and in literature, but a second and equally important literary current remains to be discussed, namely the translation of American works of fiction, which occupied much of the time of two of Italy's most important contemporary novelists in the Thirties. Cesare Pavese, who once expressed the opinion that the ten years from 1930 to 1940 would pass into the history of Italian culture as "the era of translations," was responsible with Elio Vittorini for introducing Italian readers to the characteristic works of Faulkner, Dos Passos, Hemingway, Steinbeck, Caldwell

and others, so that the American naturalist school of writing could become
a potent influence on young Italians.

In the cinema the link with America is symbolised by the fact that
Ossessione was an unacknowledged adaptation of James M. Cain's *The
Postman Always Rings Twice,* but the actual extent of the influence is hard
to assess. A man of Visconti's temperament and cultural outlook could not
for long be held by a novel as sub-literary as that of Cain, and certainly
contact with real Americans during the Liberation was bound to produce
a reaction, as was the abrupt end to the unity of the allies, as Russia and
the United States moved towards cold-war confrontation. Even in literature
the impact of America is extremely hard to pin down. In an entry in his
diary on March 9, 1940 Pavese offered an assessment of the debt to Steinbeck and Co.: "Naturalism has taught novelists—and by this time we all
have it in our blood—that nothing that is not action should come into the
story. Once it was usual to describe the setting that was part of the action,
and the events, objectively; now all that is described as seen through the
eyes of the character."[113] If this is an accurate judgement—and nobody was
in a better position than Pavese to make an assessment—then the lessons of
naturalism were largely contrary to the aspirations of filmic neo-realism.
What American literature did provide was a much needed window opening
onto a different sort of world from that provided by Fascism; it made
young artists and writers aware of the possibilities of realism but did not
inspire them to mere imitation. Pavese can be seen as speaking on behalf
of his whole generation when he says: "We discovered Italy—and here is
the central point—by seeking men and words in America, in Russia, in
France and in Spain . . . This love affair with foreigners has not been a
betrayal of our presumed social and national reality."[113]

In the Thirties young Italians looking for an alternative to Fascist
rhetoric could turn to current developments abroad—the French cinema
or American literature—but in their own cultural tradition they had to go
back to the period before D'Annunzio to find satisfactory models. As
Blasetti in *1860* had turned back to the diaries of Giuseppe Cesare Abba,
an eye-witness of Garibaldi's progress, so the young critics of *Cinema* turned
back to Giovanni Verga, who seemed to them to exemplify the true Italian
realist tradition. Questioned about the sources of his work in 1959 Giuseppe
De Santis spoke of the debt all his generation owed to Verga and it is
interesting to consider his article "Ancora di Verga e del cinema italiano"
written with Mario Alicarta and published in 1941. In it the two young
film critics advocated adaptations of the work of this great Nineteenth
century Sicilian realist on the grounds that "Verga besides a great poetic
oeuvre has created a country, a time, a society; to those of us who believe
in art, particularly as a creator of truth, Sicily . . . seems to offer the
strongest and most human, the most marvellously virgin and authentic
ambience that can inspire the imagination of a cinema seeking things and
facts in a time and space dominated by reality so as to detach itself from
facile suggestions and decadent bourgeois taste."[31] The crucial importance

of Verga in Luchino Visconti's work is discussed more fully elsewhere in this study, but it is important to realise that this is merely an exceptionally strong and lasting instance of a general intellectual trend. Many critics of the postwar Italian literary scene, among them Sergio Pacifici and Paul West, see Verga's influence as a dominant one and it is fascinating to find that even in England in the Forties V. S. Pritchett was exhorting young English novelists who wanted to shake themselves into a fresh considera- tion of the art of the novel "to get hold of Verga quickly."[116] Certainly many young Italians of the time did do precisely this, and the figure of Verga constitutes the third of the discernible if fully assimilated formative and inspirational influences on the Italian neo-realist cinema.

5. Ossessione

THE ENUMERATION of the various stylistic sources that may be said to be at the root of the neo-realist impulse would be a meaningless undertaking if one could not point to some specific results. Fortunately there exists a film which synthesises all these influences and shows clearly just how much could be achieved in the way of realism in Italy during the years 1940–42. The film in question is *Ossessione*, which was adapted from a minor American naturalist novel and yet set in an authentic Italian landscape, was directed by Luchino Visconti who was deeply influenced by Verga and had also worked in France under Renoir, and was scripted by him together with a team composed entirely of *Cinema* critics and Centro sperimentale graduates: Giuseppe De Santis, Mario Alicarta, An- tonio Pietrangeli and Gianni Puccini. *Ossessione* not only offers a summa- tion of past influences and aspirations, it also provides a first statement of virtually all the major thematic and stylistic concerns of its director, and so it is hardly surprising that it is both a key work and the crowning achieve- ment of the Italian cinema during the last years of Fascism.

Visconti had originally wanted to make his directorial *début* by adapting a story by Verga but this was turned down by the censor: "I had to present my project to the Fascist ministry. It was refused on the pretext that it was a story about bandits. One day when Gianni Puccini, one of my collaborators, had gone to see Pavolini the minister, he saw my manuscript lying on the desk. On the first page could be read the words, written in red ink, 'Enough of bandits!' It's funny, isn't it? Pavolini was certainly not thinking of himself and his Fascist pals."[52] The novel by James M. Cain which Visconti chose instead—*The Postman Always Rings Twice*—is a short, brutal tale about a tramp, Frank, who has an affair with Cora, the wife of Nick, a Greek-American restaurant owner, and is led to murder the husband. Visconti has taken over much of this basic plot, but added one major character of his own invention. He has also removed all the court scenes which figure so largely in the novel, and discarded the complicated and ponderous irony whereby a man escapes conviction for a murder he did commit only to be executed for a killing which was in fact accidental. Two short quotes will give something of the flavour of Cain's novel:

> "I went out. I had what I wanted. I had socked one in under her guard, and socked it in deep, so it hurt. From now on, it would be business between her and me. She might not say yes, but she wouldn't stall me. She knew what I meant, and she knew I had her number."

> "I took her in my arms and mashed my mouth up against hers . . . 'Bite me! Bite me!'
> I bit her. I sunk my teeth into her lips so deep I could feel the blood spurt into my mouth. It was running down her neck when I carried her upstairs."[22]

Needless to say none of this crude atmosphere of violence remains in Visconti's adaptation which is totally assimilated to an Italian setting (the Po valley) and deals with authentically Italian characters (Gino, Giovanna and Bragana). The Fascist authorities who had anticipated a harmless murder story found themselves confronted with a film that faced up to the realities of life. They reacted by attacking the director, banning the film and then releasing it in a version cut to less than half the original length. After the Liberation Visconti was able to reconstitute the film, but its commercial career was hampered by the fact that he had never owned the film rights of the novel which was filmed again in 1946 by a Hollywood company.

There is a particular appropriateness about the way in which *The Postman Always Rings Twice* had come into Visconti's hands. After the rejection of his Verga project he went through his papers and found an old and forgotten typescript of a French translation of the novel. This had been given him by Jean Renoir at the time when Visconti was working with him on *Une Partie de Campagne* as a subject which might be interesting to film. Since Visconti's return to Italy a version had in fact been made in France by Pierre Chenal and released in 1939 under the title *Le Dernier Tournant*. This direct link with France and the fact that Visconti worked there in the Thirties have led some critics to draw close parallels between *Ossessione* and Renoir's work at that time, in particular his film *Toni* (1934). There are obvious and striking similarities between Visconti's film and the French Thirties cinema in general—the sense of fatalism apparent in the defeat of two lovers united by a tragic passion, the theme of escape (typified by Gino's appearance as a tramp and by the addition of the character of the Spagnuolo) and even a few anti-clerical touches that would have delighted Jacques Prévert. With *Toni* itself, the connection is, on the surface at least, even closer. Both films are centered on a crime of passion, both depict the separation, reunion and ultimate defeat of the lovers, both contain considerable if only implicit social comment and are set in authentic surroundings while yet giving no clue to the actual date of the happenings (Renoir's film was based on a murder that took place fifteen years before). Visconti has spoken several times of his debt to Renoir in the handling of actors but in general his stylistic methods are totally different: he aims at an increased depth of character, a tighter plot line and a greater emphasis on dramatic development, and above all he makes far greater use of the possibilities of interweaving visual effect and music.

Ossessione, like all of Visconti's film work, contains a mixture of realism and formalism. The former element is particularly strong, for *Ossessione* is a film that breathes real life. The characters are living through a genuine passion which is looked at directly and honestly and portrayed without glamour. Of this aspect of the film Visconti has said: "Above all it is the intimacy of relationships between Massimo Girotti and Clara Calamai that I sought to translate with most accuracy."[21] From the opening shots of Gino's arrival at the inn and his first contact with Giovanna in the kitchen, the two are indissolubly bound together, but since she is married to the fat and gullible Bragana, their love is, from the first, tainted with deceit. Gino is repulsed by the situation of a *ménage à trois* and tries to get Giovanna to leave with him, but on the brink she hesitates and finally refuses, held back by her need for a greater security than Gino can offer. When the two meet again weeks later in Ancona, Bragana is again present, to be heard performing in the singing contest as they exchange their first private words, babbling drunkenly and repulsively about his desire for a son as they all prepare to return to the inn. The lovers kill him in a faked car crash but this act, instead of giving them their freedom, merely redoubles their need for deceit. The presence of Bragana can be felt when they return to the inn after the killing and all Giovanna's attempts to achieve normality again and make a fresh start (for example by inviting the priest to call and by hiring a band for the local fair day) are unavailing. Under the stress of events the lovers' relationship deteriorates and when they go to Ferrara to collect the insurance money, they quarrel bitterly in the street and Gino deceives Giovanna with a young whore, Anita. Already the police net is tightening and although the lovers are reunited and the baby which Giovanna is carrying seems to them both a sign of hope on which to build, fate once more intervenes in the form of a car crash in which Giovanna is killed and Gino left to face the police alone.

The course of this relationship is taken directly from the novel but given far greater depth and emphasis in the film, as the change of title indicates: where Cain is principally concerned with the ironies of fate— *The Postman Always Rings Twice*—Visconti offers a study of obsessive passion—*Ossessione.* The director has also added a quite new element in the person of the Spagnuolo, the homosexual actor-cum-salesman whom Gino meets in the train and with whom he lives and works in Ancona. The Spagnuolo's role is fully integrated into the plot—he provides a counterbalance to Giovanna and participates in the film's pattern of deceits and betrayals—but he is not handled in the same realistic manner as the other three. Whereas he is primarily a symbolic figure, they are perfectly defined in social terms. The respect that *Signor* Bragana can command, the security his money can give Giovanna, her contempt for Gino when she meets him working as a sandwich-board man, and her attempt to re-integrate herself with society after the murder—all these social elements contribute to the reactions and motivations of the characters. More remarkable still for an Italian film of this period is that no attempt is made to idealise the characters, and though Clara Calamai and Massimo Girotti who play the lovers were both popular stars of the time, there is nothing glamorous about their performances. From the very first we are aware of the sexual hunger of Giovanna and the physical repulsiveness of the fat, aging Bragana (Juan De Landa), while the homosexual inclinations of the Spagnuolo (Elio Marcuzzo) are unambiguously portrayed. Similarly all the secondary figures are realistically drawn cameos: the priest with his taste for alcohol and shooting, the pretty girl Anita drifting from chorus girl to prostitute, the sly and disagreeable policemen, the cruelly caricatured competitors in the singing contest. A further realistic element is constituted by the occasional *temps morts* when the action, which elsewhere moves forward so inexorably, is allowed to pause for a moment. Perhaps the most notable of these comes after the day of the fair when Giovanna comes into her crammed and chaotic kitchen, gets herself a bowl of lukewarm soup, sits down and tries to read the newspaper but instead falls asleep in a crumpled untidy heap. This small scene indicates one direction that neo-realism will take—the observation of everyday life—and anticipates the famous sequence of the pregnant maid getting up in *Umberto D*.

The background against which these characters are set is equally realistic, an unpicturesque provincial Italy of pubs and lorries, fair, marketplace and dockside. Only Ancona, at the moment when Gino and the Spagnuolo agree to join forces, looks at all beautiful with its church and splendid panorama. Elsewhere the landscape is bleak: the endless winding road we see behind the credit-titles and at intervals throughout the film, the sandbanks of the Po valley which offer a fitting setting for the lovers' last reunion, the bustling anonymous streets of Ancona and Ferrara. The interiors are equally authentic: the inn, its kitchen complete with fly paper over the light, the dingy hotel room shared by Gino and the Spagnuolo, or the local train on which the two first make their acquaintance. In all this Visconti is putting into practice the *Cinema* critics' theoretical concern with the problems of landscape and milieu, witnessed by an article by De Santis in 1941 in which he had maintained that the prime characteristic of the cinema "ought to be the preoccupation with an authenticity, even if it is fantastic, of gestures and atmosphere, in a word of the factors that must serve to express the totality of the world in which men live."[31] Visconti's camera style in *Ossessione*, like that of Renoir in the Thirties, constantly has the effect of linking characters and background. The film is shot almost entirely from middle distance with close-ups reserved exclusively for moments of great crisis, like the lovers' first meeting and their quarrel in Ferrara. In fact when they do occur, close-ups seem out of place in a film that for most of its length is concerned to observe the characters. The refusal to identify with Gino or Giovanna subjectively is a major difference between *Ossessione* and the original novel which, like so much American fiction of its *genre,* is told exclusively through the words and thoughts of a hero who is never seen from the outside. Like Renoir too, Visconti uses lengthy shots that link the actions of the characters and follow them in their environment. One of the longest scenes shows the police investigation after the murder of Bragana all filmed in a single take, and in this connection it is interesting to note that Visconti's editor, Mario Serandrei, has maintained that "if reels three thousand metres long had existed, he would have been capable of making a film with a single sequence."[52] The director also makes use of depth of focus and the backgrounds are always alive and important, as at the very beginning of the film when a crane shot links Gino, the lorry, the group of men by the petrol pump and the inn. Always people can be sensed pursuing their everyday activities in the background: as Gino mends the pump lorries rumble by on the highway, as Bragana boards the ferry farmers can be seen moving off in their carts, at the lovers' first separation peasants in the distance are busy with the threshing. In this way, though the motive forces of the lovers' actions are more personal than social, we are always aware of the context in which they live.

Much of the richness of *Ossessione* lies in the fact that it is not merely a slice-of-life drama but also a work of great formal complexity. Here everything has been planned to the last inch and there are none of the rough edges that a film-maker like Rossellini leaves. Mario Serandrei's account of his experience editing the film gives a clear indication of Visconti's perfectionism. "When," writes Serandrei, "I edited the first shots of *Ossessione* according to criteria I thought were determined by the shots themselves and showed this editing to Visconti on his return from Ferrara, he told me that the editing was going very well but that it would nevertheless be necessary to begin it all over again from the beginning following the criteria in accordance with which he, Visconti, had taken the shots. That meant taking up the film that had been cut, sticking together all the pieces again etc." It is a tribute to Visconti's tenacity and artistic integrity that Serandrei not only did this but has also remained his editor for nearly thirty years. For Visconti editing is, in Serandrei's words, "a *labor limae* which allows him to achieve the perfect form of the story, the one which he had already foreseen at the moment of shooting,"[52] and he has never used it as a means of changing a sequence from the preconceived pattern.

Examples of a concern with formal arrangement on Visconti's part can be found throughout *Ossessione* in the organisation of events as much as in the visual style or the use of sound. Like the novel on which it is based, the film plunges straight into the action, with the onset of a lovers' relationship that can only be resolved in death. The narrative is given its emotional pattern by the rises and falls of their love and built on elaborate series of betrayals and failures of which Giovanna and the Spagnuolo as well as Gino are guilty. This tight interconnection of events and characters is enhanced by the inner rhymes of the film, where Visconti explicitly links pairs of happenings. Thus the two car crashes occur on the same road, the friendship of Gino and the Spagnuolo begins and ends with them sitting side by side on a wall or bank, and the scene where Gino abandons Giovanna by the roadside finds an exact parallel later when the Spagnuolo angrily leaves him. Similarly, events which are only hinted at in one part of the film come to fruition later. An obvious example of this is the punch with which Gino threatens the Spagnuolo in the hotel room and which he delivers months later at their last meeting. But an even finer instance comes when the murder of Bragana is anticipated quite early in the film. The three of them—Bragana, Giovanna and Gino—are eating together in the kitchen and the tension grows unbearable when Bragana talks casually about a local murder. When he goes off with his gun to drive away a pair of cats howling outside the window, the lovers shudder, draw together and stand motionless until the shots ring out. With a sudden flash of illumination one realises that mentally they have just killed him . . .

The visual texture of the film is as rich as that of its plot and *Ossessione* is full of images that are both beautiful and meaningful. The use of the camera to link people and settings has already been mentioned, but equally significant is the positioning of characters so as to convey their inter-relationships. An early example of this occurs in the scene of Gino shaving at the inn, when a shot of his hand holding a cut-throat razor appears against a background of Bragana's bulging but terribly vulnerable naked torso. This kind of discreet symbolism occurs constantly in *Ossessione*: the first love-making of Gino and Giovanna, for instance, ends with a shot of them reflected in the mirror of the wardrobe door, which unexpectedly swings open to reveal signs of Bragana's wealth: the rows of his suits and coats. Visconti has an eye for the revealing pose—Giovanna crouching on a chair against a bare wall as she tells Gino about her life and needs—and the exact telling detail: Gino smiling happily with a seashell at his ear, listening more to its sound of waves than to her woes. In a similar way, during the sequence in Ferrara, the white swan-shaped ice-cream cart adds a note of romance to Gino's meeting with Anita (to whom he turns for escape from reality) and makes Giovanna's black mourning garb seem still more ominous. The scene of the quarrel in Ferrara is played out against the sound of a gay popular tune, and though Giuseppe Rosati's score is occasionally obtrusive in its overemphasis, there are many other instances of the inventive use of music by Visconti. This is hardly surprising in view of the fact that he studied music as a child, later went on to achieve world fame as a producer of opera, and has admitted to the opinion that "music is the noblest of all forms of art."[48] Each of the three main characters has some piece of music by which his presence can be felt even when he is in

THE ORIGINS OF NEO-REALISM

fact absent: Bragana has his aria, which he is rehearsing when Gino arrives, Giovanna the song with which she entices him into the house, and Gino the mouth organ which he can be heard playing as Bragana and Giovanna sit down to eat. The most developed use of an interaction between music and situation comes with Gino and Giovanna's meeting at the singing contest in Ancona, when Bragana sings his aria from *La Traviata*. Visconti has admitted that Verdi and the Italian melodrama were his first love and later on in his career he was to use an excerpt from *Il Trovatore* as a way of beginning his film *Senso*. Here in *Ossessione* the lovers' words of greeting and unspoken decision to kill are accompanied by Bragana singing Germont's lines: "Ma se alfin ti trovo ancor, se in me speme non falli, se la voce dell'onor in te appien non ammuti, Dio m'e sandi."

What prevents *Ossessione*, despite this intensely planned structure, from becoming a mere formal exercise is the dramatic vitality beneath the surface. Visconti admitted in 1960 that his work "almost always had a flavour of melodrama"[131] and it is this that gives force to *Ossessione*. The tensions and conflicts are always brought out clearly into the open and developed to the full. Giovanna, forced to decide between the security offered by Bragana and the love and sexual fulfillment that Gino can give her, chooses the latter even though it means committing murder. Insofar as she tries to compromise by clinging to the inn and the insurance money as well as keeping her lover, he almost loses Gino. The one possibility of a peaceful resolution—the uniting of love and security by starting a family with Gino—is offered briefly only to be snatched away almost immediately in the car crash. For Gino the dilemma is even more acute as he is torn between fulfillment with Giovanna and the fear of being tied down. He has become a tramp to avoid being caught up in society and in their first love-making Giovanna can sense the power the open road exercises over him. This conflict is by no means abstract for while Giovanna represents the call of love and family, the Spagnuolo embodies the essential male freedom, and Gino having successively achieved moments of happiness with both, betrays the two of them and himself besides. The Spagnuolo, the most complex of the characters, is clearly a key figure in the understanding of the film, and Visconti has said that through him he wanted to represent the essential elements of his work: "social problems and poetry. And whatever one may think, above all social problems. *Ossessione* was shot under a Fascist regime and at the time this character was the very symbol of revolution and freedom of thought."[21] Recalling Antonioni's words about the prestige of Carné in Italy in the Forties, we can easily find parallels to the Spagnuolo in such half-real figures as Zabel (Michel Simon) in *Quai des Brumes*, Valentin (Jules Berry) in *Le Jour se lève* or Jéricho (Pierre Renoir) in *Les Enfants du Paradis*. But the use of the Spagnuolo in *Ossessione* to convey a social message is purely Visconti's and a clear indication of the state of the times. Elsewhere in his major work the director is always careful to give an exact historical context for the conflicts of his characters, but here comment on the lovers comes through a purely negative figure who repudiates not only social hypocrisies but also the institutions of marriage, home and family. Interpreted in the light of the Spagnuolo and despite his talk in the train of solidarity and the need to help others, *Ossessione* emerges as a work totally hostile to society. For the Spagnuolo, to accept the values of society is to betray one's ideals, to become no better than Bragana, and Gino learns the truth of the incompatibility of love and society as the police hound Giovanna to her death.

Seen over twenty-five years after it was made, *Ossessione* is immediately striking in the superb technical skill it displays (it was, it must be remembered, Visconti's first film) and in the way it sets out most of the director's major stylistic and thematic concerns. It is often quoted as a forerunner of the postwar Italian cinema, as an example of neo-realism *avant la lettre*, but it is more exact to see it as the culmination of the impulses towards realism and formal perfection that can be detected throughout the Italian cinema at the end of the Fascist era. It shows the kind of realist cinema—honest, direct, technically virtuoso—that might have evolved in Italy if the events of the years 1943–45 had never happened. But it is a film made under Fascism, subject to all kinds of pressures that did not exist after the Liberation, and it lacks the burning actuality, the commitment, the preoccupation with problems seen largely in social terms that are so characteristic of neo-realism. Visconti has said that when he wants to define the true significance a film will have in his mind it is to the image that he turns. *Ossessione*, he tells us, "was born from the vision I had of a woman stretched out on the asphalt with her stockings round her ankles. This image was then to give the final scene of the film."[131] By a revealing coincidence, one of the most brilliant sequences of *Rome Open City*, the film with which the neo-realist movement proper begins, contains an almost identical image and a comparison of the two in their dramatic context is highly revealing. In both films the heroine lies on the roadway, her thighs obscenely bared in death, but whereas in *Ossessione* Giovanna is paying for a guilty passion, struck down in a car accident by an abstract retribution, in *Rome Open City* Pina dies because she has raised her voice against a specific political evil, the German tyranny, and her death is coldblooded murder of a kind calculated to turn all Italians against their erstwhile Axis partners.

Part Three

THE YEARS OF ACHIEVEMENT

When the dictatorship was overthrown, we discovered our own country. That is why the war, even if horrible in itself, was a benediction on the human level, as far as we are concerned. We could look freely around us now, and the reality appeared so extraordinary that we couldn't resist watching it and photographing it with astonished and virgin eyes.

FEDERICO FELLINI

1. The War and its Aftermath

I T IS ARGUABLE that the most important two year period in the history
of the Italian cinema is that between the showing of *Ossessione* in the
Spring of 1943 and the first presentation of *Rome Open City* in September
1945. At first sight this might seem paradoxical since no film of lasting
value was made during this time. But these years were of incalculable
significance in shaping the sensibilities of neo-realist film-makers and it is
impossible to understand the postwar cinema unless one first appreciates
the happenings of 1943–45. In view of the complexity of the circumstances
attending the Liberation of Italy, it is perhaps most appropriate to begin
by summarising these events before going on to consider their effect on
writers and directors.

When Italy entered the war in June 1940 Mussolini's position was
unchallenged in his own country and the rapid victory of the Nazi war
machine in Europe seemed assured. Indeed it was because he was "dazzled
by the mirage of a cheap triumph"[34] that the *duce* belatedly declared war
on France. But his act was a gamble from the first, since Italy was in no
position to equip and maintain an adequate fighting force. With the
obstinate resistance of the British followed by the entry of the United States
into the war and the failure of Hitler's armies in Russia, the bluff was called
and by 1942 the prospect of defeat loomed large. Under the stress of
circumstances Mussolini aged rapidly and visibly and he had little spirit
left when, in July 1943, after Sicily had been invaded and Rome bombed,
he was deposed by his own Fascist Grand Council. But his opponents
within the party had failed to appreciate that Fascism without the *duce*
was inconceivable: they found themselves without real popular support
and the initiative passed to the king who appointed not a Fascist but
Marshal Badoglio as Mussolini's successor. In the autumn of 1943 events
followed each other in swift succession: Badoglio signed an armistice with
the allies, then changed sides and declared war on Germany; allied forces
landed on the mainland of Italy; and in reply Mussolini, on his release from
captivity, set up his own Italian Social Republic (also known as the Salò
Republic) in the North.

This pattern of events left Italy in a state of utter confusion, split into
two warring factions and occupied by two foreign armies. Two separate
wars now proceeded virtually independently. There was the conventional
war, which was fought largely between the Germans and the allied invaders (both sides were hesitant to employ Italian troops whose loyalty
might be suspect and who were in any case under-equipped). Naples fell
to the allies on October 11, 1943 but progress northwards up the peninsula

was slow. It was not until June 1944 that Rome was taken and May 1945 before the final surrender took place. The progress of this war—which forms the subject matter of Rossellini's *Paisà*—was naturally of vital interest to all Italians, but there was also a second conflict into which they poured even more of their energies. In the words of Roy MacGregor-Hastie: "From September 8th (1943) until Mussolini's death in 1945, the Italians lost interest in the issues at stake in World War II and got on with the business of settling old scores and paying old political and personal debts of honour."[95] Badoglio's *coup d'état* had been no more than a palace revolution and his government soon became an irrelevance as the real battle for power was fought out behind the German lines between the supporters of Mussolini's puppet state and the partisans.

The guerilla war waged by the partisans did not decisively alter the course of the Liberation—the military historian W. G. F. Jackson in his account of *The Battle for Italy* hardly mentions it—but its psychological impact, particularly on young Italians, was enormous. The quarter of a million partisans who opposed the Germans and Fascists of the Salò Republic were men of very varied motives and backgrounds—anti-Fascists and deserters, criminals and idealists—and not surprisingly their activities ranged from acts of great heroism to outbursts of indiscriminate violence. They never really fused into a cohesive group—the Committee of National Liberation set up to co-ordinate their activities had only a shadowy command over the guerillas—and the Action Party led by Ferruccio Parri which was designed to represent their political interests and ideals had already disintegrated by 1947. There was, however, one group which stood out both by the number of participants it contributed to the struggle and by the courage and discipline with which they fought. This group was the Communist Party which emerged from the *débâcle* of Italy with an untarnished reputation and a very high esteem among artists and intellectuals. In a civil war no side can claim absolute right and to some Italians the resistance and Liberation must have seemed, as to Luigi Villari, "perhaps the most bloody and brutal 'peace-time' episode in human history."[140] But this was not the stand adopted by the creative writers and film-makers of Italy, who virtually all emerged on the side of the opposition to Fascism. The writer Italo Calvino has expressed most forcefully the importance of the partisan movement to postwar cultural life in Italy: "We had lived through the war and the younger of us—who had just been in time to serve as partisans—did not feel in the least crushed, defeated, 'burnt out,' but victorious, propelled by the impetus of the recent battle, sole trustees of its inheritance. This, however, was not easy optimism or gratuitous euphoria; on the contrary, what we felt responsible for was a sense of life as starting from scratch, a general, problematic fury and our ability to survive agony and danger; but our attitude was one of defiant gaiety."[135]

No-one was left untouched by the war and the letters and diaries of Italian writers provide an eloquent statement of the general mood in 1943–5 and supplement the less revealing accounts by Italian film-makers. The reactions were many and varied. For some, like Gaime Pintor, the war meant a new commitment: "The war has lifted men materially from their habits, it has forced them to realise with their hands and eyes the dangers which threaten the bases of all individual life, it has persuaded them that there is no possibility of salvation in neutrality and isolation. . . . Only the war has untangled the situation, sweeping away certain obstacles, removing a large number of convenient retreats and plunging me brutally into a world without precedent."[84] For Luchino Visconti, who was arrested by the Fascists two days after the Fosse Ardeatine massacre and spent some time in prison under sentence of death, the lesson was the same: "Then came the war and with it the resistance which meant for an intellectual with my background the discovery of all Italy's problems as problems of social structure as well as of cultural, spiritual or moral orientation."[55] Not all young intellectuals in Italy turned to Marxism, but the character Michele in Alberto Moravia's novel *Two Women* speaks for many of them: "Today it's the people who read and write and live in towns and are gentlefolk who are the really ignorant, the really uncultivated, the really uncivilised ones. With them there's nothing to be done, but with you peasants one can begin from the very beginning."[106]

The change is perhaps most clearly seen in writers and film-makers who had previously concerned themselves with bourgeois problems. Moravia himself, who took refuge in the mountains of Ciociara during the fighting, falls into this category. Of his own case he has said: "I had an experience which intellectuals don't usually have. I lived with peasants, ate their food, slept with them, stayed with them all day. So I conceived a great interest in the people, the people who work hard."[35] The result of this interest was the writing of two novels—*Woman of Rome* and *Two Women*—and over a hundred *Roman Tales*. Among film-makers, Cesare Zavattini shows a similar change of focus: "If the war was, for history and for the Italian conscience, a capital event influencing all forms of art it was also a capital event for each of us in particular. What was happening inside me was happening inside many others as well. If it was possible for the Italian cinema to give proof of such a complete and astonishing intimacy with the facts which each morning and evening offered themselves to us like jack-in-the-boxes opening up, then we owe this to the experience we had then."[131] Many of those who did not fight experienced agonising pangs of conscience. The novelist Cesare Pavese, for example, wrote in his diary on January 1, 1946: "You never had to fight. Remember that. You never will fight. Do you count for anything with anyone?",[113] and his commitment to the Communist party can be seen as a way of "redeeming his abstention during the war."[84] Another non-belligerent, Vittorio De Sica, shows in his postwar films a similar commitment to his fellow men and desire for truth. He has said of this period: "The experience of the war was a determining one for all of us. Everyone felt a mad desire to throw into the air all the old stories of the Italian cinema, to plant the camera in the middle of real life, in the middle of everything which struck our astonished gaze. We sought to liberate

ourselves from the weight of our faults, we wanted to look each other in
the eyes and tell the truth, discover what we really were, and seek salvation."[131]

Former supporters of the Fascist regime found their growing dissatis-
faction confirmed by the events of the war and in some cases felt a similar
link with the masses. The novelist Curzio Malaparte (later to direct an
interesting film *Il cristo proibito*) has recorded in *Kaputt* his experiences
in Naples on August 7, 1943, on his release from a Fascist prison: "I had
never felt so close to the people—I—who until then had always felt like a
stranger in Naples." When in *Kaputt* he views the Fascist society of the war
years Malaparte sees it as sick and senile: "I thought that we all had pre-
maturely aged in Italy, that the same softness, the same lassitude and bore-
dom slackened the gestures and infected the smiles and the looks of all of
us. There was nothing pure, nothing truly young any more in Italy."[96]
Renato Castellani, who considers 1944 the decisive year in which took place
for all of them "the instinctive transformation which was to lead to neo-
realism," confirms Malaparte's judgement when he defines neo-realism in
terms of a youthful revolt: "The year 1944 represented for me the explosion
of youth, although I wasn't strictly speaking a young man at the time.
Those who lived in the time of Fascism were young late, suddenly."[131]
Both Malaparte and Rossellini, the former maker of Fascist documentaries,
were fascinated by the Liberation. For Rossellini it was "an extraordinary
moment during the war when the invader arrived. We were dominated by
the Germans, the Fascists, experiencing persecutions etc. and then, one
fine day, the others arrived. Like enemies. Three days later they noticed
that we were not enemies since we were men, and their equals."[21] *Paisà*
deals largely with the complexities of the war and its aftermath, analysing
the Liberation which Malaparte characterises so bitterly in *The Skin*:
"Perhaps it was written that, just as liberation had been born of the sufferings of war and slavery, so freedom must be born of the new and terrible
sufferings caused by the plague which liberation had brought with it. The
price of freedom is high—far higher than that of slavery. And it is not paid
in gold, nor in blood, nor in the most noble sacrifices, but in cowardice, in
prostitution, in treachery and in everything that is rotten in the human
soul."[97]

The ironies and contradictions, failed dreams and all-too-present night-
mare of the struggle for Italy could not fail to engrave themselves on the
consciousness of all artists who lived through these years. But on the whole
the film-makers of Italy do not look back to analyse the causes of their
present chaos: it is enough for them to record what is there, dealing with
the Liberation only while it is part of the immediate past and then going
on to depict the prevalent poverty and injustice of postwar Italy. Their
programme has been most eloquently summed up by Alberto Lattuada:
"After the last war, especially in Italy, it was this very need for *reality*
which forced us out of the studios. It is true that our studios were partly
destroyed or occupied by refugees, but it is equally true that the decision

Roberto Rossellini's ROME OPEN CITY (1945)

The two sides—the priest (Aldo Fabrizi) and the Gestapo officers (Harry Feist and Giovanna Galetti)

The progress of Mina (Maria Michi) in ROME OPEN CITY (1945):

Top left: With her lover (Marcello Pagliero), top right: with her lesbian seducer (Giovanna Galletti), bottom left: betraying her lover, and bottom right: realizing the enormity of what she has done.

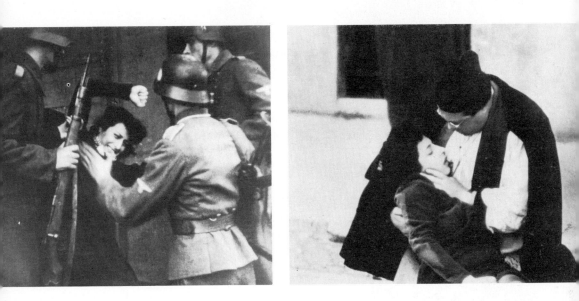

ROME OPEN CITY (1945):

Top left and right: The death of Pina (Anna Magnani)
Bottom left: The tortured Communist (Marcello Pagliero)
Bottom right: The children go down into the city after witnessing the execution
of the Priest

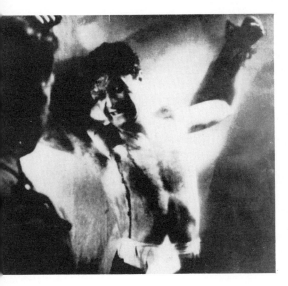

Roberto Rossellini's PAISÀ (1946)

Above and left: The Sicilian episode with Carmela Sazio and Robert Van Loon

Above and left: The Neapolitan episode with Dots M. Johnson and Alfonsino

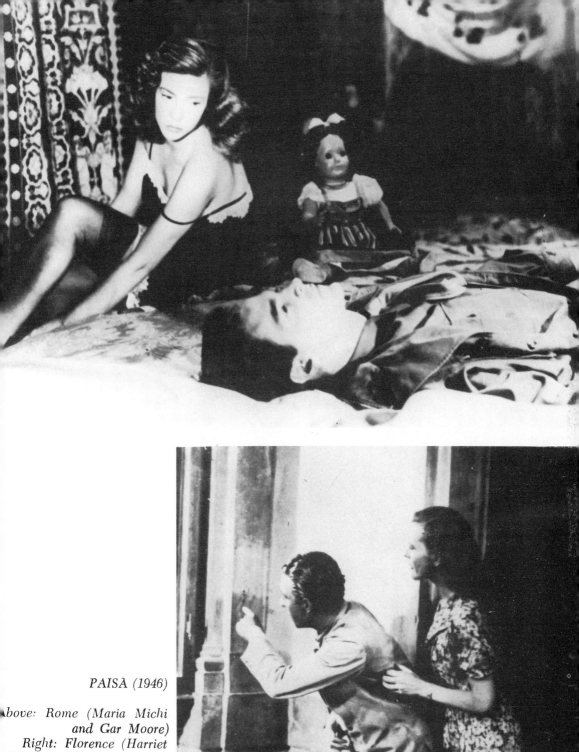

PAISÀ (1946)

*bove: Rome (Maria Michi
and Gar Moore)
Right: Florence (Harriet
White and Renzo Avanzo)*

PAISÀ (1946)

The monks

The partisans of the Po

Rossellini on location in the Po delta

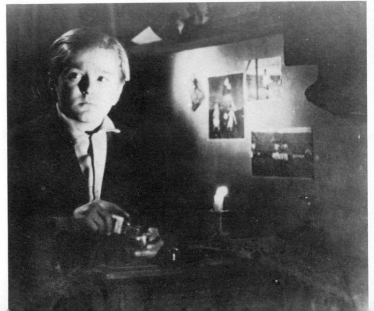

GERMANIA ANNO ZERO
(1947)

The boy (Edmund Moeschke) with his father (Werner Pittschau) (top), and his young companions (middle)

The theatrical lighting as he poisons his father (right)

Edmund's journey to death through the ruins of Berlin

to shoot everything 'on location' was above all dictated by the desire to express life in its most convincing manner and with the harshness of documentaries. The very spirit of walls corroded by time and full of the tired signs of history, took on an aesthetic consistency. The actors' costumes were those of the man in the street. Actresses became women again, for a moment. It was a poor but strong cinema, with many things to say in a hurry and in a loud voice, without hypocrisy, in a brief vacation from censorship; and it was an unprejudiced cinema, personal and not industrial, a cinema full of real faith in the language of the film, as a means of education and social progress."[55]

2. Rome Open City

ROME OPEN CITY (*Roma Città Aperta*), released in Italy towards the end of 1945, is a key film in the history of world cinema. Nothing else of any real importance was made that year in the Italian cinema so that its primacy in the neo-realist movement is unchallenged. It is a forerunner not only aesthetically, but also in a more basic and practical sense, since its success in Italy (where it was the most profitable film of the 1945–46 season) and in the United States (where it earned its distributors half a million dollars within a year) encouraged producers to finance films with contemporary subjects treated in a realistic fashion. Yet all this seemed hardly likely either when Roberto Rossellini began the film barely two months after the liberation of Rome or when it was first shown to the public. Italian critics greeted it coldly and when it was sent to the Cannes Film Festival in 1946 it won the Grand Prix but passed, according to its director, "totally unnoticed."[137] It was, however, bought by a French distributor and the chorus of praise it found in Paris was parallelled in America where James Agee, writing in *The Nation* on March 23, 1946, typified the reaction of startled critics: "Recently I saw a moving picture so much worth talking about that I am still unable to review it."[1]

By the time of the liberation of Rome, Rossellini had long since parted company with his erstwhile master Francesco De Robertis under whose aegis he had made his *début* with *La nave bianca*. Their quarrel of 1942 had in essence been about matters of aesthetic approach, but since then they had also moved apart ideologically. Whereas De Robertis had gone North to serve the film industry of the Salò Republic, the year 1944 saw Rossellini in Rome participating, as Christian Democratic representative, in the foundation of the cinema workers' branch of the Committee of National Liberation, alongside Aldo Vergano of the Action Party and the Communist Alfredo Guarini. Talking of the years which had inspired *Rome Open City*, Rossellini once said, somewhat grandiloquently: "I too have had to hide, I too have been a fugitive, I too had friends captured and killed."[15] No clearer illustration of the effect of the war years and such experiences could be gained than by a comparison of Rossellini's Fascist-inspired message of 1941 with the burning actuality of his film of 1945. A similar transformation is to be found too in the case of his principal collaborators, Sergio Amidei making the jump from films like *The Princess of Santa Cruz* and *The Son of the Red Pirate,* and Anna Magnani and Aldo Fabrizi revealing qualities scarcely hinted at in their prewar work.

The actual composition of *Rome Open City* bears out the observation of Italo Calvino to the effect that at the Liberation the Italians found themselves "face to face, on equal footing, bursting with stories for the telling; each had his own, each had lived an irregular, dramatic and adventurous life, and snatched the very words from his neighbour's mouth."[135] Rossellini was originally commissioned by a well-to-do Roman lady to make a short documentary about Don Morosini, a Roman priest shot by the Germans. Later the same woman suggested an additional short, this time about the Resistance activities of the children of Rome. Rossellini wrote a first script in collaboration with Alberto Consiglio, who had been one of the script-writers of *L'uomo della croce* in 1942. Then gradually a team was brought together and Sergio Amidei, who was to make a major contribution, joined the project. Federico Fellini, then working as a caricaturist, also became involved when Rossellini sought his help in persuading Aldo Fabrizi to play the leading part. Eventually the decision was taken to fuse the two shorts, add other material and make a feature-length film. Acquiring finance for this proved to be a major headache and at one point, when the film's private sponsors ran out of money, the director had to sell his own furniture and clothes in order to carry on. It was this aspect of the making of the film that Vittorio De Sica remembered when he came to write his memoirs:

"We came to know each other gradually. Somebody told me that Rossellini had started working again.

'A film about a priest,' they said. That was all.

Another day I saw Rossellini and Sergio Amidei, the scriptwriter, sitting on the steps of a building in the centre of Rome.

'What are you up to?' I asked.

They shook their heads sadly. 'We're looking for money. We can't go on with the film.'

'What film?' I enquired.

'The story of a priest. You know, Don Morosini, the one the Germans shot.' "[55]

The authors of *Rome Open City* drew their inspiration directly from recent events. For the role of Don Pietro they could turn to the stories of two murdered priests, Don Morosini and Don Papagallo. The character of Manfredi is said to have been inspired by one of the leading Communist figures in the Resistance, Celeste Negarville, while some of the incidents are taken from Amidei's personal experience. Aldo Fabrizi claims to have been an eye-witness of the shooting of a woman in circumstances that inspired the depiction of Pina's death in the film, and indeed he has on occasion asserted that he, not Rossellini, was the driving force behind the film.[128] This latter notion is refuted by the film's other collaborators, among them Federico Fellini, who has admitted that he himself tackled his own job as scriptwriter "in a free-and-easy, somewhat irresponsible manner" and limited himself to "a few ideas for the script."[20] A more substantial contribution was made by Sergio Amidei. It is his flat from which Manfredi escapes over the roof-tops and his own two landladies appear as themselves in the film. Knowing at first hand the life of a fugitive Amidei could draw a convincing portrait of Manfredi. Maria Michi's real life role as a contact of Amidei in the Resistance was far removed from the part of Marina she plays in the film, but Amidei tells us that on one occasion in real life, as in the film, she did phone the flat by the Piazza di Spagna at the very moment of a police raid. Rossellini himself contributed both an ideal leading lady (Anna Magnani) and, most important of all, his sense of atmosphere of the period: "*Rome Open City* is a film about fear, everyone's fear, but above all my own."[15]

As director, Rossellini was faced with enormous practical difficulties. Apart from the pressing problem of money, there was also the question of the availability of film stock. Of this latter, he has said: "When I made *Rome Open City* . . . I bought my negative from street photographers, who used 35mm negative in their Leicas. So I had one piece thirty metres long, another twenty, another fifty. I had one quality of negative for one piece, and a different quality for another." To save money and film stock all of *Rome Open City* was shot without sound or dialogue and only later dubbed by the actors, and because of the high cost of laboratory work Rossellini was unable to see the "rushes" as the work progressed. It says much for his skill and that of his director of photography, Ubaldo Arata, that all this is not more noticeable in the finished film. As far as possible, *Rome Open City* was shot on location, in the actual places where the events on which it was based occurred, and it is one of the rare films faithful to the geography of the setting. The initial sequence of Manfredi's escape was shot at Amidei's flat by the Piazza di Spagna and the scenes of Pina's apartment in a street perpendicular to the Via Casilina on which Don Pietro's church is sited.

The only studio sets in the film were the Gestapo building (a reconstruction of Kapler's notorious headquarters in the Via Tasso), Marina's flat (an enlarged version of Maria Michi's apartment) and Don Pietro's room. These were built at the tiny Via degli Avignonesi studio of Liborio Capitani which had a single stage measuring some sixty feet by twenty. Despite the many handicaps Rossellini succeeded in fusing his disparate material and combining his mixed cast of actors and non-professionals so as to give a coherent picture of the Resistance. Indeed he even used the technical limitations to advantage, achieving a unique "newsreel" quality of image which has led some critics to assert that the film was begun before the Germans left Rome and that Rossellini filmed their troop movements with a hidden camera. The director's greatest aid in his task was of course the spirit of the moment. As he himself put it: "The tragedy of war had passed. You had to avoid being a poet and everything an artist usually is, and force yourself to look around in a strictly realist fashion." Sergio Amidei was echoing these sentiments when he stressed that *Rome Open City* was shot under the impression, the power of suggestion and the influence of what they had just experienced, and in the service of the underground movement's desire to write its own page of history.[48]

Rome Open City differs from most of Rossellini's work of the Forties in its exceptionally tight construction. All the events of the film are packed into some seventy-two hours and the film concerns itself with only a small group of interrelated characters involved in varying degrees in the struggle between Italian Resistance forces and the German occupiers. The opening sequences make clear the underlying features of the period 1943–44: persecution, privation and corruption. The film begins with a police raid designed to capture a Communist leader, Giorgio Manfredi. Though he escapes this time, the net around him is steadily closing and by the end of the film he has brought others down with him. Manfredi takes refuge with his friend Francesco, a printer and fellow Communist, who is due to get married to the widow Pina next morning. The stresses of war cause quarrelling among Pina's family, particularly between her parents and her sister Lauretta, who follows a dubious career in the music hall alongside Manfredi's current mistress Marina. Unable now to appear in public, Manfredi employs the local priest, Don Pietro, to carry out the vital contacts with his fellow Resistance workers. Next morning police and troops raid the block of flats and though Manfredi escapes, Francesco is caught and loaded onto a lorry. Screaming her protest and anguish at separation from the man she is to marry, Pina rushes towards the lorry only to be brutally shot dead by the SS. But German violence merely breeds resistance and in the hills partisans attack the convoy of lorries, freeing the prisoners including Francesco. Again on the run, Manfredi and Francesco take refuge with Marina in her flat, but after the lovers have quarrelled about her drug taking, Marina passes on the details of Manfredi's whereabouts to her German lesbian friend Ingrid who works for Bergmann, the head of the Gestapo. Next morning when he goes to visit Don Pietro, Manfredi is arrested, along with the priest and an Austrian deserter whom the latter was hiding. Only Francesco escapes to carry on the struggle. Manfredi is slowly tortured to death in the Via Tasso and Don Pietro forced to witness his friend's suffering before being executed, in his case by a firing squad at dawn.

The film presents a whole range of responses to the German occupation. For all three principal figures it is a story of defeat, but despite their fate Pina, Manfredi and Don Pietro all come vividly alive as characters. In each case we see them first in a situation that typifies their whole situation and response. We first see Pina (played with splendid verve by Anna Magnani) as she heads a women's raid on a local bakery, horrified by the shop-keeper's duplicity. She faces up to the strains of living under the stress of shortages, bombing and overcrowding. She is not proud of being pregnant before her wedding but feels lucky to have Francesco. As she explains to Don Pietro: "You do things without thinking, without having the impression of doing wrong. I was so much in love, and he is so good, so strong." Despite his Communist views she wants to get married in church: "Francesco didn't want to, but I told him: it's better with Don Pietro, who is at least one of us, rather than go to the town hall and be married by a Fascist." She does not pass judgement on those around her—for her, her sister Lauretta is not wicked, just stupid—but the Fascists drive her to helpless fury. Her strength comes from her belief in God and her love for Francesco, and when he is taken from her, her grief and anguish know no bounds. She rushes blindly through the lines of troops to rejoin him only to be coldly shot down by machine gun. Her revolt against the circumstances of the time has never reached a conscious, constructive level, but her death—beautifully and economically handled by Rossellini—is one of the film's most powerful moments.

Giorgio Manfredi (played by film-director Marcello Pagliero) is a Communist Resistance leader. As the Fascists discover, his real identity is Luigi Ferraris, born at Turin October 3, 1906, arrested in Bologna February 4, 1928, and sentenced to twelve years imprisonment for conspiracy against the state. Since his escape from prison he has been a wanted man and the police raid on his flat with which the film opens must be one of the many he has experienced. But now his time is running out and unwittingly he brings death to those who help him, sparking off the Fascist raid in which Pina is killed and leading the Germans to Don Pietro. His love affair with Marina began as so many others must have done at the time: "I had just arrived in Rome. She used to eat in a little restaurant near the Piazza di Spagna. One day there was an air raid, everybody rushed off. We were the only ones left. She was laughing, she wasn't afraid." But now, four months later, the relationship has turned sour. He is revolted by her life of prostitution and drug-taking and he has resolved to leave her. Her bitterness at his treatment of her provokes her to betray him: "If you had really loved me, you would have changed me. But no, you're like all the others . . . worse even, because at least they didn't preach to me." Manfredi pays with his life at the Gestapo headquarters after a long session of torture (with instruments including a blow-lamp) which Rossellini has filmed with brutal directness. Manfredi does not indulge in false heroics but he knows exactly why he is fighting and dies without revealing the information the Germans need. As he tells the Austrian deserter captured with him: "We are not heroes. But they won't learn anything, I can assure you."

The real focus of Rome Open City is Don Pietro, played with exceptional restraint and insight by Aldo Fabrizi. Summoned by Manfredi he does not hesitate to run the risks involved in delivering money to a messenger from the partisan group in the mountains. Respected even by those like Francesco and Manfredi who do not share his religious faith, Don Pietro unobtrusively follows his own conscience: "It is my duty to give help to those who need it." He offers refuge to Manfredi and an Austrian deserter alike, and it comes as no surprise after Pina's death that it is he who cares for her son Marcello. Yet despite his evident courage he is not portrayed as an obvious hero figure and, unlike the innumerable "leader" types of Fascist-inspired films of the Thirties, he is a humble man. Our first sight of him is as he ineffectually plays football with the little boys, and his actions are for much of the film viewed in an amused, humorous way. Examples of this are the scenes in the antique shop—where he becomes embarrassed on seeing statuettes of a saint and a naked Venus facing each other—and at the police raid on the block of flats, when he has to knock out Marcello's grandfather with a frying pan to prevent the old man from revealing the presence of a machine-gun in his bed. His dislike of the Fascists is deep and sincere but he feels that the Italians are, to some extent at least, to be held responsible for their fate. As he explains to Pina: "Many ask me that question, Pina, doesn't Christ see us? But are we sure we don't deserve this scourge? Are we sure of having always lived according to His laws?" Confronted with the certainty of death he behaves with a new dignity: "I am a Catholic priest and I believe that whoever fights for justice and liberty is following in the ways of our Lord. And the ways of our Lord are infinite." Subjected to the horrifying ordeal of having to watch the torture of Manfredi, he finds comfort in prayer and when his own death finally comes, he meets it calmly: "It is not difficult to die well. It is difficult to live well."

Among those left alive at the end of the film, the two actresses Lauretta and Marina exemplify the corrupting effect of the German occupation. Lauretta, cutting herself off from her family, drifts into drinking and casual prostitution. Marina's case is graver: corrupted by her Lesbian relationship with Ingrid, she betrays her lover to the Germans—in exchange for drugs which will make her even more dependent on her "benefactor" and for a fur coat which is promptly taken away from her again. At the end she witnesses the outcome of her treachery and faints at the sight of the bloody, tortured body of Manfredi, but it is doubtful whether she still possesses the will to resist. Francesco, on the other hand, is by the end of the film a man who, having lost a wife and a friend, will fight on implacably. In the tender and beautifully realised scene between him and Pina on the stairs, after he has come home from work at the clandestine press on which *L'unità* is printed, he expresses all his faith in the future: "Spring will come back too, and it will be more beautiful than the others. You have to believe it, want it . . . I believe the thing is this . . . that we must not be afraid, not today nor later, because we are right, because we are on the right path. . . . We are fighting for something that must come, that cannot fail to come. The way will perhaps be a bit long and difficult, but we shall succeed and we shall see it, this better world; and above all our children will see it." The gang of boys led by the one-legged Romolo provides a semi-humorous parallel to the activities of the adults. They show at first little insight into the realities of the situation, Romolo wanting to machine-gun the Germans from a roof-top in broad daylight and Marcello saying to Don Pietro:

"You're a priest, you cannot understand. But we must form a compact block against the common enemy." Led by Romolo they venture out after the curfew to blow up German installations, only to revert to being little boys again when they have to face their irate parents. But at the very end, when they go back down into the city after witnessing the execution of Don Pietro, one can assume their political education to be complete.

Rossellini has frequently said that he does not allow himself to pass judgement on his characters, but here in *Rome Open City* there is no doubt about where his sympathies lie, for the Germans are depicted as vicious, drunken and sexually aberrant. Bergmann, the head of the Gestapo, is allowed an intellectual insight into the problems confronting him. He can point out to Don Pietro that he and Manfredi are not natural allies: "He is a subversive, a man who has fought with the Communists in Spain, who has dedicated his life to fighting society, religion . . . an atheist, one of your enemies." And similarly he can predict to Manfredi the eventual division of the forces at present united in the Resistance: "You are a Communist, your party has signed a pact of alliance with reactionary forces. Now you are marching together against us, but tomorrow when Rome is occupied, 'liberated' as you say, will they still be your allies, these monarchist senior officers?" But Bergmann is unable even to begin to appreciate the motives behind the Italian opposition, for he is trapped within a totally false conception of racial inequality: "If he [Manfredi] were not to talk, that would mean that an Italian is the equal of a German. That would mean there is no difference between the blood of a slave race and the blood of a master race." His total lack of human feeling is shared by his aide, the Lesbian Ingrid, who uses her power over Marina to bring about the betrayal of Manfredi, then coldly discards her. But the Germans' epitaph is provided by Hartmann, an officer who drinks in a vain attempt to keep himself from thinking and whose task it is to complete the bungled execution of Don Pietro. To Bergmann he explains the failure of the master race: "We have covered Europe with corpses. And from these tombs hate is inexorably born, hate, everywhere hate! We shall be destroyed by hate. Hopelessly!"

We have considered *Rome Open City* here principally in terms of characters because one of the film's major achievements is its creation of coherent and totally credible human beings. It differs from Rossellini's later work in the emphasis it places on this aspect and in the rigorous planning of its structure. Despite its newsreel surface, it is a film with a strong storyline building up to a number of varied climaxes. These latter are partly images of the Resistance, captured in documentary style—the raid on the two flats, the riot at the bakery, the partisan attack on the convoy or the execution of Don Pietro—and partly scenes of interaction of a more conventional kind— the quarrel over Lauretta at her parents' home, the lovers' row in Marina's flat. Despite the fragmentary method of many of its scenes, the plot element in *Rome Open City* is stronger than in any subsequent Rossellini film before *Il Generale della Rovere*. The characters' interrelationships are exactly expressed and make an unbroken chain: Manfredi seeks refuge with Francesco, who is about to be married by Don Pietro to Pina, whose sister Lauretta works in the same theatre as Manfredi's mistress Marina, whose friend Ingrid is one of Bergmann's aides. Similarly, though the film is remarkable for the authenticity of its settings, much of its action takes the form of verbal exchanges relying heavily on the quality of the dialogue. The characters gather to quarrel or confront each other on several occasions —at Pina's home, in Marina's flat and at the Gestapo headquarters—and in these key scenes the whole meaning of the film is explicitly set out.

It is a measure of the quality of *Rome Open City* that it can present so sympathetically the view-points of its two very different heroes, the Catholic and the Communist. The density of its texture is reinforced by the synthesis of varying tones, ranging from the brutally direct (the death of Pina and the torture sequences) to the almost whimsically humorous (the handling of Don Pietro and the children). Above all its characters are not merely figures caught up in the Resistance and representing varying shades of political reaction, but at the same time human beings with personal problems. In one sense indeed it would be perfectly valid to view the film as a study of the success and failure of love. Rossellini has on occasion defined neo-realism in terms of the Christian concept of love for one's neighbour and *Rome Open City* is a perfect illustration of this. The Germans are totally condemned, since their assumption of innate superiority makes them incapable of love. Don Pietro, on the other hand, emerges as the true victor —even in death—for his whole life is based on the service of others. Marina and Manfredi become involved in their story of betrayal and torture as a direct result of the failure of their love, which leaves Marina vulnerable to Ingrid's insidious machinations. Pina's love for Francesco cannot save her life, but the affection of her small son does save her lover. Francesco stays behind to talk to Marcello while Don Pietro, Manfredi and the Austrian leave. By giving him his mother's scarf, as a present, Marcello delays Francesco long enough for the latter to avoid the police ambush.

On all kinds of levels *Rome Open City* sets the pattern for the subsequent development of the neo-realist movement: in its techniques of location shooting and post-synchronisation of dialogue; in being financed largely from outside the film industry and making its profits abroad; in its closeness to life as it is lived; in its use of children; in the discovery of Anna Magnani and Aldo Fabrizi and the accommodation of them to new kinds of roles; and in its overall pattern of a story of defeat ending with a sense of the problems being not fully resolved. Thanks to Rossellini's permeability to events and the film's tone of a chronicle told as if it were happening at the very moment of shooting, it achieves a notable double focus on the German Occupation and on its immediate aftermath. On the one hand it is as vivid a portrait as one can imagine of 1943–44, a period characterised by hunger (Pina), persecution (Manfredi), self-sacrifice (Don Pietro), corruption (Marina) and the will to continue the struggle (Francesco). On the other it captures the note of hope with which the year 1945 ended. With its possibly idealised picture of Communist and Catholic working in total unison (visually the tortured Manfredi has distinct similarities with the crucified Christ), it stands witness to the beliefs of the months immediately following the Liberation when all men of good conscience felt united in one cause. As this initial unity slowly disintegrated so the neo-realist movement was extinguished as a unified entity, but *Rome Open City* itself remains as the first powerful manifestation of true freedom in the Italian cinema after the long dark years of Fascism.

3. Paisà

ROSSELLINI'S SECOND POST-WAR FILM is of wider scope than *Rome Open City*, covering the period from July 1943 until the end of 1944 and extending over the whole length of Italy from the Sicilian beaches to the marshlands of the Po delta. *Paisà* is less a conventional war film than an attempt to capture the extraordinary atmosphere of the Liberation in terms of the confrontation of Italians and Americans. As Rossellini himself put it: "In *Paisà* there were two worlds which came into contact, each with a different psychology and mental structure. From this contact was born a great confusion; so much so that in the end there were neither victors nor vanquished, there remained only the everyday heroism of the man who clings to life. And who lives, despite everything, whether he is one of the victors or one of the vanquished."[131] The extraordinary excitement aroused by this film is perhaps best captured in the words of Federico Fellini, who worked on the film as assistant director and co-scriptwriter: "With *Paisà* I went all over Italy with Rossellini, because as you know the action of the film stretches right from Sicily to the Po, and it was a very exciting discovery, because the war had just ended, and we were surrounded by a whole new race of people, who seemed to be drawing hope from the very hopelessness of their situation. There were ruins, trees, scenes of disaster and loss, and everywhere a wild spirit of reconstruction. In the midst of which we did our tour. The troupe of people working on *Paisà* travelled through an Italy they scarcely knew, because for twenty years we'd been in the grip of a political regime which had literally blindfolded us. . . . Living in amongst this mass of new impressions, which were so extraordinarily rich in suggestive power, was like filling my lungs with oxygen."[20]

For Fellini himself *Paisà* was an important experience in that working with Rossellini taught him that the cinema was the means of expression best adapted to his natural disposition but, as he is scrupulous to point out, his own contribution to the film was comparatively small. Sergio Amidei played a bigger part in the writing and Rossellini himself "had very precise ideas, he knew exactly what he wanted."[21] The director's relationship with Fellini was friendly but the film was essentially his own. To quote Fellini further: "We were like two friends chatting and exchanging their opinions:

perhaps I occasionally drew his attention to certain situations or orientated him in a certain direction, but nothing more."[21] Rossellini has given his own account of his working methods: "In *Paisà*, to choose my actors, I began by installing myself with my cameraman in the middle of the place where I hoped to shoot some episode or other of my story. Passers-by gathered around me and I chose my actors in the crowd."[45] Working in this way Rossellini was able to give his film a wealth of fresh and expressive faces, for even those Americans in the cast who claimed to be genuine actors turned out not to be so. As Rossellini has explained: "*Paisà* then is a film without actors in the true sense of the word. The American Negro claimed to have played some supporting roles but I realised that in reality he had lied to me to get a job. All the monks in the monastery scene were real, as were the Protestant and Jewish chaplains with whom they converse. It is the same with the peasants of the marshes around Ravenna who speak in the dialect of the region, just as the Sicilians at the beginning spoke their dialect. The English officers are as authentic as the German soldiers whom I chose from among the prisoners."[45] Thanks to this reliance on real locations and authentic faces Rossellini was able to give each of the six quite separate episodes that go to make up *Paisà* its own mood and tone.

The Sicilian episode begins with the landing of a party of American soldiers—part of the first invasion of the European continent by allied forces —but Rossellini gives no hint of the significance of this operation. Faithful to his ideal of de-dramatisation he shows us only a dozen or so G.I.s, a couple of explosions and a burning house. There is equally no attempt to create real tension or depict genuine heroics. Virtually the whole episode is filmed in medium or long shot and in semi-darkness, so that one has a stronger sense of being an observer than identifying with the action. The Germans and Americans never come properly face to face, though a few shots are fired and one G.I. is killed. Instead, the episode traces the effects of contact with the Americans on Sicilians. Entering the first village, the troops find not the enemy but only local villagers and are in fact taken for Germans by a Fascist villager, who proclaims his certainty that the Americans would never dare to land in Sicily. Subsequently the film concentrates on the relationship of Carmela, a sullen Italian girl who leads them through a mine field, and the G.I. left to guard her. Thrown together for a couple of hours they try to make contact. The American recites all the Italian words he knows—paisan, spaghetti, bambini, Mussolini and so on—and shows photographs of his family. But this attempt at friendship proves disastrous: flicking on his lighter, he draws fire from a German patrol and is killed. He has, however, aroused some spark in the girl who tries to avenge his death only to be killed herself at the hands of the Germans. The returning Americans find only their comrade's body and curse her as a "dirty little eyetie." This Sicilian episode demonstrates the perplexities of the position of Italians caught between the two sides and has a bitter irony in its ending, but as a comment on war it is distinctly limited, going no further than to affirm that the opposing armies are virtually the same: hardly distinguishable in their uniforms and filled with an identical longing for home.

The second episode moves to the Italian mainland to show the state of Naples as it is left in the wake of the invading armies. The situation is one of those recorded by Curzio Malaparte in his novel, *The Skin:* "The dream of all the poor people of Naples, especially the street-arabs and the boys, was to be able to hire a 'black,' if only for a few hours. Hunting Negro soldiers was the favourite sport of the boys. . . . Fifty dollars was the maximum price that was paid for the hire of a Negro for a day, that is for a few hours —the time needed to make him drunk, to strip him of everything he had on, from his cap to his shoes, and then, after nightfall, to abandon him naked on the pavement of an alley. The Negro suspects nothing. He is not conscious of being bought and resold every quarter of an hour, and he walks about innocently and happily. . . ."[97] Rossellini's subject-matter is identical with that of Malaparte and the contrast of their approaches is most instructive, for nothing could be further from *Paisà* than the sensationalised and overwritten prose of *The Skin.* In Rossellini's film the little Neapolitan boy acquires his Negro dishonestly—shouting "police!" to cause a panic instead of paying the 3,000 lire demanded—but thereafter he is drawn into a kind of friendship with his intended victim, who pours out his drunken dreams and troubles to him. He even goes so far as to warn the Negro that if he falls asleep his boots will be stolen, but to no avail. The equivocal position of the Negro is stressed throughout: the puppet play to which the boy takes him features a Moorish knight in the traditional role of the black man as villain (thus provoking the Negro to intervene), and he himself is conscious of no desire to go back to his real home, a miserable shack. Here in Naples, however, he is a man to respect, as the boy discovers when he is caught stealing from an army lorry. The Negro military policeman demands to be taken to see the boy's parents and to have his boots returned, but then finds that the boy is a war orphan living with hundreds of others in total squalour in the caves outside Naples. There is again a bitter irony here, when the boy's petty crime is weighed against the monstrous suffering caused by the war, but in general the tone is more light-hearted with the crowd scenes splendidly handled.

The Roman story that forms the third episode of *Paisà* also has its parallel in Malaparte and can almost be seen as an illustration of this bitter comment from *The Skin:* "It was enough that an allied soldier should lean out of his jeep to smile at a woman, to give her face a fleeting caress, and the same woman, who until that moment had preserved her dignity and purity, would change into a prostitute."[97] It is the most contrived of all the episodes of *Paisà*, with its remove from true neo-realist practice symbolised by the use of a flashback as an essential of narrative structure. The story is simple: a drunken soldier, Fred, is picked up by a prostitute to whom he pours out his feelings for a girl called Francesca whom he met the day his tank entered Rome to liberate the city. The prostitute is in fact that same girl and, leaving him Francesca's address, she goes off to wait for him, hoping to make a new life for herself. But next morning Fred merely screws up the paper—just some whore's address. In the Neapolitan episode some of the best scenes had been the incidental ones—as when the boy plays his mouth organ in Pied Piper fashion to lead the Negro across the empty city to a deserted ruin where he can be robbed. Here in the Roman episode the bar scenes of a corrupt, drunken mass of soldiers and whores have a real authenticity and Maria Michi (who played the corrupted Marina in *Rome Open City*) gives a fine performance as the prostitute going through the mechanical actions of her trade. Elsewhere the use of coincidence and over-simplification is shown up by Rossellini's dead-pan, semi-documentary style.

In the fourth episode, set in Florence, the tone changes once more as the focus is turned on to another kind of bitterness: the civil war between Italian Fascists and partisans. Unlike the earlier episodes this one does not deal primarily with a personal encounter: the American nurse Harriet makes her way through battle-torn Florence to meet Guido Lombardi, a painter she used to know, who is now Lupo, leader of the partisans. But before she can reach him she learns from a wounded partisan that he has been killed. Where previous episodes had shown strangers thrown together by war, in Florence we see the obverse: war's separation of those who love each other. Again we see an American and an Italian side-by-side for Harriet makes her journey in the company of a wounded ex-partisan, Massimo, but there is no real contact between them. He is as exclusively concerned for the safety of his family as she is for that of Lupo and in the end he dashes off without so much as a word of farewell. The pair's attempt to reach the San Jacopino district held by the partisans takes them through the deserted Uffizi palace, across empty squares and over roof-tops and walls. They meet those involved in the fighting and those who stand idly by. The partisans are depicted as brave and well-organised but there is no attempt to hide the brutality of the conflict. We see two Fascists dragged from a house and summarily executed by ruthless partisans indifferent to their screams for mercy. This episode, harsher than any that had preceded it, captures excellently the surface detail of confused street fighting and has an air of great authenticity. Here too, for the first time, the war is seen as a specifically Italian concern and Harriet's role as an outsider unable to influence events reflects the situation of the allied armies prevented by lack of reinforcements from crossing the river to aid the hard-pressed partisans.

In the Florentine episode Harriet and Massimo come across isolated pockets of calm, such as the two English officers studying the architecture of the city when they should be watching for enemy troop movements. The fifth episode of *Paisà* takes place in a bigger haven of peace, a remote monastery in the Apennines. Fellini played a large part in the scripting of this story and records that the original idea was a simple contrast of two types of religion: the active faith of the army chaplains and the purely meditative faith and life, filled only with prayers, of the monks. The episode emerged as much richer than this, though the plot line is quite simple. A trio of army chaplains call at a remote monastery to ask if they may stay the night. They throw the simple monks into some confusion with their army uniforms, cans of food and gifts of candy but initially all goes well— even the monks' prayers for food seem answered when a peasant brings a chicken as an offering. Then consternation reigns when the monks discover that one of the chaplains is a Lutheran and another a Jew. They cannot understand how the Catholic chaplain can have lived with them for twenty-one months without even attempting to convert them to the "true" faith. When at supper they fast and pray in the hope of saving the two "lost souls" under their roof, the Catholic priest, speaking for his colleagues as well as himself, expresses his deep emotion and acknowledges that he has received a lesson in humility, simplicity and pure faith. In this episode more than any other much of the impact comes from the personalities of the actors themselves, the monks whose artlessness sets the tone of the story, and Rossellini uses an unusual number of close-ups, no doubt aware of the power of these faces. In the loving care and gentle humour with which this episode is handled one can see the roots of both Rossellini's investigation into sainthood in *Francesco, giullare di Dio* and Fellini's concern with the "holy fool" in *La strada.*

While the roots of the monastery episode lie partly in Fellini's own childhood upbringing in Catholic boarding schools, the last and perhaps most powerful episode of *Paisà* gains richness from Rossellini's early years spent near the Po valley where his mother was born and where he used to go hunting and fishing. There is nothing tender or nostalgic about this episode, however, for the source of the story was the image with which it opens: "For the last episode of *Paisà*," Rossellini has said, "I had in my mind those corpses which passed slowly down the Po with a notice round their necks bearing the inscription 'partisan.' The river brought down these corpses for months. You could easily see several on the same day."[15] The partisans in this episode are in a perilous position. They are able to fish out and give decent burial to a dead partisan sent floating down the river but they lack food and ammunition and an attempt to drop supplies to them fails. They are completely surrounded by Germans but can expect no help from outside, for General Alexander's orders are to cease all operations. The reeds and marshlands are bleak and inhospitable but a visit to a friendly farm house merely provokes savage reprisal from the Germans who shoot all the adult inhabitants, leaving a child to cry alone among the corpses. The group is a polyglot assortment—British airmen and American O.S.S. men, soldiers from San Marco and Popsky's army as well as partisans—and the Germans make short work of their resistance. Next morning the captive allied officers have to watch as one by one the partisans, their hands tied behind their backs, are pushed into the water. The protests of the O.S.S. man Dale are unavailing: the Germans coldly shoot him down as he begins to shout. The savage pointlessness of these executions is borne out by a commentary that reminds us that four months later peace came to Italy with the German surrender. The Po episode—like the Sicilian one—is filmed almost entirely in long and medium shot (the few close-ups seem an intrusion)—and is

Rossellini's finest attempt at capturing the atmosphere of war. Again, as throughout the film, the confusion and senseless destruction brought by war is condemned and there is a bitter irony in the execution by drowning of the partisans who had lived on the water, rescued shotdown pilots and, at the beginning, fished a partisan corpse from the river.

With *Paisà* Rossellini made a most noteworthy contribution to the neo-realist movement. The film derives much of its force from its analysis of war and its aftermath, but it is important to define precisely the context in which these events are viewed. Though the allied invasion forms the back-cloth for all the stories there is no epic sweep of victory, indeed all the individual stories end in defeat of some kind—death or horror, corruption or incomprehension. Moreover the war is scaled down to a purely personal level and even in the Sicilian episode there is none of the might of naval power or rhetoric of warships at sea that had typified *La nave bianca*. The characters are not heroes or leaders but ordinary people whose involvement in war will, if they survive, be no more than an isolated episode in their lives. We get their dreams but none of the ideological conflict behind the combat of American and German, partisan and Fascist. The Florentine execution of two Fascists is shown with the same calm matter-of-factness as the murder of the partisans on the Po and is designed to arouse much the same emotions in the audience. The only episode in which a real clash of ideas occurs is the monastery sequence but even here the true issues are glossed over somewhat by the mood of gentle humour and the engaging simplicity of the monks. This reaction to events is the product of a conscious belief on the director's part: "I always try to remain impassive. I think that what is astonishing, extraordinary and moving in men is precisely that the great gestures or facts are produced in the same fashion, with the same stir, as the normal little acts of life; it is with the same humility that I try to transcribe both: there is a source of dramatic interest to be found there."[21]

The core of *Paisà* is formed by the personal interaction of the characters. The film is about the contact—often the initial meeting—of people from differing backgrounds, and in particular the impact of Americans on the Italian people (the title derives from the G.I.'s half-contemptuous slang term for an Italian). It is a film in which the use of actors from several countries speaking several languages is crucial, for the linguistic barrier limits the individual attempts at communication. The first episode sets the pattern when Joe's inability to talk about his family makes him show his photographs and so leads to his death. Only the sight of the caves outside Naples can make the Negro M.P. understand the little boy in the second episode, and the monks, lacking such concrete evidence, will never understand their guests. The tragedy of Fred and Francesca too is a failure of communication: instead of talking honestly to Fred the girl tries to "cheat," relying on a bit of paper that is simply torn up. It is hardly by chance that corruption in *Paisà* takes the form of a grotesque parody of intimacy: Francesca is a whore seducing men with meaningless words of affection and the

Neapolitan boy is a petty thief, stealing from a man who thinks of him as a friend. Communication is difficult, often nearly impossible, but the worst atrocities occur when the possibilities of dialogue are denied, as when the partisans and the Germans execute their captives without trial or explanation. Part of the failure to communicate derives from the characters' inability to come to terms with their own dreams: the G.I.'s nostalgia for home, the Negro's dream of glory, Francesca's longing for purity. Only the monks have a total serenity and this derives from their isolation from the world. Those in the forefront of the battle have no illusions and no hopes. Early on in the last episode one of the Americans remarks: "We'll all die some way or another" and subsequently the march to death has a grim inevitability.

There is little attempt in *Paisà* to link closely the six episodes which, taken together however, give a kaleidoscope of incident—invasion, partisan activity, reprisals, corruption and basic mutual incomprehension—and cover a wide range of mood from warm humour to bitter pessimism. The narrative patterns of the various episodes are quite simple, only the Roman story using a flashback, but we are never given a purely documentary slice-of-life even if shaping is minimal. The majority of episodes use a simple sequence of events in chronological order, shot with the utmost visual restraint and with music added to provide an often unnecessary emotional reinforcement. But as in a conventional short story there is usually a turning point—the shooting of the G.I. or the discovery that one chaplain is a Jew—that leads logically to an unforeseen ending in which irony predominates. Rossellini's success with this sextet of stories derives from an evasion, not a resolution, of the needs of the ninety-minute feature film which the artless contrivances and coincidences of *Paisà* would be too weak to support. The use of an episodic structure in film can give a panoramic wealth of detail but like the use of the short story in literature it can conceal a certain vagueness of thought on wider issues. Certainly *Paisà* is not particularly profound in its handling of abstract concepts and if it has a message about war it is that all soldiers are alike and that all civilians caught up in the battle suffer— a generalisation that is no more than a half truth. To compensate for any conceptual weakness, *Paisà* shows the full effectiveness of Rossellini's stylistic method: his ability to catch a seeming spontaneity, his uninhibited handling of locations, crowds and non-actors, and his sensitive reproduction of widely differing moods and atmospheres.

4. Germania Anno Zero

WHILE HE WAS IN PARIS in 1947 Rossellini decided on what he called "the third panel of the triptych on war."[21] With the authorisation of the French Government and the backing of a French production company, the Union Générale Cinématographique, he set out in March for Berlin, "not to shoot but to pay a visit and bring back the idea for a scenario."[21] The basic feeling about Germany out of which the film grew is recorded in *Cahiers du Cinéma*: "The Germans were human beings like the rest; what could have brought them to this disaster? The false morality which is the very essence of Nazism, the abandonment of humility in favour of the cult of heroism, the exaltation of forces rather than of weakness, pride against simplicity?"[21] This theme which Rossellini evolved was in many ways similar to that of *Paisà* "with the difference that this time a move to the enemy camp had been made so that observations could be carried out there and an attempt made to discover the real reasons which had driven them to act as they had done. Thus gradually there emerged from the film the problem of an erroneous education."[131] For this reason Rossellini chose as his protagonist a child, "an innocent being whom the distortion of a utopian education leads to perpetrate a crime while he believes himself to be carrying out an heroic act. But the little flame of morality is not extinguished in him: he commits suicide to escape this malaise and contradiction."[21] There is a personal note too: *Germania anno zero* is dedicated to the memory of Rossellini's son Romolo (just as De Sica later dedicated *Umberto D* to his own father).

Rome Open City began with a panoramic shot of the Italian capital, and in similar fashion *Germania anno zero* opens with a general view of Berlin. From the start there are many details serving to establish the atmosphere of the postwar period: the dead horse being cut up in the street, the queues, the bartering, the shortages and above all the desolation. The opening section of the film traces the environment in which the boy Edmund grows up. His family lives in an apartment house with five other families who collectively represent a broad cross-section of the population: the profiteering, continually moaning landlord, who cheats and bullies his way through life, a pregnant woman whose husband is in a prisoner-of-war camp, a returned refugee, a girl on the brink of prostitution, as well as Edmund's own family. Outside home the young people with whom the boy mixes are also symptomatic of the time, like the children of De Sica's *Sciuscià*. Rossellini sees the German situation as presenting a close parallel to the Italian one with the children as both wage-earners sometimes supporting a whole family and victims of the all-pervading corruption. For all their enterprise and independence, they are shaped by the blackmarket indulged in by the adults around them, by the prostitution into which circumstances push their sisters and by the petty thievery which is often the only way they can make money.

Edmund himself lives with his father, brother and sister and together these three represent, as it were, the whole history of German response to Nazism. The father—bed-ridden (with a weak heart), querulous, self-pity-ing—embodies the attitudes of the older generation. He has been, he feels, a good German: he fought in the First World War, lost his fortune in the depression, risked his son in the war. Though he contrived to keep Edmund

The study of the Resistance:
Vittorio Duse and Lea Padovani as the lovers (top) and Carlo Lizzani (bottom)
as the priest in Aldo Vergano's IL SOLE SORGE ANCORA (1946)

Massimo Serato as the Gestapo officer responsible for the sub-Wagnerian histrionics of the midnight execution in Aldo Vergano's IL SOLE SORGE ANCORA (1946)

Right: Giuseppe De Santis

Below, top: The director's characteristic cross-cutting for dramatic confrontation: Below, bottom: Massimo Girotti and Vivi Gioi in CACCIA TRAGICA (1947)

Focal points of Giuseppe De Santis's CACCIA TRAGICA (1947)

The ambush

The exploitation of the peasants

The people's trial

The earthiness of De Santis's character-drawing in CACCIA TRAGICA (1947): Vivi Gioi with Carla del Poggio and Andrea Checchi

Right: Alberto Lattuada

The drama of the ex-prisoner's return:
Below: Amideo Nazzari, Anna Magnani and
Carlo Campanini in IL BANDITO (1946)

Sensuality, corruption and solitude:
Carla del Poggio in Alberto
Lattuada's SENZA PIETÀ
(1948)

Lattuada's concern with problematic relationships:
John Kitzmiller, Pierre Claudè and Carla del Poggio in SENZA PIETÀ (1948)

out of the Hitler Youth, he could not save his elder son, Karl-Heinz, from
the poison of Nazism and all his life he has been too weak to really resist
or shape events, his impotence now symbolised by his sickness. Karl-Heinz
represents the succeeding generation, the one which grew up under Hitler's
rule, believed the propaganda and is now left to face the consequences.
Having suffered on the Eastern front, he fought until the very last in the
streets of Berlin and now hides tormented and unregistered in his room,
unable to come to terms with himself and a further burden on his family.
The daughter Eva is the one faced with the problems of survival and the
need to hold the family together. Every evening she has to go and drink
with allied soldiers in order to obtain a few cigarettes which can be bartered
for food. Naturally this existence is precarious and she is surrounded by
inducements to become a whore, but, protected by her natural virtue and
the thought of her *fiancé*, she is the foundation on which the future will
be built.

These circumstances—the need to find work instead of attending school,
the constant quarrelling and bitterness in the house, the whining self-pity
of the old man, and the general air of dishonesty—all have their effect on
the thirteen-year-old Edmund but on their own they would not have driven
him to murder and suicide. The tragedy arises only when he becomes
influenced from outside, when he turns to his former schoolmaster for
help. Herr Henning, who has been dismissed from his job because of his
unrepentant Nazi views and now makes a shady living, has been chosen
by Rossellini to serve as an example of the treacherous Nazi philosophy
that defeat in war alone cannot eradicate. As in *Rome Open City* the evil
of Nazism is equated with or at least symbolised by moral degeneracy. In
the earlier film Ingrid, the Gestapo chief's aide, was a Lesbian and in
Germania anno zero the schoolmaster is a pederast whose interest in Edmund's welfare has from the first homosexual overtones. The boy seems unaware of the implications of his mentor's gestures—the gentle stroking of his
neck as they talk in the street or the virtual embrace when they go back to
the schoolmaster's room—but the influence is nonetheless baleful. Despite his
stated eagerness to help at their first encounter, all the man does is to get
Edmund to sell a record of Hitler's speeches and then takes 190 of the 200
marks it fetches (in this he is like the landlord who gives Edmund a pair
of scales to sell and then accuses him of stealing). The schoolmaster also
introduces Edmund to the older children, Jo and Christel, whose example
can only be pernicious, for Jo is already an accomplished thief and Christel
displays in her posturings a precocious sexual awareness. The attitudes of
these two are a clear indication of the effect of Berlin's atmosphere on the
defenceless young.

But the real damage is done by the schoolmaster at his second meeting
with Edmund, when the latter approaches him in search of advice after
things have reached a climax at home. The prospect of his father's return
from the hospital in which he has found a few days' refuge has provoked
fresh rows and Edmund feels he must act to remedy the impossible situa-

tion he sees developing. Unfortunately he chooses the wrong moment for seeking advice, approaching the schoolmaster when he is obsessed with another little boy he has lured to his room. Automatically the man reels out Nazi catchwords about the need to have courage enough to let the weak die and accept the fact that only the strong deserve to survive. These words, which reinforce his father's pathetic moaning about the burden of his life and the landlord's taunts of "Why doesn't he die?" drive Edmund to his act of intended euthanasia. For all Rossellini's stated dislike of contrived and dramatic situations the scene of the murder is developed to the full and presented in such a way as to extract the maximum of emotion. As Edmund prepares the poison he has stolen from the hospital, his father mixes pitiful lament about his own condition with admonitions to his elder son to act, to be a man, to have courage—all of which cannot fail to strengthen Edmund's resolve. As he drinks the tea too the father is genuinely touched by his son's apparent solicitude, saying how he can feel the drink doing him good, how proud he is of his sons and what a good boy Edmund is.

In the opening three quarters of the film up to and including the murder, Rossellini does not show any great stylistic novelty. There are a few outstanding sequences, as when Jo and Edmund sell the Hitler record amid the ruins of the chancellery. Here, though the English soldiers to whom they play the record are stiff and totally unconvincing, the shots of the empty desolation of Berlin counterpointed by the Führer's insane assertions of pride and certainty of victory make an unforgettable moment of revelation. Equally, if the reliance on dialogue is excessive, the use of music is outstanding throughout the film: Renzo Rossellini's agitated and insidious theme tune and the drum rolls used to mark the stages of Edmund's progress: his realisation about his sister's nightly departures, the landlord's question: why doesn't your father die? the arrest of Karl-Heinz and the final decision to die. But in general, and judged by the standard of Rossellini's best work, these opening scenes are satisfactory rather than masterly, lacking the bite of similar scenes in *Rome Open City* and only adequately played—not lived—by the largely non-professional cast. One can understand that for a natural innovator like Rossellini these sequences were, as he has stated, "of absolutely no interest at all."[15] In talking about his films of this period Rossellini makes a distinction between the descriptive scenes on the one hand, and the real core of event—usually the final section of the film—on the other. It is for the latter that the film is really made and his attitude to the rest of the film is most revealing of the limitations of his style: "The other moments, the descriptive shots, make me hesitant, absent-minded, an outsider. It's no doubt a lack in me but I must confess that a scene which is not of central importance tires me, bores me, makes me incapable. I only feel sure of myself at the moment of the decisive scene."[15] Perhaps Rossellini is being excessively self-critical here, but his comments do explain the feeling one gets that these scenes are in essence merely a pretext for what follows.

The last two reels of *Germania anno zero* are a masterly piece of film-making. Rossellini once defined realism in the following terms: "It is abandoning the individual in front of the camera and letting him construct his own story. From the first day of shooting I position myself behind my characters and then I let my camera run after them."[45] This describes perfectly this final sequence of *Germania anno zero* in which the camera follows the guilt-stricken Edmund through the ruins of Berlin. The return of his father from hospital which had driven Edmund to murder had also prompted his elder brother to give himself up to the police. Karl-Heinz's return on the day after his father's death, ready now to take a full share in the upkeep of the family, reveals to Edmund the futility of his act and sends him out on his pilgrimage to death. As he plays around the fountain, hopping and balancing on walls in the twilight, his essential childishness and dependence becomes clear, and is emphasised when Jo and Christel, to whom he turns, reject him as a baby. It is dark when he returns home. He dares not go in but sits on the stairs until the darkness drives him off again in a panic. Next morning he turns to his ex-schoolmaster, confessing what he has done and expecting sympathy and understanding. But the man is horrified by the suggestion that he is responsible for this act of patricide and terrified of what the authorities will do to him if they hear of it. He slaps Edmund, who runs off, a fugitive again. His inability to cope with the enormity of what he has done is brought out when he tries instinctively to join some little children in a game of football and his isolation is clear once more when they reject him. His childish progress, as he walks on the cracks in the pavement and kicks along a stone, takes him amid ruins already overgrown with weeds and looking somehow even more menacing than ever in the bright sunlight. Suddenly he is brought to a halt by a burst of organ music from a ruined roofless church. The symbolic meaning—if any—of this surrealistic moment is not clear but it may perhaps be meant to imply a way of education and a morality that might have saved him: Christianity. But now it is too late, Edmund goes on, clambering over the rubble.

In a deserted, windowless building thoughts of death beset him, and when he finds a gun-shaped stone his first act is to hold it against his own temple and pretend to shoot himself. But soon he is caught up again in childish games shooting imaginary bullets into the shadows. Gradually he climbs higher and higher and as he looks down from a window we find that he has once more been drawn back to his home. From his lofty perch he watches his father's body collected for burial, the heap of coffins on the lorry and the casualness of the driver making clear how commonplace death has become in the city of Berlin, just as the smallness of the figures in the street emphasises Edmund's remoteness now from his family. When his name is called out by his sister, he shrinks away and hides, then continues his playing. Sliding down a beam he is confronted with a dizzying drop. He hesitates, then shuts his eyes and jumps to his death. After his body has been found, the camera swings up to capture the impersonal shapes of the ruined skyline of Berlin. This final section of the film is largely wordless and Edmund Meschke who plays the boy is hardly required to act, his face remaining a void into which we can put our feelings and all the impact coming from the flow of his aural and visual experiences. The relevance of this kind of approach outside neo-realism is clear and ten or fifteen years later the new French cinema took up its lesson. Edmund's progress has the same inevitability as that of Louis Malle's doomed socialite in *Le Feu Follet,* and it is not surprising to learn that François Truffaut drew part of his inspiration for *Les Quatre Cents Coups* from Rossellini's film.

Viewed within the context of neo-realism and indeed of realism in general, *Germania anno zero* provokes contradictory responses. Its film portrait of Germany is bare and sparse. Rossellini has made little use of the German cinema's predilection for chiaroscuro effects, and in this respect reviewers of the Forties like to contrast it with Wolfgang Staudte's *Die Mörder sind unter uns* which was made two years earlier but reached England at much the same time. If the interiors are studio-built, the exterior shots of Rossellini's film breathe authenticity and objectivity, yet the portrait it gives of Berlin has many striking omissions. Neo-realism is normally seen as a social and political form of cinema but on both these counts *Germania anno zero* is strangely silent, anticipating the director's later interest (in films like *Stromboli* and *Francesco, giullare di Dio*) in purely spiritual problems. Politically, the film makes no reference to the four-way division of Berlin or the status of the occupying powers. Indeed the appearance of the French soldiers at the drinking club comes as something of a surprise, so little have the mechanics of the Occupation been dealt with, while the English soldiers whom Edmund encounters merely seem like ill-at-ease tourists. Socially too the film's indictment of a capitalist system where everything from a pair of bathroom scales to a woman has its price and even a record of Hitler's voice finds a buyer is only implicit and never developed in any way as a conscious message. Though made in Germany two years after the defeat of Hitler's armies, *Germania anno zero* looks back at the Nazi ideals persisting into the present rather than forward to the new problems of reconstruction brought by the allied victories. The very dating of the film is ambiguous. Though made in 1947 it deals with "Germany in the year nought" which must logically mean the period immediately following the fall of Berlin. This would link it with the previous two films, both of which deal not with the circumstances of contemporary life but with the immediate past, but in this case Rossellini would be offering not a film based directly on his observations of March 1947 but his poetic reconstruction of Germany at the moment of defeat.

This is a point about which Rossellini has said surprisingly little. Writing about the film eight years later he was content to say that it had been made exactly as he wished and remained overwhelming for him, its judgement of Germany being, he felt, "just, not complete, but just."[21] The lack of strict contemporaneity and political detail strikingly reinforces the impression of subjectivity left by the film's use of its background setting.

These empty streets and grim houses where a touch of decoration is a mere anticipation of corruption (the stone nymph beside which Edmund meets his teacher) are objective correlatives of the mental landscape of the boy. Thus Rossellini's "voyage to Germany" is totally consistent with his *Viaggio in Italia* seven years later and a striking forerunner of the poetic use of landscape developed subsequently by Fellini and, more especially, Antonioni. It is also a mark of the complexity of neo-realism in the wealth of stylistic advances which it prepared that with *Germania anno zero,* made only two years after the war by the most resolutely realistic of all the Italian neo-realists, it is more appropriate to talk of poetry than of pure observation, and of a transmutation rather than a translation of reality.

5. Roberto Rossellini: The Challenge of Freedom

A NY DISCUSSION OF THE STATUS of Roberto Rossellini tends almost inevitably to leave his films in favour of other issues, for the personality of Rossellini the man is at least as fascinating and in many ways more absorbing than the filmic achievement of Rossellini the artist. His impact on those who have crossed his path—the actresses in his life like Anna Magnani and Ingrid Bergman or film-makers like Fellini or Truffaut— is clearly something that any full account of him must take into considera- tion. The view of the world press that Rossellini's private life is of more interest than his films is not wholly surprising but nor is it wholly unjust if one takes into consideration the words of François Truffaut who admires his films and at one time worked with him on a number of abortive projects: "Rossellini hardly likes the cinema any more than the arts in general. He prefers life, he prefers man."[137] At both ends of Rossellini's creative life one finds overtly documentary works—*La nave bianca* (1941) being echoed by *La Prise du Pouvoir par Louis XIV* (1966). Throughout his career the impulse towards fiction is tempered with a marked didactic urge and in the Sixties he has tended to abandon the fictional film, and indeed the cinema altogether, in favour of more direct means of persuasion. Rossellini is as much a moralist as an artist and when confronted by an interviewer he does not try to explain, clarify or justify his work; he pours out his views on life and society. Limited here to a consideration of merely three films out of an *oeuvre* extending over thirty years, we can clearly not expect to obtain a definitive judgment of his achievement, but the war trilogy of *Rome Open City, Paisà* and *Germania anno zero* does represent the least controversial part of his career. Here he was dealing directly with the key issue of his work—freedom—in a society for which this theme was totally engrossing and for almost the only time in his creative life Rossellini found himself in agreement with the mass audience. Moreover the consistency of his approach, whether he is dealing with the Resistance or Ingrid Bergman, with India or with Italian history, is such that the broad conception of realism we find in these works of 1945–48 is the one that holds good for all his creative output and constitutes his principal contribution to world cinema.

Throughout his career Rossellini has been an innovator and as such he has always been ahead of his critics. The reception of the war trilogy is symptomatic. The director himself has pointed out that the initial reaction to *Paisà* was "disastrous"[21] and that *Germania anno zero* was "very badly received"[21] on its first showing. The case of *Rome Open City* was perhaps even worse and it says much for Rossellini's strength of personality and purpose that he was in no way discouraged. He has written of this latter film: "There were no showings of 'rushes' before the end of shooting. Some time afterwards, having found a little money, I edited the film and showed it to a few people in the cinema, critics and friends. For the majority of them it was a great disillusionment . . . the reception of the critics was, one might say, frankly and unanimously unfavourable."[21] This is in some ways surprising since Rossellini, at the opposite pole to Visconti, has always been an immediate witness to contemporary events, so much so that many of his films are explicitly dated in their titles: *Germania anno zero, Europa 51, India 58*. Francesco De Robertis preceded him in the documentary but since that date Rossellini has always been in the very forefront of the struggle to free the cinema from the burden of tradition and the influence of the past. He was the first director to make an authentically neo-realist film, the first to treat the Resistance, the first to give a picture of the Liberation. With *Viaggio in Italia* in 1953 he pioneered a more introspective, analytical style of film-making which in its narrative pattern and use of background and landscape is a clear anticipation of the Antonioni of *L'avventura*. Rossellini also led the return to an historical treatment of the war years in the Italian cinema with *Il Generale della Rovere* made in 1959 and, on the debit side, one might argue that he was the first to discover the incompatability of neo-realist methods and Hollywood stars with *Stromboli*, made four years before De Sica's *Stazione Termini*. In the late Fifties too his contribution to the *nouvelle vague* was considerable. He was, according to Truffaut, "the first reader of the scripts of *Le Beau Serge* and *Les Quatre Cents Coups*"[137] and his contributions to *Cahiers du Cinéma* (four separate interviews and a three-part set of memoirs) together with his participation in *Rogopag* alongside Godard, Pasolini and Gregoretti are indications of his sympathy with the aspirations of the rising generation in the cinema.

The war, seen as the struggle for freedom from the evil and constricting forces of Fascism and Nazism, was a subject totally in accord with Rossellini's talents and it is noticeable that the years 1943–44 inspired in him his only two great popular successes, *Rome Open City* and *Il Generale della Rovere*. In 1954, at the lowest point of his career, after the succession of Ingrid Bergman films, all of which had been failures with Italian audiences and critics and at a time when he was about to go three years without directing a single film, Rossellini explained to interviewers in *Cahiers du Cinéma* that he felt the immediate postwar years to have been his period: "Life has changed, the war has gone, towns have been reconstructed. The drama of reconstruction had to be dealt with: perhaps I wasn't capable of doing it."[21] The problem of freedom exists at all times, in peace as much as in war, but the mid-Forties were a time when the problem presented itself in an acute and naturally dramatic form which allowed Rossellini to concentrate on individual characters and actions and yet provide a coherent picture of the whole. To de-dramatise the vivid actuality of war is one thing, but to deal with non-dramatic situations is quite another and throughout Rossellini's work can be traced a movement away from the vivid personal clash and towards an ever wider and more diffuse conception of reality. The tendency to generalisation is constant— from a ship in *La nave bianca* to a city in *Rome Open City* and on to a whole country in *Paisà*; from a country (*Germania anno zero*) to a continent (*Europa 51*); from a sub-continent (*India 58*) to a whole epoch of human history (the Iron Age in *L'età del ferro*)—and this naturally makes great demands on the author's narrative powers. Moreover this widening vision has been accompanied by an increased interiority, from the non-individualised sailors of his first documentary to the characters viewed in depth of *Rome Open City* to the concentration on a solitary figure, the boy Edmund, in *Germania anno zero*. As early as 1947 with *La voce umana* (the first part of *Amore*) Rossellini was filming a monologue and with the advent of Ingrid Bergman in his life this concern with the sufferings and inner torments of a single character became paramount. In following this course from *Stromboli* in 1949 to *La paura* in 1954 Rossellini was anticipating the progress of the cinema in the late Fifties, but the answers he gave to the stylistic problems raised by these films were often no more than tentative, and he left to others the task of following up and developing further the lessons of his most successful film of this period, *Viaggio in Italia*.

The power of all Rossellini's work and in particular of his war trilogy comes from the strength of his concern with human beings and their problems, or, to put it in his terms, with "man and that adventure, unique for everyone, which is life."[45] His profound respect for man which allows him to desregard any moralistic preoccupation with guilt and the attribution of blame brings us to the very root of his inspiration in a work like *Paisà*: his personal conception of humanism. Rossellini has defined this in the following words: "I continue to believe in the possibility of a humanism. I would like the cinema to serve as a means of understanding, to have a cultural value, to be a commencement of awareness."[32] To this end, the cinema must be liberated from all preconceived ideas and able to look freely and objectively at the real questions which confront man in contemporary society. But the elaboration of these questions never takes the form of a social or political analysis in Rossellini's work and it would be wrong to interpret his films—even the war trilogy—exclusively in these terms. The source of Rossellini's humanism is not a Marxist philosophy but the Catholic Faith. Unlike Visconti, who ignores the religious side of Sicilian life in *La terra trema,* he is constantly concerned with the behaviour of priests, saints and believers. Two films at least, *Stromboli* and *Viaggio in Italia,* end with what is virtually a religious conversion and the figure of Don Pietro in *Rome Open City* and the monks and army chaplains of *Paisà* are forerunners of the followers of St. Francis we see in *Francesco, giullare di Dio.* One of Rossellini's best-known definitions of neo-realism is in terms of the Christian doctrine of loving one's neighbour and for him there is no incompatibility between Christianity and freedom. In his view—and here he is furthest from the Marxist branch of neo-realism—to approach life from the standpoint of Catholicism in no way implies prejudice or lack of objectivity: "When people speak of freedom, the first thing they add is 'freedom, yes, but within certain limits.' No, they even refuse freedom in the abstract because it would be too beautiful a dream. That is why I find in Christianity an immense force, it is because the freedom is absolute."[21]

Seen through its director's eyes, the war trilogy has a precise meaning in Christian terms: "In *Rome Open City* and *Paisà,* all the acts of heroism or human kindness obviously spring from faith, and the brutalities of war from cynicism and absence of moral code. In the tragic emptiness of the postwar world shown in *Germania anno zero,* the struggle between faith and mere opportunism is still more accentuated. For the child standing unconsciously between the two extremes, it is a tightrope balancing act."[127] To a certain extent it was to counteract the blackness of these films and to answer accusations of pessimism that Rossellini moved first to the farce of *La macchina ammazzacattivi* and then to the serene world of St. Francis. *Francesco, giullare di Dio* is the most positive statement of the director's beliefs: "I am not a pessimist at all. I'm only a realist, and I'm quite prepared to portray a world full of joy and serene happiness, if only we create such a world first. That it why I turned back to the world of St. Francis, who, despite the wickedness of the world, found joy where nowadays nobody seems to seek it—in humility and service."[127] It is in the context of this view of Christianity that the realism towards which Rossellini strives is to be seen. His humanism is a Christian one and the function of the cinema is for him not to display a soulless objectivity but "to confront people with things, with realities such as they are and to make known other men, other problems."[21] Likewise neo-realism at its best "does not stop at the surface, but seeks the most subtle aspects of the soul."[15] Until 1959, the year of *Il Generale della Rovere,* it is exclusively the contemporary world and its problems that interests him, and a favourite motif of his films during this time is the voyage of discovery. *Paisà* records a journey through Italy made in the wake of the allied invaders, *Germania anno zero* describes a visit to Berlin and *India 58* chronicles his trip to the East. He has defined neo-realism as "following a human being, with love, in all its discoveries, all its impressions"[45] and *Viaggio in Italia* makes clear what he means by this. The film follows the travels of an English couple through an Italy they only begin to comprehend and, since "reality does not exist, it is always subjective,"[137] it also reveals their self-discovery. In more general terms Rossellini's films as a whole are both records of things as they really are, as captured by a film camera, and fragments of a spiritual autobiography.

Rossellini, when he enumerated the qualities of a neo-realist in an interview published in 1952, was clearly describing his own attitudes: "A greater curiosity about individuals. A need that is peculiar to modern man to say things as they are, to realise reality, I should say, in a pitilessly concrete manner, consistent with this typically contemporary interest in statistical and scientific results. A sincere need too to see men with humility, such as they are . . . A desire finally to enlighten oneself."[15] The stylistic means chosen to express these attitudes are simple and direct in the extreme. The prime requirement is a freedom from the constrictions of a conventional approach and the easiest way to begin defining Rossellini's approach is to consider its negative aspects. Firstly there is a rejection of the studio: "Basically, you see, the great enemy of the cinema is the studio. I only have recourse to it when I cannot do otherwise."[45] Secondly comes a dislike of artificiality in appearance and *décor*: "I don't like sets, I detest make-up."[45] Actors are similarly regarded with a jaundiced eye: "I prefer doing without actors . . . You see, if you are dealing with good professional artists, they never correspond exactly to the idea you had of the character you wanted to create."[45] Visual beauty is, if anything, even worse: "Beautiful shots! That's one thing that makes me ill. A film must be well directed, that's the least you can expect from a film-maker, but an individual shot does not have to be beautiful."[21] Pure technique is of little interest: "I regard the technique of film-making as something secondary and all the highly modern technical equipment I saw in Hollywood impressed me very little."[127] Nor is the preparation on paper of a script of much use: "I must confess I have never really understood the necessity of having a shooting script, unless it's to reassure the producers."[21] Even normal methods of dramatic construction are condemned, and virtually all that remains is the rhythm of the film, "the only thing that counts, and that cannot be learnt, you carry it inside you."[21] This, together with the desire to achieve realism and the willingness to improvise, constitutes the basis of Rossellini's work.

One of the driving forces of Rossellini's creative work is his desire to be free from the constraints of conventional dramatic structure. This is at the basis of one of his major achievements, his contribution to the liberation of the cinema from the stranglehold of an aesthetic based on the Nineteenth century novel and the well-made play. He is vehement in his expression of his views on structure: "I detest the logical continuity of the subject. Descriptive shots are necessary to arrive at the central event but I am by nature inclined to skip and pour scorn on them. There, I admit, is one of my limitations: the incomplete character of my language. To be frank I would like to direct only certain well defined scenes. When I feel that the shot I am directing is important for the logic of the action but not for what I urgently want to say, then my incapacity is revealed and I no longer know what to do. When, on the contrary, it is an important, essential scene then everything becomes perfectly easy."[15] This ambition is not fully realised in feature-length films like *Germania anno zero* and *Rome Open City*. Of the latter Rossellini said that he was "not at all interested in constructing a conventional story following the rules of cinematic construction, because the facts in themselves were much more forceful than any dramatic convention"[131] but in fact this film, like the German one, relies for much of the time on conventionally shot and fully dialogued scenes. Only in the final part of *Germania anno zero* does he succeed in sustaining a lengthy sequence dependent exclusively on the power of the image. Rossellini is thus by temperament nearer to a short story writer than a novelist and it is not surprising that he feels more at home with an episodic film than a normal full-length feature. Some of his more striking films, *Paisà* and *Francesco, guillare di Dio* among them, have been "sketch films" and even a work like *Viaggio in Italia* has a structure built round a journey which allows a succession of separate settings to be used. In this kind of work, which ignores logic and continuity in favour of a concentration on the decisive scenes, a certain unevenness of quality is unavoidable, even for a director like Rossellini.

Instead of placing a reliance on the tangible certainties of a detailed shooting script, Rossellini prefers the riskier course of putting his trust in the virtues of improvisation and the inspiration of the moment. He has even gone so far as to say that when he undertakes a new film he begins work on an idea without knowing where it will lead him. As he told an interviewer: "It is quite true that I sometimes start a film only with a rough outline of the script, that I often make up dialogue and change scenes as I go along. I don't see why I should change my habits . . . The content of a picture is to me infinitely more important than its technical perfection."[127] If it is fair to feel that in his neo-realist work at least he never quite solved the problems of how to replace the conventional patterns of pseudo-realism with an improvised structure capable of being sustained over ninety minutes, it is beyond doubt that in placing the emphasis on freedom to improvise he was pointing the way to the future. It is appropriate that he should have been one of the adapters of the play by Benjamino Joppolo which Jean-Luc Godard used as the basis for *Les Carabiniers*, for already in the Forties he was exploring the path which Godard was still fruitfully pursuing some twenty years later. Rossellini has always studied his subject matter thoroughly in advance (his interest in factual information aids him here) and has invariably established the outlines of his script, but he is too sensitive to his actors and settings to fix much beforehand and thereby undermine the spontaneity he hopes to achieve. Of his working methods of the Forties Rossellini said: "Amidei and I never finished our scripts before arriving at the places where we intended shooting them. Circumstances and the players which chance brought our way generally led us to modify our original canvas. And the dialogue itself, like the intonation, depends on the amateur actors who are going to speak it: you just need to give the players time to get used to the atmosphere of shooting."[45] Such a system has its limitations as well as its advantages and is more suited to the underplayed horror of the Po valley episode of *Paisà* than the elaborate force of *La macchina ammazzacattivi*, but it does serve to make the cinema once more a matter of personal expression. The neo-realists all learned from the French cinema of the Thirties but from the example of Rossellini's *Rome Open City* onwards they re-established in their own work the supremacy of the director as the creative focus of the film. Though Rossellini, like Jean Renoir in France, has never in his long career directed an absolutely faultless film, his work has constantly served to break down the barriers between the director and his material and allowed a fresh look at the creative possibilities of the film medium.

6. The Partisan Films of Vergano and De Santis

IN THE YEARS 1946–47 two films produced by the ANPI (the Italian Partisan Organisation) offer an interpretation of events from a viewpoint quite different from that of Rossellini. Aldo Vergano's *Il sole sorge ancora* and Giuseppe De Santis's *Caccia tragica* together present a picture of the war and the postwar aspirations of the left as seen through the eyes of those who, like these two directors, had actually fought in the resistance. The two films have much in common: the same producer (G. G. Agliani), the same composer (Giuseppe Rosati) and in part the same scriptwriters (De Santis and Carlo Lizzani worked on both). In more general terms they are the outcome of the same critical movement that had produced the magazines *Cinema* and *Bianco e nero* as well as the film *Ossessione*, synthesising the critical and creative impulses that lie at the very root of neo-realism and the new hopes of the radical parties in the middle and late Forties.

Aldo Vergano, the director of *Il sole sorge ancora* and the least known as well as the oldest of the directors directly connected with the neo-realist movement, was born in Rome in 1891. He grew up in Sardinia and had a number of jobs (including one selling postcards) before turning to journalism. 1920 saw him working as a journalist on the newspaper *Il popolo romano* and he spent the years 1921–23 in the Balkans as correspondent of various Italian papers. He was an outspoken opponent of Fascism and after the seizure of power by Mussolini he attacked De Bono for his complicity in the murder of Matteotti and became associated with Tito Zaniboni who was responsible for the abortive attempt to assassinate the *duce* in November 1925. Because of his views and activities Vergano found it impossible to continue working as a journalist and he was reduced to doing all kinds of odd jobs when he met Alessandro Blasetti, then the director of the film magazine *Cinematografo*, in Rome. These two totally dissimilar personalities collaborated on the film *Sole* which in 1929 launched Blasetti on a highly successful directorial career and for Vergano began a period of scriptwriting which was to last for a dozen or so years. Between 1929 and 1943 Vergano collaborated on the scripts of some thirty films, for some of which he also acted as director of production, and also directed a short documentary film, *Fore imperiali* (1932), and two features, *Pietro Micca* (1938) and *Quelli della montagna* (1943). Most of the films which Vergano scripted were purely commercial efforts by directors like Righelli, Brignone, Alessandrini, Bragaglia and Campogalliani and showed little sign of his artistic taste or social commitment. He was, it would seem, able to put more of himself into his first two feature films both of which were, Giovanni Vento tells us, "the reflection of the different historic moments during which they were shot." *Pietro Micca*, made just after the empire-building campaign in Africa, was "a resolutely patriotic and anti-monarchist film,"[32] while *Quelli della montagna*, supervised and co-scripted by Blasetti, gave a non-heroic portrayal of war by chronicling the adventures of a company of Alpine troops during the First World War.

As decisive as this extensive filmic training was Vergano's experience as a member of the Action Party fighting as a partisan in the ranks of the "Giustizia e Libertà" group. He took part in the fighting in Latium and was arrested by the Fascists after the Via Rasella incident but managed to escape and carry on the struggle. In June 1944 he helped set up the film-makers' union within the National Liberation Committee and his major work, *Il sole sorge ancora*, may be seen as a direct result of these activities. In 1946 his film work was totally in keeping with the mood of the nation but as the political climate changed he found himself increasingly isolated. In the last ten years of his life he worked on only one script (that of the re-make of *Sperduti nel buio*) and directed only four films in Italy—*I fuorilegge, Santa Lucia Lontana, La grande rinuncia, Amore rosso*—all of which were made between 1950 and 1952 but lacked the power of his partisan film. Increasingly Vergano went abroad to work: he made *Czarci Zleb* (*Il passo del diavolo*) in Poland in 1949 and *Schicksal am Lenkrad* five years later in Vienna and he was working on a film to be made in Yugoslavia when he died in 1957. The total disillusionment from which he suffered during these years can be gathered from the title planned for his memoirs: *A Chronicle of Wasted Years*.

In the speech he delivered at the Perugia conference of film-makers in 1949 Vergano defined the cinema as "an act of collaboration"[7] and for *Il sole sorge ancora* he gathered together a formidable team of writers which included the critic Guido Aristarco and two future directors Giuseppe De Santis and Carlo Lizzani. The film, dedicated to those who fell fighting in the resistance, was designed to examine not the actions of the partisans but their motives. As Vergano himself said in 1947: "There is nobody in

Italy or abroad who doubts the value of our partisans but there are few, on the contrary, who know the reasons why these 'adventurers' fought on one side rather than on the other." *Il sole sorge ancora*, which begins in September 1943 with the fall of Mussolini, takes as its subject the political education of a young soldier Cesare. In the confusion which follows the disbanding of his regiment and the Germans' "assumption of the protection of Italian soil" Cesare manages to escape from Milan and find his way back to his native Lombard village of Villavecchia in or around which most of the action of the film takes place. The choice facing a whole generation is symbolised for Cesare himself by two women. On the one hand there is Laura, a refugee looking after her dead sister's children, whose father has taken over Cesare's old job at the brick kiln. These two represent the claims of conscience and commitment and as the opposition to the Germans gradually takes shape Laura's father becomes a leading figure in the village. On the other hand there is Donna Matilde, a rich and sensual woman whose husband is the proprietor of the kiln and whose house is filled with the idle rich who have fled from Milan to avoid the bombing. She belongs to a class which has already compromised itself with the Fascists and now reacts to the problems of 1943 either by fleeing irresponsibly or by active collaboration with the Germans. The moment of truth comes when all ex-soldiers are ordered to rejoin their units to continue the fight for the Fascist cause: the rich slip off to Switzerland, the young men, encouraged by Laura's father and the village priest (played by the Marxist Carlo Lizzani), take to the hills and poor Cesare gets himself embroiled with Donna Matilde. It is only later, during a skirmish between the Fascists and partisans who are distributing hi-jacked flour to the villagers, that Cesare becomes involved in the resistance movement. But the partisan activity finds a prompt answer as the Germans under the brutal and cynical Major Heinrich move into Villavecchia.

The second half of *Il sole sorge ancora* traces the gradual growth of the resistance from the winter of 1944 onwards. While the workers organise a network of revolt, the Germans lodged in Donna Matilde's house pursue their drunken, cynical progress. Thanks to Cesare's treacherous brother Mario the two factions come face to face when the Germans uncover a planned partisan raid on an ammunition store on New Year's Eve. The night scenes after the Nazis have seized the plotters, with the darkness lit up by flares and the drunken German commander galloping round the tied-up partisans taking pot-shots at them, have an apocalyptic flavour that captures superbly the hysterical madness of Hitler's dream of world conquest. It is emphasised more strongly still by the contrasting scene next morning when the Germans lead the priest and the partisan leader to execution before the massed villagers, who signify their solidarity with the doomed men by giving in unison the responses—ora pro nobis—to the priest's prayer. Only with the actual shooting can the Germans turn this mood into one of sorrow and thereby re-establish their authority. The film's climax comes in the spring of 1945 when the Germans, faced by the threats posed

by the Milan insurrection and the flight of Mussolini, decide to blow up
the whole village as a form of reprisal. Fortunately, however, the signal for
the partisan uprising comes through—"The sun rises once more"—and the
Italian resistance men sweep down on the village to overwhelm the Germans from all sides. Mario and Matilde are killed but Cesare and Laura
are able to face the future united and in freedom.

Il sole sorge ancora remains an impressive work over twenty years after
its completion although it is hard to apportion the credit for its achievements with any degree of certainty in view of Vergano's failure (or inability) to repeat his success. The film has a fine temporal sweep in its two
year span describing the gradual change in Italian society from the confusion and uncertainty of 1943 to the final triumph of unity in 1945. It has
a certain epic quality and its impact comes much more from the scenes
of collective action than from the intimate but more conventional story
of the vicissitudes of Cesare and Laura's love. The film is undoubtedly
schematised and if Cesare's progress is hesitant and at times ambiguous,
Vergano paints with Manichean clarity the class distinctions within the
closed society of Villavecchia, portraying the effete upper bourgeoisie as
the natural allies of the Hitlerian "master race." The sharply drawn conclusions of the political analysis are parallelled by the overall stylistic pattern
of the film which derives its power from the confrontation of two women
or two ways of life and from the off-setting of the sub-Wagnerian histrionics
of the midnight slaughter by the calm-assurance of the Italian crowd next
morning. Though totally different in its tone and stylistic pattern, *Il sole
sorge ancora* shares with *Rome Open City* a closeness to the events it is
narrating, a bitterness towards the Germans and a desire to find forceful
and emphatic images to reflect the turbulent past and the uncertain but
hopeful future.

Giuseppe De Santis's *Caccia tragica*, the second film produced by the
ANPI, provides in a sense the continuation of *Il sole sorge ancora*, in that
it shows the fate of this same partisan spirit in the immediate postwar
world. But though De Santis has many attitudes in common with Vergano,
he was born some twenty-six years later and is much more typically a member of the new generation. *Caccia tragica* is not an isolated and unexpected
achievement (as Vergano's film is in many ways) but almost the natural
outcome of the director's career. De Santis had published stories "in the
manner of Verga," studied directing at the Centro sperimentale, worked as
a critic on *Cinema* and been scriptwriter for films by both Visconti (*Ossessione*) and Rossellini (the ill-fated *Desiderio*). Though in many ways overshadowed by the fluent theorising of Rossellini and Zavattini, De Santis
with *Caccia tragica* renews an authentic tradition of realism and he shares
with his fellow neo-realists the notion that "the cinema interests the artist
in so far as it gives him the possibility of making films that demand natural-
ness, simplicity and the immediate evidence of the facts which he wants to
relate."[115] Beyond this basic level of agreement, however, the divergence is

sharp as De Santis himself is aware: "My position with regard to realism implies a transfiguration of reality. I do not entirely share Rossellini's theories: placing your camera between real walls can very easily result in a mere surface realism. Art is not the reproduction of simple documents."[115] Stylistically as well as politically De Santis aligns himself far more with Visconti: "I like to immerse myself in tradition, express the current aspirations of the people through its traditions. Besides, all of us, from time to time, happen to rediscover the Italian tradition of melodrama. And of course that applies to me in particular."[32]

In the early Forties De Santis acquired a reputation in Italy as a film critic for his advocacy of Verga and the severity of his judgments. By prefacing this account of *Caccia tragica* with a brief example of De Santis's critical approach it is possible to show how far his creative achievements of 1947 echo his critical attitudes of 1941. The thoughts on the place of man in the cinema which are to be found in his review of Mario Soldati's *Piccolo mondo antico* are a fair sample of his criticism: "The cinema ought to be characterised by a preoccupation with authenticity—even if it is fantastic—of gesture and atmosphere, in a word of the factors that must serve to express the totality of the world in which men live." De Santis continues with this definition of the relationship of men and their surroundings: "But how would it be possible to understand and interpret man if he is isolated from the elements amid which he lives every day and with which he communicates every day? These are perhaps the walls of his house (which must bear the marks of his hands, his taste, his being in an unequivocal manner), or the streets of the town where he encounters other men (and such encounters cannot be chance but must indicate the particular characteristics which are inherent in him), or nature itself which surrounds him, from which he differs or, on the contrary, with which he identifies himself, because it has so much power over him that it fashions him to its own image and resemblance."[31] De Santis's first film is far removed from the everyday existence of its hero—it traces a unique occurrence in his life —but throughout one can detect a preoccupation with viewing man in his social context as he is moulded and determined by social forces.

Caccia tragica is set in the Romagna district a few months after the Liberation and has a remarkably simple narrative line. A lorry carrying a young newly-married couple, Michele and Giovanna, and the entire financial resources of the collective farm on which they want to live is ambushed by bandits who use a stolen ambulance and a false priest. The bandits ruthlessly shoot down the driver and the official with the money and also kidnap Giovanna when Michele recognises one of their number, Alberto, as a friend from the concentration camp. The remainder of the film traces the "tragic pursuit" of the gang by Michele and the members of the collective farm whose whole project will fail if the money is not recovered. As the chase unfolds the film cuts between the bandits and their pursuers so that we understand the driving forces of both groups. There are the left-wing collective ideals of the workers who want to change society and therefore get little sympathy in their plight from the hooded, fur-jacketed henchmen of the absentee landlord, whose guns and dogs are an eloquent token of the attitude of the rich. And in contrast there is the ill-fated passion that binds Alberto, despite himself, to the gang-leader Daniela, nicknamed Lili Marlene because of her association with the Germans during the war. Though he can see the life of crime and murder into which she is leading him, Alberto cannot tear himself away: even when peasants and bandits come face to face he stays with the latter who use Giovanna as a hostage to ensure their escape. But when the gang splits up and he boards a train to exchange money with a group of black-marketeers he realises the extent of his fall as ex-service men colleagues crowd around him, accept him initially as one of themselves and try to get him involved in their work of rallying the peasants to their cause. Chased and caught by Michele, Alberto redeems himself by leading him to the hideout where Daniela keeps Giovanna captive and by shooting Daniela in the final showdown. He is taken back to the collective farm and tried by the group of peasants, only to be freed when Michele and Giovanna speak in his defence. In a remarkable ending we see him walk off alone to try to reintegrate himself in society while the peasants pelt him—almost playfully—with clods of earth. Originally De Santis had planned to reinforce the political message of *Caccia tragica*: "In the initial shooting script, after having been acquitted by the peasants, the young Italian delinquent was arrested by the governmental police. This underlined the character of popular justice which sought to reintegrate into the workers' collective an individual who was certainly guilty, but equally was also a victim of social conditions."[115] This ending was rejected by the censors and so the film concludes with a scene that is more ambiguous but also far more poetically charged.

Caccia tragica is a remarkable first work which, despite its unevenness, strikingly emphasises the vitality of the director. On one level it is an exciting gangster story manipulating the conventional elements in a lively way, but it also has a quite different level of meaning and, like Visconti's original plan for the trilogy of *La terra trema*, captures the mood and atmosphere of the year 1947. In *Caccia tragica* the situation of the collective farm is shown as desperate, money and equipment are scarce and the living conditions poor, but the peasants have both a sense of purpose and a total solidarity. Though the film's plot is a simple chase we are never allowed to forget the collective force behind the surface details of the capture of the bandits and the recovery of the money. The many crowd scenes—the escape of the gang who use Giovanna as hostage, the train making its way through fields lined with peasants, the informal trial of Alberto—are handled by De Santis with a sincerity and force which recall in their mood, if not in their stylistic method, the early Soviet film. In a very real sense the enemies of the peasants are not the bandits themselves but the rich, whose agents are explicitly presented as being in league with the gang and ultimately responsible for the ambush. There is a feeling that the bandits—even Daniela—are in some ways victims of society and Alberto in particular is depicted with considerable insight and sympathy, but in no sense at all is a compromise between landlords and peasants seen as feasible. This of course does not prevent De Santis from using the sordid anti-social brutalities of the bandit gang to set off the collective ideals of the peasant workers, any more than the presentation of the happy and integrated union of Giovanna and Michele hinders an investigation of the relationship of Daniela and Alberto. The latter is a tragic passion of the kind depicted by Visconti in *Ossessione* (on which De Santis worked as co-scriptwriter) with a man driven to crime and murder by a combination of cricumstances and a fatal love for a woman. But though in this way at least there is a link between the realism of Visconti and De Santis in 1942 and *Caccia tragica* in 1947, the latter film has a whole new dimension of social analysis.

The specific political issues treated in *Caccia tragica* have lost some of their relevance in the twenty years that have passed since it was made, but the film retains its power because though the conflicts are in many ways schematised and the arguments presented with the impassioned rhetoric of a skilled polemicist, the human beings never cease to come alive. As an example of this one might cite the complicity that springs up between the two women despite their roles as kidnapper and victim and the genuine and in no way contrived sensuality with which they are endowed. There is an earthy reality about Carla del Poggio as Giovanna that recalls the playing of Clara Calamai in *Ossessione* and anticipates the more calculated eroticism of De Santis's second film *Bitter Rice*. In places De Santis has obviously experienced difficulty in putting his message into images and so resorts to overtly rhetorical speeches, and it is clear that he has tried to pack too much into one film. But throughout the whole length of *Caccia tragica* are to be found scenes that show a remarkable directorial talent at work. One instance is the confrontation of bandits and peasants when the latter, helpless despite their guns because of the threat to Giovanna, can only whistle their protest (a scene which recalls the execution episode of *Il sole sorge ancora*). Then there is the moment of horror as Daniela pushes an injured man out of the speeding ambulance and the surrealist image when the peasants visit Alberto's home only to find it full of children playing in masks. Such scenes show clearly De Santis's awareness that realism is a style demanding the transformation of reality and a heightening of its dramatic moments, not merely a pseudo-objective imitation of newsreel methods. *Il sole sorge ancora* and *Caccia tragica* show the validity of the approach worked out in the columns of the film journals of the early Forties, provided that this is combined with an historical awareness of the working of social forces, but at the same time they reveal in their less integrated moments a tendency to melodrama to which the Italian tradition is susceptible.

7. Lattuada and the Necessity of Violence

THE FULL STRENGTH OF THE IMPULSE towards realism in the early postwar years can be gauged from the emergence of Alberto Lattuada as a neo-realist director. Lattuada's cultured middle-class background and artistic inclinations were hardly of the kind one would expect to produce a social realist and when, at the age of eight, his theatrical vocation became clear to him, it was the contrivance, not the realistic possibility of the medium that attracted him: "It was in the wings of La Scala in Milan, alongside my father, the composer Felice Lattuada (who later collaborated on several of my films), that I discovered the art of directing and the power of the artifices of spectacle."[132] He tried to reconstruct at home what he has called the "magical atmosphere" in which so much of his childhood was spent, but again the reproduction of reality was furthest from his mind: "I even built a little theatre for which I also made the sets. I did not animate it. I fitted it out and then called my mother: 'Mummy, come and look at this!' The phenomenon of lighting fascinated me."[33] This interest in the mechanics of the theatrical spectacle was accompanied by a taste for the plastic arts and an abiding concern with opera. Years later he said: "When I can find a few weeks rest, so to speak, between two films, I steep myself in opera; nothing is more beneficial to me."[33] The sense of affinity with opera and melodrama at the root of Lattuada's conception of the cinema puts him, in the context of the neo-realist movement, stylistically much closer to Visconti and De Santis than to the naturalistic Zavattini, but he lacks their Marxist commitment. His own interest has always been in the arts far more than in politics though he in no way accepted the Mussolini regime. In the middle of the Fascist period he "published critical articles and short stories in the little anti-conformist Italian reviews, like *Corrente* or *Domus*"[33] and the volume of photographs, *Occhio quadrato*, which he published in 1941, had sufficient anti-government implications for him to be "summoned by the police and accused of showing only the imperfections of the regime and not its grandeurs!"[33]

At the university Lattuada qualified as an architect and his studies would seem to have reinforced his formalistic approach (as was the case too with Renato Castellani). While still studying he dabbled in the cinema, working as designer on a modestly budgeted production and as colour consultant on the first Italian color film in 1935. He was also associated with Mario Ferrari and Luigi Comencini in the founding of the Milan Cinémathèque and by the early Forties he had decided on film-making as his career. The films on which he worked in the years 1940–42 were fairly significant ones in the history of the Italian cinema but far removed from the realistic works with which he made his postwar reputation. Soldati's *Piccolo mondo antico* and Poggioli's *Sissignora* which he co-scripted and *Giacomo l'idealista,* his own feature *début* as a director, all belong to the calligraphic tendency of the wartime cinema and this form of film-making clearly seemed the one most likely to give full scope to his cultural interests and his view of the film as spectacle. The dangers of excessive detachment from reality and the use of the cinema merely to "illustrate" literary works are apparent in Lattuada at this time. In 1943 he contemplated adapting works by Robert Louis Stevenson, Dostoievski and Matilde Serao and as late as 1947 he filmed an adaptation of D'Annunzio's *Il delitto di Giovanni Episcopo* between work on the two neo-realist works *Il bandito* and *Senza pietà*. It would be wrong, however, to exaggerate the importance of Lattuada's cultural background and the significance of these works turning their back on contemporary reality. The director himself once tried to evaluate the respective weight of background and the pull of reality and while his generalisation may not hold good for all his contemporaries it certainly depicts accurately his own postwar approach: "Italian film-makers are more sensitive to reality than marked by the weight of culture. . . . Philosophy, intellectual habits and cultural preparation do not influence the birth of a work. It is while walking in the street that the Italian film-maker experiences the need to say something."[77]

In any case the cinema, as Lattuada himself has remarked, "reflects moments of crisis, that is to say, of social metamorphosis. As soon as there are reactions with regard to reality, artists react more or less. They translate these upheavals."[132] So it was that Lattuada's views underwent a gradual change and he moved away from purely calligraphic concerns: "My friends Vittorini, the painter Gottuso, Pavese, Cassola and I later felt the necessity of living outside these romantic complacencies. Our preoccupations were political and realistic."[33] In 1944 Lattuada made a documentary, *La nostra guerra*, about the events of September 8, 1943 and the activities of the National Liberation Committee and in 1945 published one of the first statements of policy of the nascent neo-realist movement. In an article entitled "Let us pay our debts" he set out the following programme: "We are in rags? Then let us show everybody our rags. We are defeated? Let us look at our disasters. This is due to the Mafia, the hypocritical bigotry, to conformism, to irresponsibility, to bad upbringing? Let us pay all our debts with a fierce love of honesty and the world will participate with emotion in this great game with truth. This confession will illuminate our crazy secret virtue, our belief in life, our superior Christian brotherhood."[53] He also showed himself aware of the need for a specifically national cinema: "I don't mean . . . that one must give up a clearly Italian character, but rather one must carry on the investigation of this character to such a depth as to find a universal interest in it, the interest of man in himself."[53]

Lattuada has often stated that in his view many of the weaknesses of the postwar Italian cinema derive from an excessive predominance of ideological preoccupations and he shows himself to be unhappy with the constraints of any one party or approach. In this respect two unrealised projects of his dating from 1944–5 are of interest, in that they show the same acceptance of the validity of both the socialist and the Catholic viewpoints such as one finds in *Rome Open City*. Indeed *Angeli neri* was in-

spired, like Rossellini's film, by the exploits of the Roman priest Don Morosini and examined the crisis of conscience that led this man actively to
oppose the Nazis. *Il ferroviere,* on the other hand, dealt with the problems
of workers' solidarity and treated the efforts of railway workers to by-pass
government bureaucracy and themselves organise the reconstruction of a
damaged railway line. The two realistic studies of contemporary society
that Lattuada was able to realise in the years 1946–47 are both more
ambiguous works. Though firmly rooted in a social context both are concerned more with the notion of solitude—the isolation of man from his
fellows—that with the workings of society. (In this way these films link up
with the rest of Lattuada's work for the theme of solitude is a constant
from *Giacomo l'idealista* onwards). *Il bandito* and *Senza pietà* are also
of necessity complex works in that they deal with the phenomenon of violence which was both inevitable and fatal to those caught up in the turmoil
of postwar Italy. The two films are a penetrating treatment of "uncertainty
and social instability, violence and revolt," and in the context of the potentially revolutionary situation in which Italy found itself in the Forties
Lattuada examines the necessity of violence which, in his view, ensues when
"the lack of balance at the heart of society pushes man into unaccustomed
paths and compels him to confront conflicts which upset and break his
life."[131]

Il bandito is an excellent illustration of Lattuada's thesis. The early
scenes are firmly rooted in contemporary circumstances: two friends return
from a prisoner-of-war camp to war-torn Italy. The one, a farmer, has a
home and a young daughter, Rosetta, to return to and can successfully
reintegrate himself into society, but the other, the film's hero Ernesto,
arrives in Turin to find his home in ruins, his mother dead and his sister
missing. The only person left who knows him is a neighbour who is herself
mourning a son shot while fighting with the partisans. Ernesto's subsequent
encounters are all disastrous: his impatience with bureaucrats loses him
the money due to him from the state, the prostitute he follows to a brothel
turns out to be his sister Maria and the elegant woman, Lydia, whose purse
he finds is, in reality, a ruthless gang leader. After he has seen his sister die
in a brawl and has killed her pimp, Ernesto is a man on the run. Inevitably
he turns to the seductive Lydia and from this point onwards the film
becomes a fairly routine crime melodrama. There are similarities with the
defeatist atmosphere of prewar French works like Carné's *Quai des Brumes*
but the Prévert poetry is missing. Ernesto tries to maintain a sense of honour, helping the poor and ruthlessly executing those who traffic in women,
but becomes involved in the struggle for power within the gang. When he
quarrels with Lydia she doublecrosses him by revealing his movements to
the police. Ernesto has always preserved the thought of little Rosetta—
whom he has never seen but to whom he has written several times—as a
symbol of innocence and he is able to save her life before dying amid
the snow.

In this final scene the little toy goose which Ernesto bought for Rosetta and which she has given back to him as a present is used to represent the values of which his life of crime has deprived him and functions as a symbol in the literary sense. This is a clue to Lattuada's basic approach which is to create drama and significance out of material extracted from life rather than to seek an authentic and direct documentary-style transcription of reality. His use of professional players like Amedeo Nazzari as Ernesto and Anna Magnani as Lydia is a further instance of the same stylistic attitude, as is the insistence on scenes of violent action (Ernesto's fight with the pimp and flight from the police) and on vivid confrontations and flamboyant gestures (the startlingly theatrical jewel robbery or the bitter quarrels over gang leadership). In this context the warm sentiment of the scenes involving the child Rosetta can be seen as designed to bring into sharp relief these dramatic elements. What *Il bandito* lacks is an adequate social analytical perspective. Maria's decline to prostitution is not used as a starting point for an examination of social problems but as a pretext for a scene of high drama when Ernesto follows a pair of shapely legs into a brothel and, coming face to face with the whore, discovers that she is his own sister. Similarly Ernesto's progress as a gangster is to some extent a deflation of the Robin Hood myth but serves equally as an excuse for scenes of violent action, pursuits and gun-fights. Lattuada has always worked strictly within the commercial structure of the film industry and the original and penetrating insights of *Il bandito* are set firmly in the context of a conventional gangster plot.

Some of the same criticisms have been raised against Lattuada's second neo-realist film, *Senza pietà*. Again there is a close link with immediate contemporary reality with the film set in the port of Leghorn, the debarkation point for American army supplies and for this reason a centre of black-marketeering and prostitution. Like *Il bandito* it paints a vivid picture of one of the least pleasant aspects of liberated Italy: the violence and crime that flourished in the wake of the allied armies and brought corruption to all who came into contact with them. There are also perhaps echoes of the fatalistic French cinema of the Thirties for which Lattuada has such admiration in *Senza pietà*'s tragic love story of two social outcasts, Angela and Jerry. Angela, an Italian girl who has been abandoned by the man she loved, lost her child and been driven to prostitution, finds new hope in her love for Jerry, a Negro who has come to Italy with the American army. He falls in love with her and wishes to rescue her from her present life and take her back to the United States. His efforts to do this involve stealing American supplies and throw him into contact with gangsters. Instead of escape, the result for Angela is death and Jerry, in despair, kills himself by driving the truck containing her body over a cliff. The violently anti-Catholic critics Borde and Bouissy detect the hands of Federico Fellini and Tullio Pinelli, who both worked with Lattuada on the script, in the film's emphasis on redemption (Angela is shot after she and Jerry have stopped to pray in church). But it would be quite contrary to Lattuada's deepest convictions for him to offer a single propagandist message, whether Catholic or Marxist, and during his involvement with the neo-realist movement the director seems to have tried systematically to avoid making films that could be given any ideological label. In his view the artist should limit himself to "presenting elements for judgement, in such a way that the events of the story trace a path which always leads away from error and moves in the direction of truth,"[131] and it is fairer to see *Senza pietà* as a further variation on Lattuada's perennial theme of solitude: "After many struggles and efforts and loves man finds himself alone with himself once more." Angela and Jerry, whose love allows them to overcome the barriers of race, long for the reintegration with society which her profession and his colour deny them. But in the bleak world of Lattuada the only outcome for them—as for Ernesto in *Il bandito,* another basically good man corrupted by his environment—is death.

Contradictions abound in the work of Alberto Lattuada, as both *Il bandito* and *Senza pietà* amply reveal. Throughout his work there is a conflict between his lofty view of the film-maker's mission and the concessions to commercial pressures apparent in his own films. In his opinion, the artist "must work towards authenticity and the clarification of ideas, must contribute to progress, struggle against conformity, seek modestly and humbly —that goes without saying—to say the things he feels capable of contributing to the redressing of errors, must be a guide, a 'detector' for society, but must in no case be transformed into a mere instrument of political propaganda."[15] At the same time, because such a message needs an audience and "the cinema is contact with the masses,"[77] Lattuada has been compelled to submit to commercial pressures. He believes it wrong to "cut yourself off from the mass audience, for if you make a film to be shown only to a few friends, it would be better to write a pamphlet,"[77] and as a result his output contains films like *Anna* (1951) and *The Tempest* (1958) which were clearly designed to obtain popular success and most of his other works—like *Il bandito*—are flawed by scenes which he now disowns and "concessions coldly agreed to."[77] To most critics the major strength of Lattuada's neo-realist work lies in its precise and forceful capturing of the realities of the postwar situation, though he is clearly never content merely to record with newsreel style photography. But when he himself, in 1963, came to evaluate his own past achievements he found that the principal weaknesses lay precisely in these social aspects: "If I think back to *Il bandito* and *Senza pietà* I'd say that the most valuable parts of these films are also those most detached from events and from actuality. They are the most symbolic, with a significance intended to be universal. While the most decrepit parts are those most firmly anchored in the documentary. I have made films which are more harmonious but those two illustrate very well my defects."[78] With regard to the symbolic aspects of, say, *Il bandito* it is hard to see how they can be said to outweigh the sense of reality present in the scenes depicting Ernesto's arrival in the shattered ruins of his home town, but the second half of Lattuada's statement is valid—if one adds a corollary that *Il bandito* and *Senza pietà* illustrate very well his outstanding virtues as a director too.

8. Myth and Reality of the Mezzogiorno

SINCE THE UNIFICATION OF ITALY a century or so ago, successive generations of politicians have been confronted with the intractable complex of problems posed by the South, the *Mezzogiorno:* the stagnation of an unbalanced agricultural economy, over-population and grinding poverty, the violence of banditry and the contradictions of the mafia code of honour. The most obvious approach to Sicily for an outsider would therefore seem to be the path of reality, social concern and documentation followed by such men as Danilo Dolci and Carlo Levi. But this underdevelopment is only one part of the story, for the South has also given Italy some of its most impressive cultural achievements. Sergio Pacifici, who makes a most interesting comparison of the *Mezzogiorno* with the American South in its combination of "an extraordinarily rich cultural heritage" with "awesome social and economic backwardness and lack of educational opportunities,"[110] produces a notable list of Southern poets and novelists: Giovanni Verga, Luigi Capuana, Salvatore di Giacomo, Grazia Deledda, Luigi Pirandello, Salvatore Quasimodo, Corrado Alvaro, Elio Vittorini, Eduardo de Filippo. To these names one might add the politician Gramsci, the philosopher Benedetto Croce and a further novelist, Tomasi di Lampedusa. In this way a second possible means of access presents itself to the outsider: the path of Myth, or the South seen through its cultural heritage. The importance of Luchino Visconti derives from the fact that, as a Marxist follower of Antonio Gramsci and a lifelong admirer of Verga's novels, he synthesises the two approaches, thereby capturing in his work something of the intricate self-contradiction that is Sicily.

Giovanni Verga (1840–1922), though little known in England except as author of the story on which Mascagni's opera *Cavalleria Rusticana* was based, is generally considered one of the greatest Italian novelists. Born in Catania, in Sicily, of a land-owning family, Verga went away in his twenties to Florence and Milan where he wrote his first, somewhat modish novels. But then, around 1880, came the turning point of his career: he returned to his native Sicily and began to write about local themes in a new realistic style. He himself has described for us the origin of this latter approach: "I had published several of my first novels. They went well: I was preparing others. One day, I don't know how, there came into my hand a sort of broadside, a halfpenny sheet sufficiently ungrammatical and disconnected, in which a sea-captain succinctly related all the vicissitudes through which his sailing ship had passed. Seaman's language, short, without an unnecessary phrase. It struck me, and I read it again; it was what I was looking for, without definitely knowing it. Sometimes, you know, just a sign, an indication, is enough. It was a revelation."[138] The outcome was several collections of stories, including *Vita dei campi* (*Cavalleria Rusticana*) in 1880, and *Novelle rusticane* (*Little Novels of Sicily*) in 1883, and two great novels of a projected series to be known as *I vinti: I Malavoglia*

(*The House by the Medlar Tree*) in 1881 and *Mastro-Don Gesualdo* in 1888.

In an earlier chapter we have already seen how Verga captured the imaginations of quite a number of young film critics in Italy in the early Forties. But the most powerful impact he had was on Luchino Visconti. Perhaps initially this was because of the two men's shared origins: Visconti, like Verga, was of aristocratic birth and had toyed successfully with a worldly career (in his case the breeding of race-horses) before a startling revelation changed the whole pattern of his life. For Visconti, the equivalent of the sea-captain's pamphlet was a month's stay abroad. As he tells us: "It was precisely my stay in France and meeting with a man like Renoir, which opened my eyes to many things. It made me understand that the cinema could be the means of approaching certain truths from which we were very far, especially in Italy."[52] But the affinities also go deeper than this. Both men display an abiding sympathy for the poor and choose as their favourite material the progress of a family: Verga in his two principal novels and Visconti in such works as *La terra trema, Rocco and his Brothers, The Leopard* and *Vaghe stelle dell'orsa*. Above all both take, as their central theme, the notion of defeat and the title of Verga's projected series of Sicilian novels—*The Vanquished* could serve equally well to cover Visconti's *oeuvre*.

The latter's discovery of Verga began to make itself felt in the early Forties and helped to shape his conception of *Ossessione:* "I have always considered the problem of Southern Italy as one of the principal inspirations for my work. I must stress that I first became aware of this problem, indeed I may say that I discovered it for myself, thanks to a purely literary revelation: the novels of Verga. That happened to me in the years 1940–41 while I was preparing *Ossessione.* Within the framework of the Italian novel, the only narrative literature which I felt able to take inspiration from at the moment of starting work on my first film in which, in spite of Fascism, I was affronting a theme of contemporary Italian life, was in fact that of Verga and his novels *Mastro-Don Gesualdo* and *I Malavoglia*."[55] Even earlier Visconti's first project had been an adaptation of Verga's *L'amante di Gramigna* (*Gramigna's Lover*), which he wrote with Giuseppe De Santis and Gianni Puccini but which was banned by the Ministry of Culture. In the opening pages of this short story Visconti could find a statement of aims that prefigures much of neo-realism. Verga wrote: "I am sending you here not a story but the outlines of a story. . . . I'll tell it you just as I picked it up in the lanes among the fields, more or less in the same simple and picturesque words of the people who told it me, and you, I am sure, will prefer to stand face to face with the naked honest fact rather than have to look for it between the lines of the book, or to see it through the author's lens. The simple human fact will always set us thinking; it will always have the virtue of *having really happened,* the virtue of real tears, of fevers and sensations which have really passed through the flesh."[138] According to Verga, the triumph of the novel will come when "the harmony of its form will be so perfect, the sincerity of its content so evident, its method and its *raison d'être* so necessary, that the hand of the artist will remain absolutely invisible, and the novel will have the effect of real happening, and the work of art will seem *to have made itself*, to have matured and come forth spontaneously like a natural event, without preserving any point of contact with its author."[138]

Clearly there is much here that ties in better with other neo-realists, such as Rossellini, than with Visconti himself but the basic lesson of realism proved enormously valuable. The culmination of the Verga influence is, of course, constituted by *La terra trema* and it was as early as 1941 that Visconti first decided on an adaptation of *I Malavoglia*, while on a visit to Catania. That year he wrote: "To me, a reader from Lombardy, accustomed by tradition to the limpid rigour of Manzoni's imagination, the primitive and gigantic world of the fishermen of Aci-Trezza and the herdsmen of Marineo had always seemed as if raised by the picturesque and violent tone of the epic: to my Lombard eyes . . . Verga's Sicily appeared like a veritable island of Ulysses, an island of adventures and boiling passions. I thought therefore of a film taken from *I Malavoglia*."[48] The director has returned again and again to the Sicilian novelist in search of inspiration or enlightenment. In 1957, for instance, while hunting for a new subject and before deciding on Dostoievski's *White Nights*, he and his scriptwriter Suso Cecchi d'Amico considered a Verga story, *E andato cosi*. In 1960, when he was preparing *Rocco and His Brothers*, Verga again came to occupy his mind, as he records in his foreword to the published script: "For *Rocco*, a story I had already been thinking about for a long time, the essential influence that I underwent is perhaps that of Giovanni Verga: indeed *I Malavoglia* has obsessed me since my first reading of it. When I come to think about, the principal theme of *Rocco* is the same as that of Verga's novel . . . This film is related to *La terra trema*—which is my interpretation of *I Malavoglia* —of which it constitutes, to a certain degree, the second episode."[142] When Visconti returned to Sicily in 1962 to make *The Leopard*, the influence of Verga again made itself felt, as he pointed out to an interviewer who suggested that his films gravitated towards dream rather than towards social reality. "I am in complete agreement," said Visconti, "if, on the contrary, you say that in Lampedusa's work the particular ways of tackling the themes of social life and existence that were the realism of Verga and the 'memory' of Proust find their meeting point and unison. The strongest ambition that I felt was to have recalled Odette and Swann in the persons of Tancredi and Angelica on the night of the ball and Mastro-Don Gesualdo in the figure of Don Calogero Sedara in his relations with the peasants and on the night of the plebiscite."[32]

As durable as this twenty-year fascination with Verga has been Visconti's adherence to Marxist doctrines. It was the writings of Antonio Gramsci that allowed Visconti to bring the strictly apolitical Verga into a dialectical context and provided a framework in which the novel *I Malavoglia*, and with it the South, could be viewed. In Visconti's own words: "The mythological vein which I had found in Verga no longer seemed adequate to me. I felt an impellent urge to find out for myself what were the historic, economic and social foundations on which that Southern drama had been built. Reading Gramsci I learned the truth that is still waiting to be resolved. Gramsci did not only convince me by the acuteness of his historical and political analysis but his teaching also explained to me the character of Southern Italy as a great social rupture and as a market for a colonialist type of exploitation by the ruling classes of the North. I saw in Gramsci, the founder of the Italian Communist Party, something that is not to be found in other studies of the South's problems: the indications of a realistic, practical solution, in terms of the overall problem of the unity of our country: an alliance between the workers of the North and the peasants of the South, in order to break up the power of the agricultural and industrial capitalist block."[55]

It is interesting to note that Visconti's discovery of Communism and his first awareness of the potentialities of the cinema date from the same year and the same encounter, namely his work as Jean Renoir's assistant on *Partie de Campagne* in France in 1936. Visconti has recorded his debt to the great French director and to the spirit of France in the Thirties: "During that ardent period—it was the time of the Popular Front—I adhered to all the aesthetic ideas and principles and not only those, but the political ones as well. Renoir's group was sharply left-wing and Renoir himself, even if not a member, was certainly very close to the Communist Party. My eyes were really opened then: I came from a Fascist country where you could not know anything, read anything, become acquainted with anything, nor have any precise personal experiences. The impact was very great and when I returned to Italy I was really much changed."[52] Visconti still sees Communism as the only force capable of radically changing Italian society and avoiding mere "transformism," that is to say surface modification and reconciliation that leaves the essence of the problem untouched: "My adhesion to the action and programme of the Italian Communists is dictated by the knowledge that in Italy a new, autonomous, historic force has formed which is not corrupted by transformism but is capable of working to transcend that sterile but ever-present compromise between right and left which, from Crispi to Giolitti, ends by producing Fascism. This new historic force has its roots in the unity of all the workers."[32]

Visconti's Marxism gives his work a dimension lacking in that of Rossellini or De Sica in that he shows concern with establishing the economic and social causes of his tragedies that are moreover viewed in an historical context. The fate of the Valstro family in *La terra trema*, like that of the Parondis in *Rocco and his Brothers*, grows out of the lasting division of Italy into a wealthy North and a poverty-stricken South. The lovers of *Senso* and the Prince in *The Leopard* are alike representatives of a dying class. In the often quoted words of Franz Mahler, the "hero" of *Senso*: "What does it matter to me that my compatriots have won a battle today in a place called Custoza . . . when I know that they'll lose the war . . . and not only the war. And Austria within a few years will be finished. And a whole world will disappear. The world to which you and I belong. And the new world which your cousin speaks about has no interest for me. It's better not to be involved in these matters and take one's own pleasure where one finds it."[143] Here Visconti is presenting both a view radically different from his own and a statement that sums up a whole class at a given moment of history. Almost all his films are set in their precise historical context, often by the use of a kind of "double focus." *La terra trema,* more especially in its planned form of a trilogy, records conditions prevalent for well over three quarters of a century—the novel after all was published in 1881—and yet at the same time reflects the particular aspirations of the Left in 1947. Even more striking are Visconti's interpretations of Italian history. *Senso* is both an examination of a phenomenon of considerable actuality for those who fought in the partisan movement—the motives behind collaboration with the enemy—and a study of the causes for the resounding Italian defeat at Custoza in 1866. If this suggestion seems to exaggerate elements only lightly sketched in the distributed version of the film, it must be recalled that this version is the result of extensive cuts by producers and censors. Visconti's original intentions were more explicit: "It is towards the historical aspect that it was orientated first of all. I even wanted to call it *Custoza* after the name of a great Italian defeat . . . The battle therefore had originally a much greater importance. My idea was to draw a comprehensive portrait of Italian history against which the personal adventures of Countess Sapieri would stand out, though she was, basically, no more than the representative of a certain class. What interested me was to tell the story of a badly-waged war, fought by a single class and leading to disaster."[21] In a similar manner, *The Leopard,* in which Visconti again deals with Sicily, is both a treatment of the transformism that in the director's eyes characterises contemporary society and the specific study of the Risorgimento viewed as a revolution that failed. Thus the concern with Marxist approaches to history and society extends outside Visconti's neo-realist work, just as the influence of Verga permeates his films up to the Sixties. But one film in which the two interests are perfectly fused is Visconti's masterpiece of 1948, *La terra trema.*

9. La Terra Trema

THE MARXIST TEACHINGS OF GRAMSCI are perhaps more apparent than the lessons of Verga in the vast project that Visconti had in mind when he went to Sicily in 1947. Although the final film of *La terra trema* is technically a production of Universalia (a large but short-lived company with close Catholic connections founded by Salvo D'Angelo), it was initially sponsored by the Italian Communist Party which provided the first few million lire that allowed Visconti to begin work. Starting out fom his twin sources, Visconti conceived a plan for making a film which would deal with three of the principal economic problems confronting postwar Sicily: fishing, mining and agriculture. The only remaining trace of this triadic structure in the finished film of *La terra trema* is the subtitle, *Episodio del mare*, but originally the three episodes, though complete in themselves, were to be intercut so as to trace the rise and growth of unity among the workers of the island. The details were not fixed beforehand but the broad outlines were: three stories, each of four parts, interwoven and building up from defeat, through partial success to a real victory.

In Visconti's original plan, the projected first episode, dealing with the fishermen, was to follow much the same pattern as the completed *La terra trema* as we know it. At dawn the boats return and the fishermen receive their meagre earnings, but the young men led by Antonio are increasingly frustrated and turn to attack their "enemy." On his return from prison Antonio makes his attempt to achieve independence and enjoys an initial success. But in a stormy night his boat is smashed and all is lost. Antonio is defeated and resumes work under humiliating conditions and the message is clear: "He has lost because he was isolated."[141] The only major divergence of *La terra trema* from this first pattern lies in the identity of the "enemy." In the original script this was to be a big motor trawler which was ruining the coastal fishing, but in *La terra trema* the social focus is sharper and the "enemy" is clearly seen as the group of wholesalers. The second episode was to begin with a crowd of miners protesting about short working at the sulphur mine at Giove. They find a leader in the thirty-year-old Cataldo who persuades fifty or so to join him in taking over a disused mine and working it co-operatively. But the vein gives out and they face ruin. Then a new vein is found and they are able to continue their joint efforts for a while at least: "They know that the new vein will not signify victory . . . They will continue their hard life of toil as before."[141] In the third episode we were to see peasants awaiting the arrival of an organiser who will help them to take over the uncultivated land, but he does not arrive for he has been shot by the Mafia. Under the leadership of a second organiser, nicknamed "il Saracino" (the Saracen), the peasants decide to oppose the old semi-feudal order. A co-operative is organised to take over the land and plans are made to impress the landowners by a show of strength and unity. The peasants' open-air celebration is broken up by machine-gun fire from the hills but the Mafia has miscalculated, since the funeral of the victims becomes a massive demonstration of solidarity and leads to the land being occupied nonetheless. When the authorities oppose this move, help from towns and villages pours in: "The battle is won thanks to the solidarity of all the workers of the island (fishermen, farm labourers, industrial workers, etc.). The government is forced to intervene to resolve the dispute."[141]

The planned trilogy, then, had a strongly revolutionary content. Visconti did not underestimate the difficulties—his notes refer to the final victory as "a miracle" but the tone is positive and progressive. The pronounced Marxist flavour of his approach comes clear from his own account of his intentions: "I was seeking to express the whole dramatic theme as a direct outcome of an economic conflict. The key to the understanding of the spiritual and psychological conflicts is always social, even if the conclusions I reach are always those which concern the individuals whose cases I am describing."[55] Unfortunately for him, however, production difficulties allowed only the first episode to be made and this on its own runs for some two hours forty minutes. The "Episode of the Sea" is the least revolutionary and the most pessimistic of the three parts planned and it brings Visconti very close to Giovanni Verga, whose account of his own approach to the material of the novel *I Malavoglia* provides a fascinating contrast to that of Visconti quoted above. In his short story *Caprice* Verga wrote about his forthcoming novel: "I have tried to decipher the modest and obscure drama . . . whose whole point seems to me to lie in this:— that when one of those little beings, either more weak, or more incautious, or more egotistic than the others, tries to detach himself from the group, in order to follow the allure of the unknown, or out of desire to better himself, or out of curiosity to know the world, then the world of sharks, such as it is, swallows him and his kin along with him."[138] Visconti's own film differs from Verga's novel in many ways but nevertheless, and against his original intentions, *La terra trema* emerged as a study of defeat and not as an affirmation of victory through class-solidarity.

To recapture the tone of the missing portions of the trilogy we have to look outside the cinema to a book by Carlo Levi, about his journey through Sicily in 1951, entitled *Words Are Stones*. The central part of this book describes a visit to some sulphur mines near Palermo where the miners have come out on strike against the archaic and inhuman methods of the owner. One evening Levi visits the headquarters of the miners' league and talks to the strikers: "They told me their stories, the evils they had to endure, the hunger, the tyrannies, the hardships—the whole life of the poverty-stricken sulphur miner. But that was not what counted, either for them or for me, at the moment. When they spoke of their misfortunes, their eyes and their expressions were cheerful, open and smiling. They were thin, some of them disfigured by accidents, and many of them, both children and men, have on their faces the signs of disease, of tuberculosis and prolonged undernourishment. But it seemed as though they had all of them forgotten these things, moved by a flood of enthusiasm for what was happening, for what they were doing, all of them together, all of them in unison. They were proud, sure of victory, and happy to have discovered themselves as human beings and free men, happy with a new kind of happiness which showed itself in the expression, both touched and touching, on all their faces. They were new faces, faces of today, eyes which, today, saw things that until yesterday had been hidden, eyes which saw themselves."[89] Trying to understand their feelings Levi concludes that "the pleasure they have at feeling themselves alive, and their sureness of victory, derive from an ineffable, unconscious sense of having undertaken a role in a real adventure, of having plunged into the moving stream of history."[89]

Many commentators writing about *La terra trema* give the impression that it was improvised by Visconti during the six months he spent in Sicily or that it grew spontaneously out of the lives of the fishermen who act in it. This is, however, to underestimate both the degree of formal planning behind the film and its very close relationship with Verga's novel *I Malavoglia*. This latter is quite remarkable when one takes into consideration the fact that the novel was published in 1881, whereas Visconti was filming in 1947–48. That the director could take over so much unchanged is of itself a revealing comment on the stagnation of Sicilian society. Visconti filmed at the very village of Aci-Trezza in which Verga had set his story and took over the central motif of a failed attempt by a family of fishermen to break out of poverty. The stages of the decline are inevitably simplified and much of the motivation significantly altered but the focus of attention in the film, as in the novel, is the family. Many of the characters too—virtually all the principal ones in fact—come straight from *I Malavoglia*, though in most cases they have been given new names, the family surname, for example, becoming Valastro. The patterns of personal relationships are largely those of the book, in some instances with the dialogue virtually unchanged: the unrealised relationship of the eldest daughter Mara with the bricklayer Niccola echoes that of Mena and Alfio in Verga's work, while the police officer Don Salvatore's seduction of the second daughter Lucia follows the same course as Don Michele's affair with Lia in the novel. The secondary themes too recur: emigration to seek fortune (Cola Valastro is a new character but he has many traits of the original 'Ntoni Malavoglia), the grandfather's death in hospital, 'Ntoni's unsuccessful wooing of Nedda (renamed after the heroine of one of Verga's best-known stories), and the decline to drink and then eventual rehabilitation, united in the figure of 'Ntoni Valastro in the film, but split between the brothers 'Ntoni (the failure) and Alessi (the restorer of the family fortune) in the book.

Equally important is the new perspective of the film. Whereas in Verga's work the plight of the poor is hopeless and the tone therefore fatalistic, with Visconti there exists a possibility of changing the social pattern and if 'Ntoni fails, others coming after him may succeed. This is reflected in the way in which the focus has shifted from the grandfather and mother who typify acceptance in the book, to the grandson 'Ntoni who represents the new order in the film. In *I Malavoglia* the only representative of "progress," the chemist who advocates revolution, is a comic figure, afraid of his wife and terrified by a visit to the lawcourts. But in *La terra trema* 'Ntoni is a most forceful young representative of the rising working class who suffers defeat but ends with an awareness of the chances of ultimate success. In line with this new perspective, the gossip-ridden village of Verga's novel with its local notables bound up intimately with the poor families in a unified community is replaced by a society split between rich and poor on

Marxist lines. Vividly drawn characters like the money-lender Uncle Croce-
fiso and his aide Paedipepera are replaced by the fish-wholesalers Raimondo
and Lorenzo who are little more than typical representatives of the exploiting classes. Visconti also falsifies the picture of Sicily to a certain extent
by reducing the place of religion in society. In his film there are a few
references to "the will of God" but not a single scene of church-going,
though at the end of the film, when the wholesalers' new boats are blessed
by the priest, Visconti does indicate discreetly the links he sees between
church and aristocracy, wholesalers and Fascism.

La terra trema is by no means an episodic film but its action falls into
four phases which, though separate in themselves, grow logically the one
out of the other, like the successive acts of a play. The first phase traces
the hero 'Ntoni's realisation of the situation facing him and the other
fishermen and leads to a first purely negative but partially successful
rebellion. The film opens at dawn. As Mara Valastro and her sister Lucia
begin the day's housework, the fishermen come home from their night's
work. On the beach they repair their nets before going home to wash and
eat. In the few hours break in the routine of work and sleep, the family
carry on with their personal affairs. 'Ntoni goes off happily to meet his
flirtatious girl friend Nedda, Lucia, walking through the village, is eyed
by the *maresciallo* of police, Don Salvatore, and from her window Mara
talks to the bricklayer Niccola with whom she has a shy, unspoken understanding. But all too soon the round of work begins again and the men
of the Valastro family go off with their nets taking with them a meagre meal
of wine, bread and anchovies. In the course of this time we see three distinct stages in the growth to self awareness of 'Ntoni Valastro and since the
only copy of *La terra trema* available in this country lacks subtitles, it seems
worthwhile to record these important passages of dialogue.

COLA: The tackle's all damaged this morning. It'll take a month
to repair.

'NTONI: Not a month, but a week at any rate.

FISHERMAN: It was a rotten night. Ours is all in pieces too.

'NTONI: And what do you think? Do you think that certain "friends"
can understand these things? *They* don't care a damn!
We're donkeys, good for nothing but work!

BANDIERA (*a friend of 'Ntoni*): And in the morning, when we bring the fish,
how they hurry to get here and wait on the quay.

'NTONI: If it wouldn't be too difficult, the thing to do would be to
transport it ourselves, the fish that is, to Catania, instead
of letting them grow fat.

COLA: Did you hear how Raimondo and Nino Nasca were quarrelling this morning when we landed? Raimondo said that
he'd arranged to buy ours.

FISHERMAN: Don't you worry, Cola. They never really quarrel. They do
it to give themselves airs. They argue, they come to blows
but they're always in agreement against us.

'NTONI: We are the ones who are never in agreement. Because everyone only looks after his own interests, and for a penny we sell our souls as well.

COLA: We can't carry on like this.

        Later, at home, the dissatisfaction of 'Ntoni and Cola becomes clearer and contrasts strongly with the acceptance of life as it is shown by the grandfather:

'NTONI: Here we are again. We work all night and the others take our fish.

GRANDFATHER: It's always been like this, as long as I can remember, at Trezza, Castello, Capo Mulini.

'NTONI: It shouldn't be like this any more (*he calls to Lucia to bring him a jug of water for washing*). It cannot go on like this. I've often told you so, Grandfather.

GRANDFATHER: Cola, what's the matter with 'Ntoni?

COLA: Grandfather, do you know what it's all about? 'Ntoni has been on the mainland, to be a soldier, and he cannot stand injustice. Now he doesn't reason like us anymore, he reasons in another way. Isn't that right, 'Ntoni?

GRANDFATHER: I'm seventy years old and I've always reasoned in one way and everything's gone well for me. 'Ntoni should listen to the old men. An old head on young shoulders, that's what they say.[141]

        On the boats at night a new conversation springs up as the men pause for a smoke or a drink and 'Ntoni's influence on his fellow fishermen becomes apparent:

'NTONI: It's no good struggling. The sea's dry and the night's dark. There are too many of us in the boats—there's nothing to be done. Even if you all worked together. The sea of Trezza would have to be as big as the city of Catania.

COLA: Oh yes? What would we need then? The fishermen of Trezza would be able to look at their own reflections in it!

GRANDFATHER: This is the sea that God gave us, and we must be content with it.

'NTONI: Yes, Grandfather, God gave us this piece of sea beyond the faraglioni and he also gave us these boats . . . in which we cannot go far . . . but, Grandfather, the Lord didn't invent these dealers who always exploit us fishermen.

COLA: I see what Grandfather means. When a thing doesn't go right, it's no use blaming the others.

'NTONI: Yes, that's it. It turns my stomach to see anything as rotten as this. They simply grow rich on our backs.

PEPPINO (*an old fisherman on Bandiera's boat*): I tell you youngsters, these are the terms . . . You talk, but we have to get the fish out whether we like it or not.

BANDIERA: Eh. Whether we like it or not, up to a certain point. Whether

The realists of the South:
Antonio Gramsci (top left), Danilo Dolci (top right), Carlo Levi (middle left)

The mythical South and its cultural heritage:
Giovanni Verga (middle right), Luigi Pirandello (bottom left), Giuseppe Tomasi
di Lampedusa (bottom right)

Luchino Visconti directing Katina Paxinou in ROCCO AND HIS BROTHERS
(1960) (top left) and Burt Lancaster in THE LEOPARD *(1963) (top right)*

THE LEOPARD:
The last ball (bottom left) and the revolution that fails (bottom right)

Alida Valli as the Countess, representative of a dying class, in Visconti's SENSO (1954)

The family and the community in harmony in the opening scenes of Luchir
Visconti's LA TERRA TREMA (1948):

Mara and Niccola (top), 'Ntoni with his family (middle) and his friends (bottom

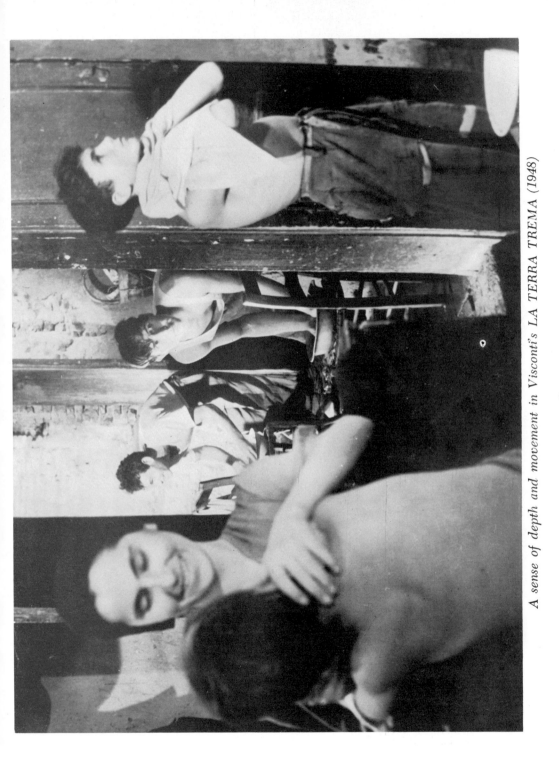

A sense of depth and movement in Visconti's LA TERRA TREMA (1948)

*The disintegration of the family in LA TERRA TREMA (1948):
The women's vigil, the seduction of Lucia, poverty and the mocking, triumphant
wholesalers*

Luchino Visconti   *Suso Cecchi d'Amico*

Maria Schell and Jean Marais in Visconti's WHITE NIGHTS

203

Luchino Visconti's
BELLISSIMA (1951):
Alessandro Blasetti as the film
director (top) and Anna
Magnani as the hopeful
mother

we like it or not, until you old men go to sell the fish. On account of you, things always end with them getting the better of you . . . Isn't that right, 'Ntoni, what I'm saying?

GRANDFATHER: Don't say such things, Bandiera.

BOY: You're too good, you are.

PEPPINO: You talk and talk and always worry about us old 'uns. Instead of worrying about the old 'uns, why don't you go onto the quay? Let's see what you're capable of.

COLA: Uncle Peppino, you shouldn't get offended if we tell you things like this. You know what us young people are like. We want to put our finger on the injustice . . . like St. Thomas. So, if Grandfather allows us, we'll go there, we will, to the quay.

GRANDFATHER: I've never seen things like this as long as I've lived: the young people doing what the old 'uns do. All the same, if you want to go there, then go. But remember, they're always right.[141]

So it is agreed and when at dawn the boats return, it is 'Ntoni who confronts the wholesalers. In the turmoil of buying and selling he suddenly intervenes to seize the scales and hurl them into the sea, shouting at the top of his voice as he does so. A general fight ensues with men tumbling over propped-up bicycles and into the water, and the first phase ends with Don Salvatore's policemen intervening to break up the fighting and arrest the ringleaders. The second part of the film appears to confirm 'Ntoni's belief that the time to act has come. The wholesalers, deprived of their best fishermen, capitulate and withdraw their charges against 'Ntoni and his friends. By mortgaging the house 'Ntoni can raise the capital that allows him to work independently of the middlemen and his venture reaches its climax when the Valastros, their friends and neighbours, salt the anchovies they have caught which are to be the basis of their fortune. This sequence with its fast crosscutting and close-ups of grinning faces shows Visconti at his closest to the great Russian directors of the silent era. But already the warning signs of 'Ntoni's failure are apparent. On a personal level we sense the terrible vulnerability of these unsophisticated people, witnessed most touchingly in the little fairy tale Lucia is telling her baby sister Lia at the moment when Don Salvatore comes to call. The contrast of her childish dreams and his all-too-obvious intent is clear and moving: "And the king's son, handsome as the sun, rides for a year and a month and a day on a fine white horse, until he arrives at an enchanted fountain, full of milk and honey. He gets off his horse to drink, and what do you think he finds? My thimble! Taken there by the fairies. And the king's son sees my thimble and falls in love with me. He rides and he rides and he rides and finally reaches Trezza! To look for me! He takes me, puts me on his fine white horse and takes me far, far, far away with him."

'Ntoni comes back from prison having learned a further lesson:

GRANDFATHER: What's it all about, 'Ntoni?

'NTONI: Did you see? They put us in prison because the law says we have committed a crime . . . Yet when it suits them, the law doesn't count any more. And they let us out. Do you understand what that means? I'll tell you! . . . It means that they need us.

COLA: But how can they possibly needs us . . . We are work-horses, like Cousin Jano's donkey. Who could need us? The fish, to get caught.

'NTONI: I'll tell you who needs us! And then, why always stay subject to them. Let's leave them alone. And let's see where they finish up. Let's see how they eat without our help!

GRANDFATHER: 'Ntoni, a man who chooses a new road in place of an old one often finds himself worse off.

'NTONI: Grandfather, your proverbs were good one time but not anymore. Don't think that I'm mad. I think with my head, not with my feet. I don't want to hurt anybody . . . yet I can tell you that we didn't come into the world to lead the lives of beggars, without being able to hope for better . . . but to be at least masters of our own lives and those of our families.

GRANDFATHER: Your father used to work all the time and he didn't grumble like you.

COLA: Yes, yet our father died at sea, beyond Capo Mulini. Who thanked him for it? After he'd worked all his life for the others! Who thinks about him any more now and all the others who died like him at sea, working for the others? . . . 'Ntoni is right.[141]

What 'Ntoni has failed to see is the absolute need for solidarity: it is because *all* the best young fishermen had been arrested that the wholesalers had to secure their release. Now, although the nerve of the other fishermen fails despite his passionate harangue, 'Ntoni thinks that he can win with merely his family as a unit. The wholesaler Raimondo has a truer awareness of the situation and sums it up in one of his proverbs: "as the worm says to the stone, give me time and I'll riddle you with holes."

The third phase of *La terra trema* traces the disintegration of the family when 'Ntoni's project fails. The family now have to fish in all weathers and a single storm washes out all their hopes by tearing away their nets and ruining the boat. For a long time in fact it seems certain that the men have lost their lives too and for hours the black-garbed women stand on the rocks, straining their eyes for a sight of the boat. When 'Ntoni does land to the mocking laughter of the wholesaler Lorenzo, he knows that he has lost. Gradually the family's ties with the community outside are broken: they are turned out of their house, 'Ntoni loses his girl friend Nedda to Lorenzo, Mara renounces Niccola, Cola, unable to find work is tempted away to the mainland and Lucia is seduced by Don Salvatore. With the grandfather's death and 'Ntoni's decline to drunkenness the outlook seems hopeless. The key scenes of this section are two confrontations. The first is that between 'Ntoni and Cola on the eve of the latter's departure:

COLA: Do you know what it's all about? I'm tired of living here (*standing in front of the chest-of-drawers he lights the lamp and fixes the photograph of 'Ntoni in his sailor's uniform to the mirror. Then turning to his brother*) I can't believe that in the rest of the world men are as bad as the ones living in Trezza! So much that I am even fed up with living here.

'NTONI: (*reflected in the mirror, sitting on the bed with his face in his hands, stirs at Cola's words and raises his head*):
You shouldn't say things like that.
(*sets up and goes up to his brother, still reflected in the mirror*)
Because we were born at Trezza, and at Trezza we must die.
(*puts his hand on his brother's back*)
Even if we suffer, Cola.

COLA: (*his face now reflected in the mirror, looks at the photograph of 'Ntoni*) You can talk like that, 'Ntoni, because you know the world (*smiles*) Taranto . . . Bari . . . Spezia, you've even been there. There are so many places outside this district . . . a man could make his fortune. I want to help you 'Ntoni and I want to help the family as well.

'NTONI: Cola (*both their faces are reflected in the mirror. 'Ntoni goes nearer to his brother*) in all the world (*resting his face on Cola's back*) the water is salty . . . as soon as you get beyond the Faraglioni the current will wash you away (*lowers his face to weep and leaves his brother. Goes to the door then turns back*) Cola, always remember this, it's here that we must fight.[141]

The second major confrontation is the mid-night one between Mara and Lucia:

MARA: Where have you been?

LUCIA: Sh. Sh, 'Ntoni may hear us.

MARA: 'Ntoni isn't here, he hasn't come in yet. Nowadays he doesn't come back anymore at night, and I stay here waiting for him.

LUCIA: Then you've been waiting for me too?

MARA: If Mother knew . . . She would die of shame . . . With all the worries she's had.

LUCIA: And me? What have I done? I haven't done anything wrong. Mother can know about it for all I care. Tell her. I do what I want. And nobody's going to tell me what to do. After all, what does it matter to me. Staying indoors all the time, hidden like a treasure. Some treasure. Nobody would want to marry us. Do you know that?

MARA: Don't say things like that, Lucia. Now that we are poor, we must think of saving our honour. And we must work as well to help 'Ntoni.

LUCIA: (*shouting*) It was 'Ntoni who brought this misery on us. And now we're in this state, what does 'Ntoni do? He's out all night and doesn't do a stroke of work. Cola's gone off. Grandfather's been taken to hospital. Do you want to know the truth. Someone told me they ought to keep an eye on 'Ntoni, otherwise he'll be committing some stupid act.

MARA: (*rushing at her sister, slapping and shaking her violently*) Who? Who told you that? Don Salvatore, I suppose. And that, what's that? (*she points at Lucia's necklace and tries to grab it*)

LUCIA: Nothing, nothing. Don't touch it. It's mine.

MARA: It's yours? Really? Shame on you. Shame on you.

LUCIA: Let me go. Let me go. (*She runs outside knocking over the lamp. Mara sits down at the table, puts her head on her arms and begins to sob.*)[141]

Finally, however, 'Ntoni finds the strength to face up to his responsibilities once more. His regeneration begins when he goes to look at his old boat which he can no longer afford to repair and a little girl, Rosa, asks if she can help him: "Help me? How could you help me? Those who could do it don't, because they are just envious . . . And yet they should understand that what I did I did for everyone, not for myself alone. And now? You can see they have all abandoned me. And as for me, what are my flesh and bones worth?

That's my old family boat. Look at the state it's in. They all say it's my fault that it's in this state. But the day will come when they all understand that I was right. That day, losing everything like I've done will be a blessing for all of us.

We must learn to love one another and all be united. Yes, then we'll be able to make progress."

'Ntoni has learned the lesson of what happens to the poor if they are not united. Swallowing his pride, he goes with his younger brothers Vanni and Alfio to seek work under humiliating circumstances from Lorenzo and Raimondo. That evening the three of them set off to recommence the Valastros' struggle against the sea.

10. The Critical Realism of Luchino Visconti

I T IS PERHAPS ONLY IN ITALY, where appearance and reality are so often at odds, that one would find such a character as Luchino Visconti. It is perfectly credible that, as Duke of Modrone and son of a nobleman who dabbled in the theatre but married the daughter of a millionaire industrialist, Visconti should turn his attention from the breeding of racehorses to work in the theatre. Equally it is quite feasible that he should make a name for himself as a theatrical director with such productions as a version of Shakespeare's *As You Like It* with sets by Salvador Dali and later move on to opera to achieve great success at La Scala Milan with Maria Callas. All this seems quite compatible with his aristocratic origins, even if his ruthless professionalism in theatre and opera-house is unexpected. What is hard to believe is that this Visconti co-exists with another, totally different one: the Visconti who is a Marxist and an admirer of Antonio Gramsci and whose work in the cinema bears witness to a life-time's concern with the poor and underprivileged. It was this latter Visconti who forged a totally new style with *Ossessione* in 1942 from the twin sources of Jean Renoir and the American naturalist novel and who, under the influence of Verga, gave the Italian cinema one of its masterpieces with *La terra trema* in 1948. It is hardly surprising that at first the two streams ran separately side by side in Visconti, the Dali experience following immediately after *La terra trema* without either one influencing the other. But in time a fusion ws established, in the theatre with a realistic production of Chekov's *Three Sisters* in 1952 and in the cinema with the operatic *Senso* in 1954. This new and enriched style took Visconti far beyond the bounds of neo-realism, though his characteristic themes and obsessions remained the same and the chosen means of expression were still realistic in the wider sense of the word. Visconti's film work in the Fifties and Sixties has been more complex and spectacular, but it is possible to feel that it has lacked the supreme cohesion of his Sicilian masterpiece.

Most discussions of Visconti's work are centred on the relationship between his films and his theatrical and operatic experiences, and clearly this is in many ways a valid approach. *Senso* is indeed a *melodramma* (to use the Italian term since the equivalent English word has acquired a quite unjustified pejorative sense) and the subsequent works follow the same trend. But all this is quite irrelevant to *La terra trema*. On the one hand we have the director's own explicit assurance: "*La terra trema* is a film made after my first theatrical experiences and I cannot say it was influenced by the theatre;"[21] on the other the most cursory examination would show the futility of seeking analogies with the theatre. What *La terra trema* does show more clearly than the later films—and this underlines its importance as a key work in his development—is that the source of Visconti's narrative style lies in inspiration drawn from the novel. Like the great critic Georg Lukács, whose Marxism existed alongside a deep love for so bourgeois a writer as Thomas Mann, Visconti draws many of his standards from the novel of critical realism as it evolves in the Nineteenth century.

In his approach to film structure, Visconti has many affinities with the novelist. Unlike Rossellini, he believes in the shaped narrative that shows development of plot and character over a period of time, not in the anecdote or tightly sprung *conte*. His editor, Mario Serandrei, has aptly said that "two hours are never enough for Visconti"[52] for his films are planned in terms of sequence rather than of shot and he needs time above all else for his narrative to grow and reach its climax. Several of Visconti's finest films—*Ossessione*, *La terra trema*, *The Leopard*—have been based on novels but, as he reminded an interviewer regarding this latter work, he is never a mere adaptor: "My film is not and could not be a transcription into images of the novel. . . . Even while maintaining a great fidelity to the novel which has inspired it (as will, I hope, be the case with *The Leopard*) a film must have its own expressive originality. And not only from the visual side."[32] Inspiration from the novel is always there, however, even when Visconti is writing an original script. In the case of *Senso*, for which Camillo Boito's short story is no more than a pretext, Visconti turned to Stendhal whom Auerbach, it may be recalled, saw as the father of the modern realist novel. Visconti has admitted that he thought all the time of Stendhal: "I should have liked to make *La Chartreuse de Parme*—that was my ideal. If my film had not been cut, and if it had been edited as I wanted, it would have really been Fabrice at the battle of Waterloo. Fabrice passing *behind* the battle. And the Countess Serpieri had as a model La Sanseverina. My ideal, I confess, would be to film one of Stendhal's great novels."[21] *White Nights* was adapted from a story by another major novelist, Dostoievsky, while the shadow of Verga hangs, as we have seen, over much of Visconti's work. With regard to Twentieth century novelists, Visconti has drawn inspiration from Proust and Lampedusa in *The Leopard*, adapted Albert Camus's *L'Etranger* and made *Rocco and His Brothers*, the title of which is a discreet homage to Thomas Mann whose novels *Buddenbrooks* and *Joseph and His*

Brothers are, according to the scriptwriter Suso Cecchi d'Amico, among his favourite books.[52]

Visconti's deep and lasting concern with the novel allows him to avoid both the theatrical artifice to which the Italian cinema is so prone and the photographic naturalism, on the brink of which neo-realism always hovers. *La terra trema* has a deep stylistic unity that is greatly aided by its classic simplicity of form. To bind his work together Visconti uses basically simple devices like repetition and the spacing of scenes to great effect. There is a rhythm of recurrence of certain scenes—the arrival and departure of the boats for instance—and the film's power is such that a whole lifetime of experience seems to lie between the two symmetrically placed appearances of the little boy selling oranges. Similarly the three meetings of Mara and Niccola spread out over the whole length of the film hold together thanks to their repetition of words, gestures and muted emotions, and come to imply a whole relationship stifled by social pressures. The same purpose of coherence is served by the constant use of stock figures—the grandfather who is so out of tune with the new ideas and bewildered by change, and the self-effacing mother almost invariably depicted carrying the smallest baby—her eighth child—in her arms. A discreet use is made too of symbolism. The *faraglioni,* the twin rocks guarding the entrance to the bay, are seen again and again in the film and gradually, though not explicitly, acquire a certain symbolic value. They mark the limits of man's control: beyond them lie the hostile sea and an ensnaring outside world. In the black immobility of these rocks lie too a sense of foreboding and a reminder of the harshness of life in Aci-Trezza. Equally important is the family portrait that serves to introduce us to the family at the beginning of the film. The strength of the Valastros resides in their sense of unity and the film becomes tragic when, under the stress of circumstances, this is broken. When, at the very end, Mara hangs up the portrait once more, we know that the Valastros are not beaten: Life has begun again. None of these stylistic devices is over-emphasised, for rhetoric is not part of Visconti's aesthetic concern. The lessons he has drawn from literature are quite the opposite: "It seems to me that one must simplify the style to the maximum extent. Because the style of a great novelist is the barest possible, it contains the least adjectives, the least punctuation, the least superlatives, and is the plainest of all."[52]

The underlying unity of *La terra trema* does not imply monotony, indeed the very visual texture of the work is matched to the various phases of development. The opening shots of the fishing boats returning before dawn are both beautiful and sombre and set the key for the film's mood. The scenes of 'Ntoni's formulation of his ideas form a methodical succession and take place in the open air—on the beach or at sea—where the Valastros work with their neighbours and friends. Their house in these early scenes shares the same atmosphere: doors and windows are open, allowing background and foreground to be linked by the flow of people moving to and fro, depth and movement being admirably caught by G. R. Aldo's camera. The Valastros are integrated into the community and one senses the easy interchange between them and their neighbours. The brief period of success is admirably reflected in the faster rhythm of the salting scene with its quick succession of grinning, laughing, chattering faces, young and old, neighbours and friends. Then with the defeat that comes midway through the film the rhythm changes again and the mood becomes melancholy, reinforced by the highly effective but sparsely used music. The Valastro home is closed up now, half prison, half refuge for the family, and when Don Salvatore comes wooing Lucia he has to force open the shutters closed by Mara to keep out the world. The key scenes of this section take place in the semi-darkness of the home—'Ntoni pleading with Cola to stay, Mara angrily confronting the errant Lucia. When fate strikes, events hammer down on the family leaving it no respite—Cola's departure coincides with the arrival of the bank officials and Lucia returns from her seduction by Don Salvatore to find her grandfather being taken off to hospital. In the earlier part of the film when the camera had lingered, it had been on scenes of bustling activity such as the daily fish auction, but now the long-held scenes all have a desolate air: the black-clad women standing motionless on the rocks, straining their eyes for a glimpse of the Valastro boat, or the empty windswept beach where Cola seeks a means of escape. Only in the final scene of renewed struggle do the Valastros go out among the people again.

Visconti's concern with the formal aspects of La terra trema was not limited to the visual side and he took great care with the soundtrack. The music, which was arranged by Visconti and Willy Ferrero from Sicilian melodies is used sparingly and, perhaps for that reason always to good effect. It is saved for the latter part of the film, where it serves to emphasise the magnitude of the disaster facing the Valastros. Almost the only reminder in the score of the director's interest in opera occurs in the triumphant fish-salting scene when music from Bellini's La Sonnambula is used for ironic comment, in much the same way that the "charlatan" theme from Donizetti's L'Elisir d'Amore is used in Bellissima to underline the appearances of the film director played by Alessandro Blasetti.

Despite the sparseness of the actual musical accompaniment considerable use is made of natural and informal music-making: there is the singing of the workman that draws Mara to the window to meet Nicola, the gloating, self-satisfied whistling of Don Salvatore and the harmonica playing of 'Ntoni's drunken companion. There is also the use of sound itself: the bells and shouts that go with the opening dawn shots, the turmoil of the fish auction and the joyous sounds that accompany the blessing of the wholesalers' boats and drift up to the defeated 'Ntoni. The spoken language too is boldly used. Only the bank officials consistently speak Italian which, as Visconti tells us in his introduction to the film, is not the language of the poor. 'Ntoni, his friends and his enemies all speak a Sicilian dialect which is so broad as to be incomprehensible to Italians elsewhere, so that even in

Italy the film had to be accompanied by an explanatory commentary. The effect of this use of dialect is both realistic and poetic: it allowed the use of improvisation and actors drawn from real life and also constituted a tongue that Visconti found both "very beautiful" and archaic "like Greek."[21]

The formal perfection of *La terra trema* is in no way sterile for it is balanced by Visconti's constant preoccupation with the human element in film-making, the actors. This was the great lesson that Jean Renoir gave him: "It was Renoir who taught me to work with actors. That brief contact of a month was sufficient, so much did his personality fascinate me."[21] Actors already occupied a dominant place in his conception of the cinema as early as 1943 when he wrote his celebrated article on an "anthropomorphic cinema": "Of all the tasks that fall to me as director, the one that excites me most is working on the actors, the human material with which one constructs these new men who engender the new reality that they are destined to bring to life, the reality of art. Because the actor is above all a man. He possesses the key human qualities. On these I try to build by graduating them in the construction of the character to the point when the man-as-actor and the man-as-character manage, at a certain point, to form only a single unit."[31] For Visconti the actors, whether they are stars, professionals or amateurs are all subjected to the same discipline and his success with non-professionals may be attributed to his ability to turn them swiftly into actors and make them embody the conception of their parts that is already clear in his mind.

Visconti himself has given the best analysis of the use of fishermen and peasants in *La terra trema*: "Employing non-professionals is not in any way an indispensable condition of neo-realism. True, it is possible to find in the street 'real' people who fit the characters in question exactly but the real work is then to make them into actors. I spent hours and hours with my fishermen for *La terra trema* just to make them say a tiny piece of dialogue. I wanted to get from them the same result as I would have got from an actor. If they were talented, and indeed they were (they had one extraordinary quality above all: a lack of complexes in front of the camera), they could achieve this very quickly. The real job with actors is making them overcome their complexes and modesty. But these people had no modesty. I obtained from them what I would have obtained from actors after a much longer time."[21] The standard of acting in the film is extraordinarily high. Visconti's hand is apparent in the controlled *mise en scène* displayed in the crowd scenes and in the organisation of the hustle and bustle of the Valastro home. But frequently he uses long takes for quite complicated pieces of acting—the principal confrontations of brothers and sisters in the latter part of the film or such passages as 'Ntoni's return to find the bank officials measuring the family home or Lucia's reactions after her seduction by Don Salvatore. The latter scene, for instance, needs no word of dialogue. As the grandfather is carried out to the car that will take him to hospital, Lucia arrives home, excited and clasping something in her hand. She moves towards the house with a guilty look to either side, then reveals the glass trinket. Tears come to her eyes, but she smiles as she holds the necklace against her throat.

The actors in *La terra trema* were in many ways as subordinate to the will of the director as are the non-professionals in a film by Robert Bresson. But even if the overall conception of the film depended little on them, they were able to make an important contribution to the dialogue. In some cases this was taken almost word for word from Verga's novel, his literary transcription of the language of the people being "translated" as it were back into Sicilian. Elsewhere, as Visconti has explained, the actors themselves made a major contribution: "The text was not a preconceived text. I made them make it up themselves. For example, I took the two brothers and said to them: 'Now the situation is this. You have lost the boat, you are living in poverty, you have nothing to eat, you don't know what to do any more. You, you want to go away, you're young and your brother wants to keep you here. Tell him what's drawing you away from here.' He replied: 'To see Naples, I don't know, really.' 'Good, that's it, but why don't you want to stay here?' He told me then exactly what he says in the film: 'Because here we are like animals. They don't give us anything. Then I'd like to see the world quickly.' For him the world was Naples, it was far away, it was the North Pole. Then I went to the other: 'What would you say to your brother, your real brother, to keep him here?' He was already moved, with tears in his eyes. He thought it was his own brother. That's what you want from actors but never get. With tears in his eyes, then, he said: 'If you go beyond the *faraglioni* (that's the name of the two rocks) the storms will carry you off.' Who could have written that? No-one . . . The dialogue was born like that then. I only furnished the preliminary sketch. They brought images, ideas, flourishes. Then I made them rehearse the text, sometimes for three or four hours, just as you do with actors. But we didn't change the words anymore. They were fixed, as if they had been written. And yet it was not written, it was invented by the fishermen."[21]

In one instance the effect of this improvisation of dialogue can be measured with real accuracy, for the published script of *La terra trema* contains an appendix in which Visconti's original notes for one scene are printed. A comparison of these notes for the scene when 'Ntoni puts his plan to his fellow workers with what is actually said in the film is most instructive:

| Here is what 'Ntoni wants to propose to his friends: | 'NTONI: |
| To open their eyes. Liberate themselves from the system in which they live and work which results only in their being exploited by the wholesalers. | Listen to me, lads, then I'll tell you what I've thought of doing. |

For too many years—centuries perhaps —they have supported them. And their fathers too, and the fathers of their fathers. So much that one is born a slave. If one of us had the courage and knowledge to give the example and rebel, all would follow him.

They have all seen it and quite recently. Why contrive to work for the Raimondos and Lorenzos? What do they risk? They alone have the advantages and the profits. And they themselves the risks, the dangers. And the families they support—their families who must eat—and the risks of the boats and their lives, the lives of their younger brothers, and all suffocated, without hope—trapped in the circle of poverty. He knows that all of them have thought, are thinking about these arguments.

He too, 'Ntoni, has done that so many times. But then it reaches a point where there is no way out. The ideas become confused. And the habit . . . and then everything becomes obscure, like a fog, and if you do not want to beat your head against the walls you have to leave things alone and resign yourself.

Oh yes. They threaten reprisals. They seek to frighten the weaker, the more timid and fearful. . . . We must not let ourselves be impressed. Let's remain strong and united! We must not let ourselves be intimidated. For the rest, if they threaten, what does it mean? That they are afraid: they know that a change would be a defeat. They will not recover again. They will have to accept the new reality. Work will be a noble sacred thing.[141]

For so many, so many years, perhaps centuries even, we have all had our eyes closed . . . and our fathers, and the fathers of our fathers, so much so that we can't see ourselves any more.

You all saw what happened a couple of days ago. . . . Why continue to work for Raimondo, Lorenzo and co.? What do they pay back to us? They have all the profit and none of the risk. The risks and the dangers, we have them: we risk the boats and the tackle, and our younger brothers run the risk of ending their lives prisoners in a cage of poverty. I know you have all thought about these arguments.

I've done the same as well, many times. I know it's reached the point where everything gets confused in our heads . . . like in the basket where the fish twist and turn without finding the way out . . . then we resign ourselves. We must put an end to that state of affairs at all costs.

Of course they threaten us. They try to frighten us. But whom exactly? The stupidest of us! But we mustn't be afraid of them. It's enough if some of us begin to work on our own, because the others will find their courage and follow our example. And then they'll thank us.

❀   ❀   ❀

Visconti's aim when he set out to make *La terra trema* was to achieve absolute realism: "The causes of *La terra trema* stemmed too, basically, from the perplexity which increased day by day within me, when I saw the movement going off course, losing its prestige. From which, at a certain moment, came the need to begin again from scratch, from pure truth, without any trickery. Without a pre-established script, without any real actors, relying completely on reality and truth. . . . At the time of *La terra trema* I remember that my professional conscience told me: you must do that, you must take the method to its extreme limit, you must make *no concessions.* You must demonstrate that this is the right course. . . . With *La terra trema* it seems to me that I really achieved realism."[52] This is a judgement with which it is difficult to quarrel, and a measure of the film's achievement is its complexity. It is, first of all, a totally personal work and much of its homogeneity derives from the consciously implanted imprint of Visconti's personality that it bears. "It seems to me," the director said, "that the most important thing is for a work always to bear the mark of a personality."[52] This mark can be traced in every aspect of *La terra trema*: in the overall conception of the film as much as in the acting, in the visual style as much as in the soundtrack. On another level the film fulfils the Marxist aim of art, as defined by Ernst Fischer: "The essential function of art for a class destined to change the world is not that of making magic, but of enlightening and stimulating action."[57] *La terra trema* is an object lesson for Socialists in that the reasons for 'Ntoni's failure are clearly attributed to the fact of his being alone. But at the same time, being so close to Verga's fatalistic novel *I Malavoglia*, it never falls into the trap of becoming a mere *film à thèse;* indeed the somewhat doctrinaire Marxist historians of neo-realism, Raymond Borde and André Bouissy, talk sourly of "les self-made men du Reader's Digest"[17] when discussing 'Ntoni. From an artistic point of view, however, *La terra trema* can only gain from such ambiguity. Though the work of a Marxist, it has as its real subject pride, not solidarity, and it sees the essential unit of society as the family, not the social class. The hero is no proletarian—at one point he talks of the humiliation of working for others —and his aspirations are largely personally motivated, and yet his struggle is viewed with a sympathy worthy of Verga himself. Though reference to religion is minimised, there is no real condemnation of Mara's fatalistic resignation when she tells Niccola that they must do God's will and part. The bricklayer Niccola too is by no means an unsympathetic character yet he accepts his social role as preordained. Even 'Ntoni at one point says to Cola: "With God's grace and our work we will move forward." This is not to imply that a religious interpretation fits the film better than a Marxist one —the sense of impending social change is deeply embedded in the film— yet it is a measure of Visconti's realism that he does not try to impose a rigid Socialist pattern of progressive thought on his film.

Perhaps the most common criticism of *La terra trema* is that its formal perfection is somehow gratuitous. Whether it is Orson Welles complaining tersely that Visconti photographs starving peasants like fashion models in *Vogue* or Geoffrey Nowell-Smith becoming perturbed at "the faint aura of aesthetic indulgence with which the film is beset,"[108] these antagonistic comments have essentially one thing in common: the belief that it is somehow wrong for a realist film to be beautiful. This puritanical notion fails to take into account the fact that realism in the cinema is a style, not a mere transcription of reality and that accordingly an ugly shot is no more real than a grammatical error. Moreover it would seem that poverty, in Aci-Trezza at least, is not always unaesthetic. Carlo Levi, in *Words Are Stones*, records a conversation about Aci-Trezza he had with a foreign lady whose enthusiasm "was quite natural and direct. She knew nothing of classical mythology, nor had she ever heard of Verga or Visconti." Her comment on the village and its inhabitants is worth reporting at length since it bears out the validity of Visconti's vision: "They don't seem to me to be men and women and children of today, but trees in a forest, or antique beings like the gods. Their looks and their gestures are like those of statues: the fishermen, both young and old, have necks like statues. It seems to me that everything here must always have been thus and always will be thus. . . . They will have the same gestures, the same way of accepting things, the same way of wrapping themselves in their shawls and walking with the grace of animals or of princes. That is why this little village seems to me eternal and wonderfully beautiful."[89]

The richness of *La terra trema* lies in its successful synthesis of seeming incompatibilities: it is in part a documentary on crafts and faces in the manner of Georges Rouquier and yet it has a plot development that requires over two and a half hours to unfold; it relies strongly on words for its arguments, yet the dialogue was improvised by fishermen in a Sicilian dialect largely incomprehensible even to educated Italians; it was shot on a small budget in the open air and on location but the clarity and depth of its photography could not be bettered in any studio; it is a completely truthful study of poverty and also a polished and beautiful work of art; it is Verga plus Gramsci, the aristocratic Visconti plus the fishermen of Aci-Trezza. As such it is complex enough to encompass the reality of Sicily as few other works have done but at the same time—and this is perhaps its greatest achievement—it fulfils totally Luchino Visconti's stated first aim in the cinema: "to tell stories of living men."[31]

11. The Agrarian Problem: De Santis and Lattuada

THOUGH THE NEO-REALIST DIRECTORS are largely town-bred and university educated, the problems of city life find surprisingly little expression in their films and Vittorio De Sica's primacy in the depiction of urban corruption, unemployment and isolation is unchallenged. In general terms—De Sica apart—the works that are given urban settings are of less interest than those examining rural conditions and problems. Visconti's *Bellissima* (1951), for example, is set in Rome but its social insights are peripheral to the description of a woman's obsession with making a film star of her young daughter. The situation gives Anna Magnani the opportunity for a virtuoso performance but does not produce drama to match the Sicilian *La terra trema.* Similarly it was not until the virtual end of neo-realism and after three films with rural settings that De Santis made *Roma ore undici* (1952), based on a real-life incident, the collapse of a staircase on which two hundred girls all seeking the same vacancy were crammed together. De Santis researched his material thoroughly: "For days and days I galloped around Rome questioning everyone directly or indirectly connected with the tragic event. I spoke to a great number of those girls. I spoke to the people living in the block of flats. I spoke to the firemen and the police. The result of all this was an enormous dossier of accounts, incredibly rich in humanity."[17] The script that he elaborated with Cesare Zavattini reflected his discovery that "today unemployment strikes not only the working class but also the middle and lower middle classes,"[17] and traced the stories of half-a-dozen of those involved, ranging from a prostitute who wants to change her life to a rich girl who has left home out of love for a painter. No answer could be given to the question raised of which individuals were responsible for the catastrophe, because the blame clearly lies with the organisation of a society that allows millions to go unemployed.

By contrast there are numerous films dealing with the agrarian problems and indeed the late Forties in Italy are marked by the general revival of interest in the life of the peasant and the problem of the South which had too long been ignored. Writing in *Christ Stopped at Eboli* Carlo Levi had described the South as, "that other world, hedged in by custom and sorrow, cut off from History and the State, eternally patient . . . that land without comfort or solace, where the peasant lives out his motionless civilisation on barren ground in remote poverty, and in the presence of death." The situation in the late Thirties, when he was banished to a remote corner of Lucania, was characterised by Levi in these words: "To the peasants the State is more distant than heaven and far more of a scourge, because it is always against them. Its political tags and platforms and, indeed, the whole structure of it do not matter. . . . Their only defence against the State is resignation, the same gloomy resignation, alleviated by no hope of paradise, that bows their shoulders under the scourges of nature."[88] But this centuries-old neglect was partially remedied in the postwar period, thanks to the efforts of writers like Levi himself, social workers like Danilo Dolci and one politician above all, Antonio Gramsci. The founder of the Communist party, who died shortly after his release from a Fascist prison in 1937, had seen the unity of the industrial workers from the North and the peasantry of the South as the main hope for a Communist revolution. In the late Forties it seemed possible that events would bear out his analysis, as the peasants turned more and more to the parties of the left, the Communists and Socialists. Muriel Grindrod, who has no particular liking for the Communists, admits that it was they who "penetrated remote hamlets, setting up their own local organisations and staging congresses for the 're-birth of the

Mezzogiorno.' In the pre-land-reform years they untiringly advocated such a reform and encouraged peasants to occupy land, proclaiming that the Government would never take the initiative and that only a completely revolutionary policy could 'free the peasants from their serfdom' and bring about the radical changes needed."[63]

To the rising pressure from the Communists and Socialists, the Right replied with violence, of a kind typified by the events of May Day 1947 at Portella della Ginestra when a peasant rally was broken up by machine-gun fire from the gang led by the bandit Giuliano. But action of this type ran the risk of proving counter-productive, for the combined impact of the American invasion and compulsory military service had widened the horizons of the young men and made change of some sort inevitable. Against the background of violence and poverty a new social conscience developed, not only in the North but in the remoter regions of the South as well, and the neo-realist films dealing with the South and with agrarian problems are unusually closely linked to current events. A publicity brochure put out with *Il cammino della speranza* records that "when Pietro Germi arrived, the workers of the Ciavalotta mine—where filming was to take place —had been on strike for several days for the self-same reasons which provoke the events of the film story. This gave Germi the chance to film some of the most impressive scenes 'from life,' in a genuinely tense atmosphere."[61] Similarly Alberto Lattuada has said, with regard to his film *Il mulino del Po* that "the peasants could say their dialogue with great truth for, at the time when I was shooting the first peasant strikes at the end of the last century, other strikes, very real ones this time, were breaking out."[117]

Not all the concern with the problems of the countryside was purely disinterested, as Giuseppe De Santis's film *Riso amaro* (*Bitter Rice*) shows. This, the director's second film, made in 1948, was scripted by three men with impeccable credentials, all of them ex-critics of *Cinema:* De Santis himself, Carlo Lizzani and Gianni Puccini. The writers apparently spent weeks among the workers of the Po valley, studying their problems, listening to their stories and sharing their hardships. The subject is of considerable social interest—the thousands of girls who flock annually to the rice fields to work for forty days or so under appalling conditions for forty kilos of rice and a payment of forty thousand lire. They are treated as a kind of rural sub-proletariat, herded into barracks behind walls guarded at night and with their wages depressed by the employment of "irregulars" without proper contracts who will accept a cut rate. With this material there is clearly scope for an uncompromising social study but judging from the film it is evident that someone in the course of the production saw the commercial possibilities of a film featuring several hundred naked-thighed young women. The plot too is far removed from sober documentation, being a melodramatic story involving two interacting couples and illustrating the same kind of tragic passion as that of Alberto and Daniela in *Caccia tragica* or Gino and Giovanna in *Ossessione*. Francesca (Doris Dowling), a basically good girl in love with a crook, Walter (Vittorio Gassman), who exploits her, joins the train carrying women to the rice fields. She becomes involved in friendship and rivalry with Silvana (Silvana Mangano) who is herself on close terms with the police sergeant Marco (Raf Vallone). When Walter arrives to join Francesca, he is immediately attracted by the beautiful Silvana and has little difficulty in seducing her, in view of her cheap romanticism fostered by her predilection for pulp fiction, pop music and commercial movies. He persuades her to help him steal the rice by flooding the fields as a diversion, but his efforts are foiled by Francesca and Marco. After an indecisive gun-battle, the film reaches its climax with Silvana shooting her deceitful lover and then going to throw herself off the high watch tower overlooking the camp.

There is an epic sweep and plenty of violent action in *Bitter Rice:* quarrels among the girls in the rice fields, a seduction in a thunderstorm, a gun battle amid rotting carcasses in the refrigeration plant and a spectacular suicide. There are also several typical De Santis touches. The women, though forced to toil for hours on end at the back-breaking work, are not allowed to talk to each other, and the director makes full use of the lyrical and dramatic possibilities offered by their chanted communication of news and emotion. The ending of the film also recalls *Caccia tragica* as the rice girls file past the body of the dead Silvana and signify their forgiveness by scattering over her body a handful of their precious rice. De Santis seems particularly fond of this kind of unexpected symbolic gesture: a sign of his discontent with the recording of unheightened reality. Silvana is undoubtedly the most interesting character in *Bitter Rice* and was intended by De Santis to "criticize alienation, the American morality of *Readers Digest* and pin-up films."[45] He has always denied any erotic intent, explaining that in this film he was thinking not so much of eroticism as of liberation, wanting "to express man, woman and society in their . . . natural primitive integrity."[32] For him eroticism is only acceptable as "a total interpretation of nature, outside social or moral habits, a total sense of nature, a . . . cosmic sense of nature."[32] If this is the case, De Santis has not really succeeded in *Bitter Rice* for Silvana Mangano dominates the film with her physical presence, establishing an international reputation for herself as the kind of pin-up the film was supposed to denounce and opening the way for such Italian sex symbols as Gina Lollobrigida and Sophia Loren.

A much more uncompromising work is *Non c'e pace tra gli ulivi* (1949) generally regarded as De Santis's masterpiece. Again the director, working with his usual writers, has shown his fondness for a strong story line and for passions taken to extremes. Francesco (Raf Vallone), a young farmer, returns from the war to find that his flock has been stolen by Bonfiglio (Folco Lulli) who has also become engaged to the girl he loves, Laura (Lucia Bosé). Bonfiglio is powerful enough to impose silence on those who might tell the truth about his actions, so Francesco takes the law into his own hands by attempting to recover both Laura and his flock. Bonfiglio responds by raping his sister and having him imprisoned on false charges,

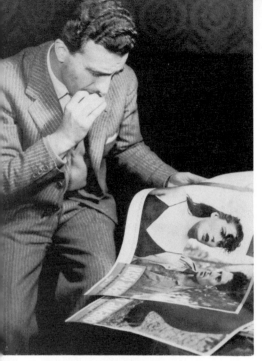

Massimo Girotti and Carla del Poggio in De Santis's ROME ELEVEN O'CLOCK (1952)

Giuseppe De Santis inspecting posters for BITTER RICE

Vittorio Gassmann in De Santis's BITTER RICE (1948)

Silvana Mangano as the de-luded heroine of Giuseppe De Santis's BITTER RICE (1948)

BITTER RICE (1948): the
work in the rice fields

Raf Vallone and Lucia Bosé in Giuseppe De Santis's NON C'E PACE TRA GLI ULIVI (1949)

The statuesque nobility of De Santis's peasants:
Raf Vallone and Lucia Bosé in NON C'E PACE TRA GLI ULIVI (1949)

Alberto Lattuada's IL MULINO DEL PO (1948):
The mill (top), the simple Princivale (middle), the thwarted lovers mocked by
the crowd (bottom left), the failed peasant revolt (bottom right)

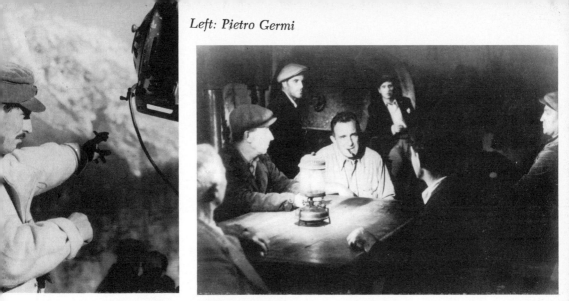

Left: Pietro Germi

Germi's IN NOME DELLA LEGGE (1948):
Above right: The Mafia leader (Charles Vanel) and the violence his rule creates
(below)

Pietro Germi's IL CAMMINO DELLA SPERANZA (1950):
The miners' defeat (top left), the hope of a new life (top right), the final duel in the snow (above)

Germi's later comedy style:
Marcello Mastroianni and Daniella Rocca in DIVORZIO ALL'ITALIANA (1961) (below)

compelling Laura (as a final turn of the screw) to give perjured evidence
against him. Francesco escapes from prison, however, and, helped by the
peasants who have now fully appreciated the extent of Bonfiglio's ambition
to dominate their lives and lands, he succeeds in evading the police and
coming face to face with Bonfiglio. After the latter's death he and Laura
can build a new life together for themselves. The relationship of this film
to *Caccia tragica* is evident and once more it is shown that success can only
come from collective effort by the whole community against those who try
to impose their will by force.

The setting is of crucial importance in *Non c'e pace tra gli ulivi* and De
Santis has placed the action in his own native region of Ciociara, basing
the film initially on a real-life incident which had made the headlines in
the local papers. His concern, however, is with more than a recording of
regional folk dance and song, and his view of peasant character has helped
to shape the dramatic pattern of the film. Replying to an interviewer who
commented on the melodramatic performances of the actors, De Santis replied that in directing them like that he "did no more than respect local
customs. The peasants of the region are proud and distant, they have a
natural tendency to pose, they don't like to look each other straight in the
eye, and that is why in the film they sometimes deliver their dialogue while
facing the camera."[32] Far from trying to simplify or pare down his visual
style to bring it into line with newsreel austerity, De Santis aimed at "developing the architectural side, composition, formal beauty"[32] which he admits
was very important for him. He also turned for inspiration to the works of
Gabriele D'Annunzio, notably to *I pastori*, but found little that accorded
with his own personality. The director wanted neither to record simply
what he saw nor to create a falsely melodramatic "dannunzianism." What
he had in mind would seem to have been not pure neo-realism but the kind
of fusion experienced by Carlo Levi and recorded in *Christ Stopped at
Eboli*. Attending a performance of a D'Annunzio play put on by a troupe
of wandering actors, Levi found that the plot, far from seeming far-fetched
"was true to life, for the audience endowed it with its real atmosphere,
that of the closed, hopeless, mute world of the peasants." In this performance, as in De Santis's film, "all the rhetoric, affectation and pomposity
of the tragedy vanished," leaving just what it should have been in the first
place, "a bare tale of immutable passions against the background of a land
that knows no time."[88]

Alberto Lattuada's *Il mulino del Po* (1948), possibly his finest film and
certainly his own favourite, is a complex work tracing the fortunes of two
families against a background of social change and political unrest amid
the peasants in the year 1876. The film was adapted from a long historical
novel by the contemporary novelist Riccardo Bacchelli, who worked on the
scenario alongside Lattuada's customary collaborators Federico Fellini and
Tullio Pinelli. This use of an historical setting allowed the director to fuse
the two previous disparate elements of his style: the urge for formal perfection most evident in his calligraphist works and the involvement with

the problems of personal revolt in his own age, which he had already treated in melodramatic form and a contemporary setting in *Il bandito* and *Senza pietà*. *Il mulino del Po* is a crucial film in the development of neo-realism, a most striking and successful attempt to unite formalism and the study of the poor, contemporaneity and an awareness of the historical process. The lives of the film's protagonists are shaped by a number of forces. The family of millers, to which the heroine Berta (Carla Del Poggio) and her brother Princivalle (Giacomo Giuradei) belong, is part of the traditional working class which has remained proud of its ancient independence but now finds itself beaten down by government pressure in the form of the excise men who rigorously extract the milling taxes. As a result Princivalle's boast that he is master of his own mill and grinds corn for whom he pleases becomes the empty bragging of a man who is unwittingly betraying his own interests, which in fact lie with the farmers he basically despises. On the land, the tenant farmers of whom the hero Orbino (Jacques Sernas) is one are caught in a deadly struggle between Clapasson their landlord, who believes in progress even at the cost of traditional customs, and Raibolini, the Socialist political organiser who proclaims that the land belongs to those who work it and tries to make the farm workers aware of the political strength which lies in unity.

This clash of interests reaches its climax in the scene during the agricultural strike when in a confrontation on the open fields both Clapasson and Raibolini show themselves willing to allow the soldiers to fire on defenceless women and children if, as they think, this will serve their political ends. In the final outcome neither side emerges as wholly victorious: Clapasson has found that he cannot ride rough-shod over his farmers, he has gained no allies and his crops and cattle have been lost, while Raibolini, his adversary, has been forced to call off the farmers' strike. The mass of ordinary people are organised as never before and the last we see of them is when they march off in a body behind their banner in search of justice for their imprisoned womenfolk. The outcome of this act of revolt is left in doubt but it is clear that collectively they have lost much and gained little, for the film is set, as Lattuada himself explained, "at a time when Socialism is becoming aware of its strength but without succeeding in renewing the structure of Italian society."[32] While making the film Lattuada was constantly reminded that the problems he was evoking had still not been resolved over fifty years later and were the subject of renewed strikes and disorders at the moment of shooting. The director's refusal to draw conclusions unjustified by the facts or to make concessions to either side naturally pleased neither political faction and he has recorded with evident pride that "in *Il mulino del Po* the Communists found that the strike was not used to maximum effect" while the Right said that he "had attacked the order of the middle classes by showing peasants affirming their rights in the face of authority."[77] Lattuada is an authentic neo-realist in that he sees problems in terms which do not allow neat formulas or glib assertions of right and wrong, and his comments on this aspect of his work are strikingly reminiscent of Cesare Zavattini's: "I have doubts, and as I am not a philosopher, I have indicated problems and not solutions."[77]

In part this refusal of political answers derives from the artist's deep concern with his characters whose situation he has himself defined with great precision: "The protagonists of my films are, for the most part, I won't say anarchists, but rebels who find themselves in a situation of revolt and polemic and it would be equally fair to say that in the heart of this struggle they find themselves somewhat isolated."[15] The path from passive acceptance to political awareness and action followed by the uncles of the hero in *Il mulino del Po* recalls words used by Carlo Levi to characterise the peasants: "They have gentle hearts and patient souls; centuries of resignation weigh on their shoulders, together with a feeling of the vanity of all things and of the overbearing power of fate. But when, after their infinite endurance, they are shaken to the depths of their beings and are driven by an instinct of self-defence or justice, their revolt knows no bounds and no measure. It is an inhuman revolt whose point of departure and final end alike are death, in which ferocity is born of despair."[88] Where Lattuada annoyed the political parties of the left was in the recognition—again shared with Carlo Levi—that as the peasant world "has neither government nor armies, its wars are only sporadic outbursts of revolt, doomed to repression."[88] Despite his concern with social issues and with the political attitudes of his characters, Lattuada's prime interest remains not commitment but solitude. He has defined his approach on numerous occasions, claiming that the one constant of his work is "the state of solitude of the individual faced with society, a solitude inseparable from the individual's aspiration to rejoin in the heart of society all those who hope and struggle with him. An attitude of rebellion, engendered by solitude and directed against it but resulting, in most cases, only in the confirmation of this solitude."[15]

This conception of solitude lies at the root of Lattuada's view of freedom: "A free, isolated, independent man, recognising neither parties nor dictatorships, neither fanaticisms nor religions, an individual man struggles, and the army of free men becomes more and more numerous."[77] It is in this sense that the figures of Orbino and Berta who form the foreground of the film are to be interpreted. Their tragic love story is not an irrelevance or a concession to popular taste but the very core of the film, for love is perhaps man's only way of overcoming his innate solitude and by destroying this, society destroys all men's hopes of a better future. Berta and Orbino come, like Romeo and Juliet, from warring factions, her family struggling to maintain the millers' traditional aloofness while his throws in its lot with the Socialist league. Economic pressures from outside prevent them from marrying or securing any kind of future for themselves, and their attempts to stand above the bitter disputes which tear the agricultural community apart merely result in their being denigrated as traitors and blacklegs. The destruction of their love with the murder of Orbino comes as a result of the pressures brought to bear on Berta's brother Princivalle. Duped by Clapasson into betraying his class and tricked by one of Raibolini's lieutenants who has a personal grudge against him, this basically good-natured young giant of a man is driven to kill Orbino because of a fictitious insult. In a situation in which even the lucid and open-minded Orbino cannot make a place for himself in the community, a man like Princivalle who thinks with his fists is obviously doomed.

Like De Santis and Germi, Alberto Lattuada has aspirations to create works of epic proportions and in *Il mulino del Po* these ambitions are masterfully fulfilled. The film contains the flow of violent incident customary in Lattuada's work with fights and confrontations in abundance. As a piece of pure action the scene where Princivalle sets fire to the mill to hide evidence from the excise men is an outstanding amalgam of hubbub and chaos, fire and darkness. The architectural, formalistic sense evident in Lattuada's handling of his crowd scenes is nowhere more apparent than in the scenes confronting peasant women and soldiers amid the half-cut field of corn. There is no attempt at a purely realistic picture of the clash, instead Lattuada draws his camera back from the participants to set the black and menacing line of soldiers against the ragged groups of peasant women in a manner reminiscent of Eisenstein's treatment of the Odessa steps sequence in *Battleship Potemkin*. Here the emphasis is on the courage of the women who win a moral victory, only to throw it away senselessly by attacking with their fists and nails the retreating troops. Seldom has the need for discipline and unity among the poor been more poignantly demonstrated. But Lattuada is not content with a mere violent surface. As the true protagonist of the film is the Italian people buffeted by forces beyond its control, so the action is given a cosmic meaning through its links with nature. Nature is used to comment on the action: the millers' disaster comes after a night of rising flood, and a storm is in the air as Clapasson decides to dispossess Orbino's family. Above all there is the river Po itself, given a lyrical theme by the composer Ildebrando Pizetti who was born on its banks. It is with shots of the Po that the film opens and closes, and the gulf separating Berta and Orbino is defined initially by the difference of their attitudes to the river. Orbino fears the river and it is ironic that after his death his body should be unceremoniously thrown into the Po. After all the violence of fire, revolt and murder, *Il mulino del Po* comes to an elegiac ending with the black clad Berta and her mother waiting for dawn and for Orbino's body to rise from the depths of the Po.

12. Pietro Germi's Sicily

ESSENTIALLY THE PROBLEM OF THE SOUTH arises from the persistence into modern times and in the context of a modern state of an alien, in many ways feudal, culture with its own attitudes and reaction patterns. Pietro Germi himself spoke of Sicily as a "land of limitless solitude, withered beneath a relentless sun. It is a land which is not only a smiling paradise of oranges, olive groves, flowers and blue seas—but a land which is inscrutable, mysterious, splendid and possessed of a tragic primitive loneliness. For the great part it is scorched and arid—a land where men live like anchorites in accordance with ancient changeless customs."[61] One cause often singled out to explain the circumstances of the South in general and of Sicily in particular is the social and economic system that has favoured the underdevelopment of industrial resources and the preservation of large estates. The latter are often deliberately and systematically underworked by their absentee owners and left largely in the hands of farm managers more concerned with their own positions of power and authority than with the living standards of the landless peasants hired as day labourers. Such a system is clearly open to abuse, particularly as there is no incentive to achieve efficiency and a better use of land resources. As a result the peasants find themselves forming a pool of unwanted labour, permanently under-employed if not totally unemployed (the official figure for the latter was 12% in 1950). Moreover there has been no increased development of industry to compensate for this agricultural stagnation, and a survey carried out in the Fifties pointed out that industrial development in the South was in fact lower in 1950 than at the time of the unification in 1861. These circumstances, aggravated by Sicily's lack of exploitable natural resources and its high birth rate, have given rise to a situation where abject poverty is almost the norm: a survey of 1952 classified the living standards of half the inhabitants of the South as "low" or "very low," and enlightened investigators from the North found unbelievable living conditions prevalent everywhere.

The face of the *Mezzogiorno* has hardly changed in a hundred years. Describing the Sicily of 1860 in *The Leopard*, Giuseppe Di Lampedusa wrote "In the vivid light of five-thirty in the morning, Donnafugata was deserted and seemed despairing. In front of every house the refuse of squalid meals accumulated along leprous walls; trembling dogs were routing about with a greed that was always disappointed. An occasional door was already open and the smell of sleep spread out into the street; by glimmering wicks mothers scrutinised the lids of their children for trachoma; almost all were in mourning and many had been the wives of those carcasses one stumbles over on the turns of mountain tracks. The men were coming out gripping their hoes to look for someone who might give them work, God willing . . ."[134] Against this one may set the account of the town of Matera at the time of Mussolini's Abyssinian war given by the narrator's sister in *Christ Stopped at Eboli*: "The houses were open on account of the heat, and as I went by I could see into the caves, whose only light came in through the front doors. Some of them had no entrance but a trapdoor and ladder. In these dark holes with walls cut out of the earth I saw a few pieces of miserable furniture, beds, and some ragged clothes hanging up to dry. On the floor lay dogs, sheep, goats, and pigs. Most families have just one cave to live in and there they sleep all together; men, women, children, and animals. This is how twenty thousand people live . . . I saw children sitting on the doorsteps, in the dirt, while the sun beat down on them, with their eyes half closed and their eyelids red and swollen; flies crawled across the lids, but the children stayed quite still, without raising a hand to brush them away. Yes, flies crawled across their eyelids, and they seemed not even to feel them. They had trachoma."[88]

This then was the Sicily to which Germi went in 1948. With *In nome della legge* he set out to investigate one of the most perplexing features of this society, the non-Christian Mafia code of honour and manliness. The Mafia would seem to have evolved originally as the poor man's defence against brutal tyranny and oppression and in the course of time it developed its own iron morality. As Norman Lewis explains: "No *mafioso* sees himself as a criminal, and the Mafia has always been the enemy of petty crime—and therefore, to a limited extent, the ally of the police . . . The *capo-mafia* considers himself a lawgiver, concerned with the welfare of his people, and prides himself on watching over the advancement of deserving juniors in the organisation with the assiduousness of the master of novices of a religious order. In his own eyes, he never steals from the community, but he can see no objection to exploiting his power over men to enrich himself. To delinquents he awards only one punishment, usually after a warning: death."[90] Such a code, demanding killing as of right, must inevitably degenerate into meaningless violence and as a result banditry has always been prevalent in Sicily. At the end of the Second World War there were two or three dozen armed gangs of bandits in the hills of Sicily of which Salvatore Giuliano's was only the best known. Moreover in the course of time the Mafia had changed from being the defender of the poor to becoming the most efficient instrument of their oppressors. The only man to cower the Mafia had been Mussolini who, by giving his ruthless police chief Mori free rein to torture and intimidate, at least drove the organisation underground. Ironically it was the American liberating forces who, using the Mafia network to aid their invasion of Sicily in 1943, restored its fortunes and those of its head, Don Calogero Vizzini.

In nome della legge, Germi's film about the Mafia, displayed great technical polish, for the director had already had considerable cinematic experience. A graduate of the *Centro sperimentale*, he had worked as Alessandro Blasetti's assistant and directed two films on his own: *Il testimone*, a thriller, in 1945, and *Gioventù perduta*, a study of juvenile delinquency, in 1947. Turning to the problems of the South he chose to confront social issues of great importance to those concerned with the development of Sicily and it is unfortunate that the treatment he gave them was flawed by concessions. The story is that of Guido Schiavi (played by Massimo Girotti), a young judge who comes to the Scilian village of Capodarso and struggles to apply the principles of law to a community which is used to Mafia rule. He uncovers corruption and neglect, compels the Baron to heed a court order demanding the re-opening of the sulphur mine, but fails to win the love or trust of the people. A combination of intrigue and disappointment turns the whole town against him and the pattern of Mafia killings continues. Guido's only powerful ally is the Baroness, with whom he falls in love and, getting no support from his superiors, he is on the point of resigning when a young lad he has befriended is shot dead. Angered, Guido summons the whole village to an open trial, turns on the Mafia and wins a resounding victory. The Mafia chief, reminded of his own son by Guido's impetuous burst of idealism, hands over the culprit to him and submits to rule "in the name of the law."

This is clearly a trite conclusion, accepting uncritically the Mafia's own estimation of its actions and pretending that age-old customs rooted in the very fabric of Sicilian culture can be eradicated by one public speech. Passalacqua, the Mafia leader, is played by an actor of considerable presence, Charles Vanel, who stands out from the mass with a strong personal authority. He is depicted as calm, reasonable, slow to take offence and always in command of the situation, and the connections between the presence of his Mafia men and the persistence of the corrupt system personified by the Baron are carefully understated. It would be understandable if *In nome della legge* had been given simply a compromise ending as a concession to the producers, but in fact the whole film is bent on establishing the Mafia leader as a legendary figure. The first shot of Passalacqua shows him and his men silhouetted heroically on the skyline and all the subsequent appearances of the armed Mafia killers riding on horseback are accompanied by stirring, triumphal music. Charles Vanel, like so many screen villains before him, dominates the film, but Germi's own sympathies lie no doubt with Guido. Initially seen in longshot, a lone figure on a deserted station, the young judge is treated with great scepticism by his associates, the clerk of the court, the mayor and the local gentry. Gradually, however, he manages to impose his will on those around him, winning the devotion of the *maresciallo* and the love of the Baroness and outfacing the notorious Passalacqua. Though he falters when the workers desert him, it comes as little surprise when finally he stands up to the crowd and the Mafia to establish the rule of law.

In nome della legge has other flaws, even if these pale to insignificance beside the major defect of the handling of the Mafia. The love affair between Guido and the Baroness, for example, adds little to our understanding either of Sicily or of the workings of passion and has clearly been inserted to give audiences a conventional romantic interest. But the film also contains many incidental indications of the director's talent. The action sequences are well handled: the tense atmosphere surrounding Guido when he stands up to Passalacqua or the sudden void that opens up around a man known to be under sentence of death by the Mafia when he enters the bar. Equally successful is the depiction of the "law of silence" which operates when a dying man knows the name of his killer but refuses to denounce him for fear that the Mafia will take revenge on his family. As he tells Guido: "If I die I forgive my murderer, if I live I shall kill him." Germi also contrives to touch briefly on a number of important social issues. The only court scene we witness deals with two workers, both of whom have been unemployed for three years, who have come to blows when one of them accepted a job at cut rates. More striking still is the story of the sulphur mine, closed by the Baron who prefers watching two hundred families starve to trying to run the mine efficiently—an example of the deliberate underemployment of resources on which Sicilian society is built and amid which the Mafia flourishes. But the deepest impression left by *In nome della legge* is the quality of its visual style, its bold use of contrast, making full use of the possibilities offered by the arid Sicilian landscape, setting the black-garbed figures of the women against the dazzling white-ness of sun-drenched walls and focusing on the care-worn faces of authentic Sicilian workers.

Il cammino della speranza (1950), Germi's second Sicilian film, grows out of the first but is an infinitely superior work, containing all the commit-ment lacking in *In nome della legge*. The publicity material put out with the film tells us that while waiting for the ferry to take them to Sicily in 1948, Germi and his producer Luigi Rovere had been struck by "a group of third class passengers arriving from the island. Among them old men, women, children; loaded with their wretched bundles, they looked the typical poor emigrants leaving their native land. What would their fate be? What adventures, sufferings and trials would these people have to go through before settling at last in some corner of the earth that offered them a means of livelihood?"[61] Further inspiration for the new film came during the actual making of *In nome della legge*: "While exteriors . . . were being shot near Agrigento, the sudden closing down of the sulphur mines provoked lively resentment among the local population. Talking to one of them, Pietro Germi learned about the misfortunes of a group of miners, thrown out of work some while before. Attracted by the mirage of well paid jobs in French mines, they later discovered that they had been tricked by the machinations of a shady adventurer."[61] The links between the two films are stressed by the fact that Germi used largely the same technical team, and a number of actors from the earlier work reappeared in *Il cammino della speranza*: Saro Urzi, Saro Arcidiacono and Franco Navarra.

In this new film Germi examined, more honestly and penetratingly this time, a second major Sicilian theme, the question of emigration and the dream of a better life. In the course of time various responses have been evolved by the peasants to the grinding poverty that is their lot. For some the answer has been the Mafia, for others popular revolt (of the kind depicted in Giovanni Verga's story *Liberty*), while others again have turned to the politics of social revolution (Raibolini in Lattuada's *Il mulino del Po* for instance). But one constant has been the lure of emigration: in 1913, for example, well over three-quarters of a million people left Italy and a high proportion of these came from the poverty-stricken South. In the early part of this century the promised land was America but more recently it has been simply the industrial centres of Northern Italy, with the kind of results chronicled by Luchino Visconti in *Rocco and His Brothers*. *Il cammino della speranza* treats a transitional situation: the

attraction of France and the French mines. It begins at the heart of the
problem with a strike by workers in a sulphur mine threatened with
closure because the company is bankrupt. The men's attempt to influence
events by staging a sit-in at the bottom of the mine ends ignominiously
in defeat when fumes drive them back above ground after forty-eight
hours. These opening images—the motionless black figures of the women
waiting in the bright Southern sunlight for the return of their men folk
immured in their gloomy, fume-laden voluntary prison below—show Germi
at his best and stand comparison with visual compositions in *La terra trema*.
As in Visconti's film, the futility of isolated protest against the shortcomings
of a whole social system is pitilessly delineated.

The workers' plight seems hopeless until a stranger, Ciccio, arrives
in the village with the offer of an apparent way out. For twenty thousand
lire apiece, to be paid in advance of course, he will smuggle as many of
the villagers as wish to go into France where work is plentiful. Many of
the men, led by Saro (Raf Vallone), a widower with three small children,
accept and their surge of hopeful anticipation and joyful singing recall the
initial optimism of the migrant workers in Jean Renoir's *Toni*, made sixteen
years earlier. The trek across Italy of the party of miners and their families,
joined by a prostitute Barbara (Elena Varzi) and her gangster lover Vanni,
occupies the rest of the film. The guide Ciccio turns out to be a crook who,
after having vainly tried to give the party the slip in Naples, succeeds in
absconding at the main station in Rome by provoking a gun battle between
Vanni and the police. The miners are warned by the authorities to go back
home or to face imprisonment but many of them decide to carry on. In
the course of the journey some get lost or become discouraged and turn
back and some die, but a small party survives the perils of workers' hostility,
sickness and bitter quarrels to reach the border. There the guards take pity
on them and they cross into France to seek the chance, if not the certainty,
of a new life.

Il cammino della speranza is basically an epic film, narrating a journey
across the whole length of Italy completed only after innumerable hardships and requiring a great strength of character. In the success of the film
the awareness of open space and the sensitive employment of landscape are
key features and, from the hot, bleak Sicilian setting of the film's opening
to the icy, snow-covered mountain slopes of the finale, the background
serves as reflection of and commentary on the action. The characters too
fit an epic pattern. They represent basically a cross-section of the community, types neatly differentiated and with their emotions clearly defined.
They work according to accepted patterns, offering few surprises and the
two key characters, the widower Saro and Barbara, the prostitute in search
of a new life, are romanticised larger-than-life figures. The love of these
two provides the romantic interest conventional in a film of this kind but
it is integrated into the film in a way that the relationship of Guido and
the Baroness in *In nome della legge* was not. *Il cammino della speranza* is
about the finding of new hope by a small group of men, women and children,

and it is appropriate that its emotional core should be formed by the reintegration into the community of a woman whose original family ties in Sicily had been broken by her fall from virtue.

As in the films of Lattuada and De Santis there is in *Il cammino della speranza* a strong element of melodrama. If the early mine sequences constitute an underplayed tragedy, the later confrontations and clashes are all developed to extremes. The gun fight at the railway station in Rome is constructed in true gangster film fashion, while the ritualistic element is stressed in the knife fight to the death which takes place in the snow between Saro and Vanni for the possession of Barbara. The lovers are brought together by the injury to Saro's daughter which prompts Barbara to an act of heroic proportions when she braves the bitterly hostile crowds in the nearby town to fetch a doctor. Yet despite the emphasis laid on the violence of the conflicts and the over-simplified distinction between the good (Saro and Barbara) and the evil (Vanni and the guide Ciccio), the social message of the film is not distorted. The miners who, at the beginning of the film, have been seen on strike against the closure of the mine, are driven by events to become unwitting blacklegs, breaking a strike by farm workers and thus arousing the hatred and hostility of men who should be their allies. There is no attempt to gloss over the bitterness produced by political unrest or to pretend that there are any easy solutions to the problems raised. The film depicts the path of hope, not the certitude of success for those who follow it.

Pietro Germi has expressed his debt to two great film-makers, René Clair and John Ford, and his Sicilian films clearly follow the Ford pattern. Like many of the American director's works, *In nome della legge* and *Il cammino della speranza* are built around the performance of an indestructible hero, played by an actor with star quality. The landscape plays an important part in expressing and visualising the essential conflicts, and both Germi and Ford show the same appreciation of the qualities of a life lived out-of-doors. In many ways these Sicilian films of Germi are best regarded not as works in a pure realistic tradition but as stylised Italian equivalents to the American Western. In *In nome della legge*, for example, Guido arrives in Capodarso like a new sheriff aiming to clean up the town. Friendless and alone, he finds himself confronted by a smiling villain on a white horse. Unarmed he faces the armed gang which opposes his right to establish the rule of law and, with the aid of a faithful henchman and the love of a good woman, he wins through in the end. In *Il cammino della speranza* too there are similarities with the western pattern: Barbara, like the golden-hearted saloon girl, involves the hero in a battle which is fought with the same concern for direct confrontation and fair play as any western gun duel. The comparison with Ford also holds good if one relates the social message of *Il cammino della speranza* to that contained in *The Grapes of Wrath*. The two films share a commitment to the poor, the use of types and a central theme of the journey across a whole country in pursuit of a promised prosperity, and in both works circumstances set workers against workers and lead honest men to become strike-breakers.

Il cammino della speranza is possibly Germi's best film but it did not open the way to further advances. In the late Fifties and early Sixties Germi's career followed a pattern remarkably similar to that of Vittorio De Sica: a number of films in which the director himself played the lead— *Il ferroviere, L'uomo di paglia* and *Un maledetto imbroglio*—followed by a series of comedies designed for the international market—*Divorzio all'Italiana, Sedotta e abbandonata* and *Signore e signori.* From 1950 onwards the South ceases to be a source of inspiration for film-makers and becomes instead a central preoccupation of Italian politicians. Film-makers like Germi and Visconti played a vital part in bringing to the fore the problems of the South, but the issues they raised found their answers not within the realm of art but with political action, like the setting up of the *Cassa per il mezzogiorno* in 1950, to finance the modernisation of Southern Italy.

13. The Story of a Friendship: De Sica and Zavattini

EVERYTHING IN THE CAREER of Vittorio De Sica fits satisfactorily into a neat pattern—except for the works he produced during the period covered by this book. His early career points to exactly the kind of director he has finally become—one whose forte is comedy and who views the cinema as a medium based on acting performance—just as the *carabinere* hero of *Bread, Love and Dreams* in 1954 exhibits the same charm and assurance as the matinee idol of *Gli uomini, che mascalzoni* in 1932. We have seen in an earlier chapter how his first films as a director are a natural outcome of his success on the music hall stage and in Camerini's film comedies. Indeed his real reason for turning to directing was because he wanted to assume responsibility for his acting performance after being attacked by critics for certain aspects of his interpretation of Des Grieux in Carmine Gallone's *Manon Lescaut,* which he had known from the first to be wrong. De Sica's progress in the Fifties and Sixties is consistent with these beginnings. Despite the "sense of dread"[55] with which Hollywood filled him on his visit there in 1952, *Stazione Termini,* made the following year, featured Jennifer Jones and Montgomery Clift and showed a willingness to come to terms with the Hollywood star system. *L'oro di Napoli* (1954), his next film, marked a return to the Italian tradition of good-humoured comedy gliding lightly over the surface of life, and was the first film of his own that he had appeared in as an actor since 1941. The Fifties offered him few chances to direct but innumerable opportunities to act in other people's films. He appeared in well over fifty films during this period and re-established his reputation as a light-comedy actor, partnering firstly Gina Lollobrigida and then Sophia Loren. When, in 1961, he returned to directing after a five year break it was merely as Loren's director in a series of works designed for international distribution.

The overall pattern of De Sica's career as debonair actor and comedy director is clear and consistent, though it in no way explains the fact that between 1942 and 1951 he made a major contribution to the creation and development of the neo-realist movement, which he was still attempting to keep alive as late as 1956, the year of *Il tetto*. It is clearly pointless to use films like *Bicycle Thieves* or *Umberto D* as sticks with which to beat the later "commercial" De Sica, just as it is wrong to doubt the qualities of the neo-realist works because of the inadequacies of *Yesterday, Today and Tomorrow* (1963) or *Marriage Italian Style* (1964). Rather, one should marvel that the works of 1945–51 were ever made at all, given that the producer Rizzoli pestered De Sica for a year to make *Don Camillo*, that De Sica himself once planned a three-language version of *Bicycle Thieves* starring Jean Gabin (French version) and Henry Fonda (English version) and that the material of *Umberto D* was originally conceived to star Barry Fitzgerald in a London setting.

There can be little doubt that it was his scriptwriter Cesare Zavattini who encouraged and sustained De Sica during the difficult years of neo-realism. This is not to say that Zavattini contributed all that was most valuable to the partnership, for *Sciuscià* was predominantly De Sica's in conception as well as execution, while the writer had at that time shown little sign of becoming the great advocate of screen realism. The truth is rather that like Jacques Prévert and Marcel Carné in the partnership which produced such works as *Le Jour se lève* and *Les Enfants du Paradis*, Zavattini and De Sica complemented each other perfectly. As the latter expressed it: "With my lazy, timid and pessimistic character I constantly take a step backward and lack the courage to undertake anything adventurous. Zavattini is quite the opposite, so he was just the man I needed."[131] The two first met in Verona in 1935 when they were both working on Mario Camerini's *Darò un milione*, the one as leading actor, the other as scriptwriter. A friendship developed between them and in 1939 and again in 1940 they vainly sought backing for a film based on a synopsis written by Zavattini for the comedian Totò and entitled successively *Diamo a tutti un cavallo a dondolo* and *Totò il buono*. Eventually this material, after being published in novel form, served as the basis for *Miracle in Milan*, but meanwhile they had begun their collaboration with *I bambini ci guardano* in 1942 which, as De Sica has said, represented "a compromise between the old formula and the new."[55] Subsequently they made *Sciuscià*, based largely on De Sica's experience but with a script revised by Zavattini, and the enormously successful *Bicycle Thieves* from a subject suggested to De Sica by Zavattini. The depth of their friendship is shown by the fact that their next two films, *Miracle in Milan* and *Umberto D* were, in a sense, mutual tokens of esteem. De Sica has expressed his feeling of being profoundly linked to the first of these "because I had conceived the whole film as a homage to my friend, Cesare Zavattini. A long time before, since we first met in fact, I knew how fond he was of a little book called *Totò il buono* which he had written for children. I knew furthermore that his secret wish was to see it made into a film. So I conceived *Miracle in Milan* as a film that would be entirely Zavattini's. A year later Za said to me: 'I want to write a film about an old man called Umberto D.' Umberto De Sica is my father's name; but Zavattini never said that he thought of my father in writing the idea of that film, nor did I ask him whether he was returning the gesture that I had made in filming the Totò story. Good friendships always thrive on sentiments and gestures silently expressed."[55]

For ten years, from 1942 until December 1951 when De Sica paid his first visit to Hollywood, he and Zavattini moved in perfect harmony and caught the precise tone of the period. For the writer *Umberto D* was "not as you think a conclusion, but a point of departure"[3] and he was already working on the virtually plotless *Italia mia* which was to mark the next advance. Everything had been fixed when suddenly and unexpectedly De Sica abandoned the project. Of this Zavattini has written: "I could say then that *Italia mia* represented for us a film of great importance and responsibility. We had reached a good point: De Sica and I were to start shooting, and had agreed on the end of February for our trip. Then a bomb (let's call it that) blew up in connection with another trip, that of De Sica to the United States . . . De Sica left and, after about a month in the United States, he freed me from the obligation I had with him regarding *Italia mia*."[21] This was the decisive break, with De Sica returning to the light-hearted, actor-dominated comedy in which he had begun his career, while Zavattini, as his theoretical writings show, wanted to develop a more spontaneous kind of cinema in which actors and plot would have little place. In the Fifties Zavattini's most cherished propects—*L'amore in città*, *Mexico mio* and *Le italiane e l'amore*—were all planned with other directors and *Il tetto*, their major collaboration of the mid-Fifties, represents more a return to a formula of neo-realism than a creative advance. The personal friendship of the two is still strong and Zavattini has remained De Sica's inseparable scriptwriter, but their co-operation is no longer mutually enriching and they have become no more than a routine, if enormously successful partnership producing star-vehicles tailored for the international market. To characterise the quality of their collaboration in its heyday one cannot do better than quote De Sica's reply to their critics in his open letter to Zavattini published in 1953. "It is certain that none of these critics encouraged us ten years ago, at the time of *I bambini ci guardano* or *La porta del cielo*, when the community of our inspiration was already apparent and we were already giving proof of an agreement that could never be more total. No-one encouraged us, let me repeat, and we were really alone, you and I, each putting his confidence in the other, and it was in this way that *Bicycle Thieves* was born . . . For my part, I have never had doubts, and I don't believe that in the wartime and postwar years two brothers could have been more united than we were, moving towards the same goal."[21]

After the break in the early Fifties Zavattini continued to plan and theorise, and indeed his most notable accounts of neo-realism date from this time. But much of this theoretical writing deals with the way he thought the movement ought to develop rather than with what it actually was, and therefore demands to be treated separately. In the case of De Sica, however, *Umberto D* is in a very real sense a culmination, for nothing he has done since merits the same kind of attention and analysis. He is not a theorist and all his principal ideas and concerns are implicit in his films and best discussed in the context of them. But before we proceed to *Sciuscià* we need to examine briefly the basic assumptions on which De Sica's film work rests. It is important to remember that his work has its roots not in social analysis or commitment but in comedy. Asked by an interviewer in 1950 who, in his opinion, had contributed most to the renaissance of the cinema since the end of the war, he replied without hesitation: "Charlie Chaplin, of course."[127] He must have been delighted when René Clair described him in his book *Réflexion Faite* as "Chaplin's most authentic successor," for Clair is another of his idols. Of these two he once said to an interviewer: "Do you know that I am obsessed by two 'monsters'? They make life completely impossible. They are Charlie Chaplin and René Clair . . . After them the cinema has become almost impossible! Those two discovered everything."[45] Interestingly enough this formation in comedy was shared by Zavattini who has admitted that before the war he had felt that "the 'bright idea' and the 'gag' were the essential thing in the cinema and that they represented the fundamental function of the film writer."[131] The war gave both De Sica and Zavattini a new perspective, but something of their initial way of looking at the cinema must have persisted, if we are to believe De Sica when he says that one of the difficulties of preparing *Bicycle Thieves* was "the necessity of fighting against situations that are too funny, words that are too witty, everything there is in fact above (or below) the line separating realism from filmed comedy."[45]

De Sica sees himself as a realist and his work bears witness to a profound sense of concern with humanity: "It is perhaps presumption on my part but I would find it hard to give up my conviction that I am capable of understanding men, their feelings, their sorrows and their dramas."[86] For him the true path of the modern cinema is realism and those who prepared the way are men like Chaplin, Donskoi and Flaherty. These are significant names, for Chaplin made his statements about mankind almost exclusively through the medium of comedy, Donskoi made films "to tell the universe that life is beautiful, if living means working for the happiness of others, for their right to be happy,"[28] and Flaherty remained, as Roger Manvell has pointed out, an interpreter of humanity not of social phenomena and made his films by living happily among people whose lives are governed by an isolated existence in natural surroundings. In terms of his own work

De Sica could justly claim to have taken his cameras into the streets to lay bare the face of poverty and suffering in postwar Italy. His great discovery outside the studios was the extent of human solitude and, as he has said, the real meaning of his films is "the search for human solidarity, the struggle against egotism and indifference."[45] The tragic note of so much of his work, deriving from the failure to achieve this, may be attributed to his scriptwriter Zavattini who has explicitly stated that in his belief "solidarity is not within us . . . Even children are alone and must seek refuge in the dream embodied by the white horse of *Sciuscià*."[45] In De Sica's view of art there is no room for an expression of political commitment, as he made clear at the time of *Il tetto*: "If with the excuse of neo-realism one wanted to make political propaganda, these would be the first films I personally would refuse to have anything to do with. Propaganda should be left to the newspapers, posters and election speakers."[55] His own definition of neo-realism is quite different from that of Zavattini, in that for him "neo-realism is poetry, the poetry of real life."[55] Whereas the writer in his later statements is intent on blurring the boundaries dividing film and reality, De Sica himself draws a clear distinction between realism and naturalism, seeing the latter as "a banal documentary," whereas realism is a "transposition of reality," a "poetic transposition"[45] which for him forms the point of departure for his work.

Despite their ultimate divergence De Sica and Zavattini were agreed, in the years preceding *Umberto D*, on the need to link their films to the reality of postwar Italy, which offered ample scope for the treatment of social problems. Initially the economic situation was grave, industry was slow to recover from the war and unemployment faced those returning from the war and the prisoner-of-war camps. With rationing proving inefficient, the black market flourished, aided by a fall in the value of money. As Muriel Grindrod records: "Between June 1946 and September 1947 prices rose by 150 per cent; the cost of living doubled and by mid-1947 the lira had lost over 98 per cent of its pre-war value."[63] Urban life in Italy cried out for film-makers to record its problems but strangely enough De Sica and Zavattini were almost alone in their choice of material, for Rossellini followed his war trilogy with a series of investigations into Divine Grace (of which *Francesco, giullare di Dio* is the most significant) and into conjugal problems (the Ingrid Bergman films), while the Marxist and Socialist directors were, as we have seen, particularly attracted by the question of agrarian reform and the *Mezzogiorno*. In view of De Sica's pronounced repugnance towards explicit political commitment, it is not surprising that he should choose his characters from those on the margins of society—the child, the unemployed, the old-age pensioner—but nonetheless the link with current events is close. George Huaco points out of *Bicycle Thieves* that "its reflection of the actual social situation seems to be fairly accurate . . . Figures show that officially registered urban unemployment reached a peak in 1948, the year *Bicycle Thieves* was released. Since the official 1948 figure probably represents something over 11 per cent of the work force, the actual total unemployment was probably above 22 per cent of the work force."[75]

Films like those made by the De Sica-Zavattini team clearly need a climate of opinion favourable to the investigation of social problems and in which the voice of the left is heeded. But in fact this was not the way in which postwar Italy developed. The potentially revolutionary situation of the immediate end of Fascism evaporated as the Communist party under Togliatti sought electoral respectability rather than revolution and the prime minister Alcide De Gasperi successfully contrived a consensus of centre-aligned parties so as to isolate the Communists. On one level both sides gained by these manoeuvres. The Communists maintained and enhanced their strength so as to take a quarter of the votes by the time of the 1963 elections and to remain the strongest Communist party in Western Europe. De Gasperi was able to obtain massive American aid for Italy and so prepare the way for the subsequent Italian "economic miracle" and for major schemes of re-development. But in the process the ideals of the partisan movement which lay behind the shortlived Parri government after the war and the renaissance of Italian culture were lost. As the rise of neo-realism can be seen as a product of the resistance to Fascism in 1943, so its demise can be charted in the neo-Fascist upsurge of the early Fifties. In this connection Muriel Grindrod's comments on the Italian neo-Fascist party, the *Movimento Sociale Italiano* are of great interest. This party, she writes, "made no significant showing in the 1948 election, when persons prominently associated with Fascism were still debarred from voting or standing as candidates. But by 1952, despite its lack of outstanding leadership, it had built up some sort of status for itself with the aid of a few powerful backers. The climate of the country had changed since the immediate post-war days when the whole subject of the Fascist regime was anathema. Former Fascists were no longer boycotted to the same extent. Practically all those imprisoned after the war had been released, and Italian tolerance towards individuals had paved the way for their return to circulation."[63]

14. Sciuscià

THE ORIGIN OF *SCIUSCIÀ* is to be found in *Film d'oggi* on which De Sica worked for a short time in 1945 before deciding that "the magazine was becoming too political and calling for the shooting of this person and then that."[55] De Sica's view was that instead of shooting people they should shoot film and in the third number he wrote about a film project: "In contrast to adults, children are ashamed. I notice in their eyes a sort of sense of shame which irritates them and forces them to talk of something else or to run away ... The starting point of the film would be this: children and only they feel that the life they lead is not the one they ought to live."[53]

Vittorio De Sica as actor:
Top: With Maria Mercader in Gianni Franciolini's BUON GIORNO
ELEFANTE! (1952)
Middle left: With Eduardo De Filippo and Maria Fiore in Alessandro Blasetti's
TEMPI NOSTRI (1953)
Middle right: In Luigi Comencini's PANE, AMORE E FANTASIA (1953)
Bottom left: In Alessandro Blasetti's E PECCATO CHE SIA UNA CANAGLIA
(1954)
Bottom right: With Piero Bilancioni in his own L'ORO DI NAPOLI (1954)

Vittorio De Sica's later commercial career:

Top: De Sica directing Sophia Loren in YESTERDAY, TODAY AND TOMORROW (1953)
Middle: Marcello Mastroianni in a scene from YESTERDAY, TODAY AND TOMORROW
Bottom: Sophia Loren and Eleonora Brown in De Sica's TWO WOMEN (1960)

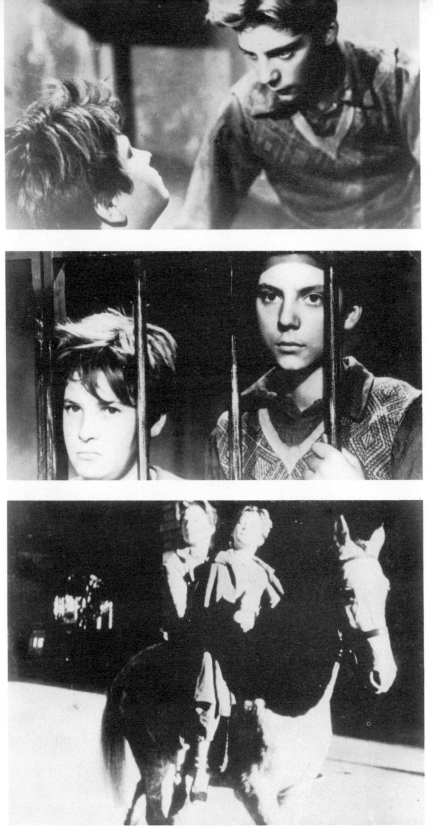

The two shoe shine boys and their dream of escape:

Rinaldo Smordoni and Franco Interlenghi in Vittorio De Sica's SCIUSCIÀ (1946)

The innocence of the boys in an indifferent adult world:

Rinaldo Smordoni and Franco Interlenghi in Vittorio De Sica's SCIUSCIÀ (1946)

The prison world in Vittorio De Sica's SCIUSCIÀ (1946)

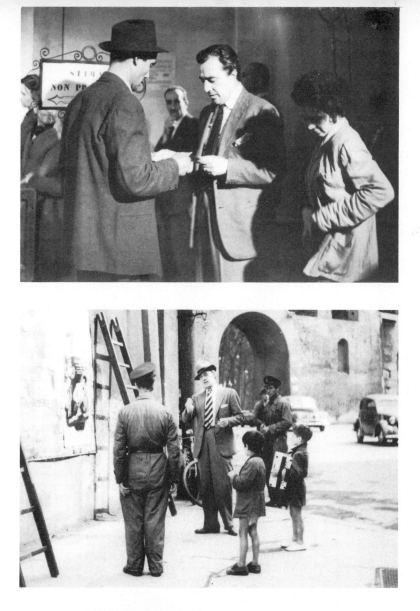

Top and middle: Vittorio De Sica directing BICYCLE THIEVES (1948)

Left: Lamberto Maggiorani who plays Antonio, the bill poster

Antonio with his son (Enzo Staiola) and his precious bicycle in Vittorio De Sica's
BICYCLE THIEVES (1948)

Antonio's vain search for his stolen cycle

Lamberto Maggiorani in Vittorio De Sica's BICYCLE THIEVES (1948)

Looking back ten years later De Sica found it easy to see why he had turned to children rather than to adults. The latter, he felt, "had lost all sense of proportion" and this was "truly the moment when the children were watching us. They gave me the true picture of how our country was morally destroyed."[55] It is clear even from these two brief comments that De Sica already felt the sense of moral concern, shared indeed by all the great neo-realists, on which his collaboration with Zavattini was to be founded. It is also noticeable that the problems are not formulated in specifically social terms for throughout his career, (although his characters are always seen in a precise social context), De Sica is more concerned with human emotions and relationships than with socio-economic issues.

The film was based on De Sica's personal experience of the *sciuscià*, the shoeshine boys: "I knew two of them, Scimmietta (little monkey) and Capellone (big cap). Scimmietta slept in a lift in Via Lombardia, and he was lucky to have a grandfather who loved him. This family warmth saved him. Capellone was nobody's child, completely alone in the world, with his big head deformed by rickets. Eventually he stole and ended up in jail. They were twelve and thirteen respectively. Scimmietta wore a weird cloak and nothing underneath except a pair of torn pants. As soon as they earned three or four hundred lire from cleaning shoes, they ran to the nearby Villa Borghese park and hired a horse."[55] The link between this subject and *I bambini ci guardano*, made in 1942, is emphasised by the fact that an early and not wholly successful scenario was prepared by Cesare Giulio Viola, co-scriptwriter of the earlier film and author of the novel on which it had been based. Other writers—Adolfo Franci and Sergio Amidei—were also involved in the project but the most important intervention was that of Cesare Zavattini. The latter's contribution was a minor one, as he has admitted: "To tell the truth I didn't attach a great deal of importance to the first film of the series, *Sciuscià*, at the beginning. The original subject hadn't been written by me. I intervened at the request of De Sica for a revision of the script which I had to carry out in record time."[45] With this short collaboration (four hours work according to one interview, forty-eight according to another) was established one of the most vital writer-director partnerships in the history of the cinema.

Sciuscià describes more sharply than *I bambini ci guardano* the end of innocence. The two young heroes, Pasquale and Giuseppe, are linked by a deep and pure friendship which is symbolised by their purchase of a horse. But under the pressure of circumstances they are led from shoe-cleaning to the black-market and petty crime, when they become the unwitting accomplices of Giuseppe's elder brother in a scheme to rob an old fortune teller. In this way they are thrown into conflict with the adult world—policemen, lawyers and prison officials—and meet men only too willing to use any means, however base, to further the course of "justice" as they see it. As a result of the deceit and callous misunderstanding that surrounds them, the boys' friendship is shattered and Giuseppe, the weaker of the two, comes under the influence of older, nastier boys with whom he takes part in an escape from the boys' prison. The climax comes with a quarrel on a bridge when Pasquale in his anger inadvertently pushes his smaller friend to his death. The horse which Giuseppe had planned to sell vanishes into the darkness as a dream of happiness is broken. *I bambini ci guardano* had dealt with the moral problem of adultery only obliquely, through the eyes of a child who is incapable of offering a true evaluation of it, so that the film's centre of attention was thereby shifted to the less controversial topic of the effects of adultery on a small child. Something similar happens with *Sciuscià* where judgement is passed on the adult world not by analysing it in its own terms but by contrasting it with the innocence and purity of childhood.

Comparatively little of the specific atmosphere of 1946 comes through in the film (a lack emphasised by the rather glossy photographic style) and the tragedy does not derive in essence from the war and its aftermath. The principal targets for attack—the bureaucrats and petty officials—are not unique to the immediate postwar period and indeed are attacked equally vigorously in *Bicycle Thieves* and *Umberto D*. As a social document (which it was not really intended to be in the first place) *Sciuscià* also suffers from the idealisation of the two boys, who avoid the corruption undergone by, for instance, the young delinquents of Luis Buñuel's *Los Olvidados* and remain clean, well-scrubbed and sensitive characters. In this connection the choice of young actors is significant. De Sica never considered solving the casting problem by using the boys who had inspired the film. In his memoirs he writes: "Indeed it was difficult to find two boys for *Sciuscià*. Capellone and Scimmietta would not do: they were too ugly, almost deformed."[55] In this way any idea of absolute authenticity was rejected from the start and the children De Sica in fact chose—Rinaldo Smordoni and Franco Interlenghi—are, like Luciano De Ambrosis in *I bambini ci guardano,* pleasant and attractive boys whose sufferings can be counted on to touch the heart of the stoniest spectator. Indeed many commentators have commented on the handsomeness of Pasquale (Henri Agel talks of his "princely and seraphic beauty"[3]) and it is unsurprising that Franco Interlenghi who played the part should later have made a notable career as a film actor.

With the children depicted as innocent victims, the blame in the film rests squarely on the shoulders of the adults whose actions are indeed often mean and spiteful. Giuseppe's brother callously involves them in crime, while the police use underhand methods to make Pasquale confess by pretending to beat Giuseppe (we see what is really happening in the next room: a policeman is beating a sack while a boy shrieks convincingly). The lawyers are cheaply opportunistic, suggesting that Giuseppe puts all the blame on his friend, and the prison officials act foolishly and split up the pair (so that Giuseppe is left a prey to bad influences) and then punish Pasquale for fighting a bully. None of this casts much light on the social system but it does serve to break up the friendship of the two boys which forms the real core of the film. If the crucial importance of friendship in

Sciuscià is understood, the inclusion of the scenes featuring the horse—
described by De Sica as an "exquisitely poetic touch"[55] on Zavattini's part—
becomes more easily explicable. Purchased jointly it stands for the essential
unity of the two boys (hence its appearance at the beginning) but also
it serves as a more general symbol of the longing to escape from the sordid-
ness of everyday life. When, as in so many prewar films of Marcel Carné,
the dream turns sour and the outcome is death and not escape, it is wholly
appropriate that the horse should be seen again, vanishing this time into
the night. The mixing of poetry and realism does not have the subtlety in
Sciuscià that it acquires in some of De Sica's later films, but this film of 1946
indicates clearly how far removed from mere social analysis the director's
deepest preoccupations are.

For both De Sica and Zavattini *Sciuscià* was a real landmark. It gave
the director the first real proof of his powers, as he told an interviewer:
"Before *Sciuscià* I didn't have as much confidence in my abilities as I have
had since the film came out. The press has helped me a lot."[45] Zavattini, who
had begun the collaboration fairly lightly, began to see the possibilities of
further films on the same theme, the solitude of man. Zavattini also became
aware for perhaps the first time of the split in his nature between imagination and the quest for reality: "There too you could see my double nature:
on the one hand I sought bitter and painful contact with reality, on the
other I could not free myself from my imagination which overflowed with
fantasy."[131] This basic dichotomy within Zavattini will be considered more
fully later on when we come to deal with *Miracle in Milan* and his theoretical writings. As far as *Sciuscià* is concerned, though the poetic-symbolic
passages derive from him, it was the aspiration towards greater realism that
attracted him more. More specifically, *Sciuscià* sets the pattern to be followed with even greater artistic success in *Bicycle Thieves* and *Umberto D:*
into a social setting of harsh reality and an unsympathetic world dominated
by unfeeling functionaries is placed a pure and deeply felt emotion of a
warm and sentimental kind which events threaten with destruction. Where
Sciuscià differs from the later films is in the bitterness of its ending which
is rather uncharacteristic of De Sica, who has said that if the end of the
film had been fully foreseen by him it would not have had such a desperate
air. Zavattini's reaction was somewhat different in that with this film he
came to see the positive value of an inconclusive ending: "For the first
time I had the intuition that sad, negative final scenes would be a polemical
manifestation against those gay ones which in the cinema represented and
still represents a certain way of conceiving life. I felt that a final scene which
was not gay—this kind of desperate echo which is awakened in the spectator
as if a stone were thrown into water—would be just and moral. It was necessary to adopt it at all costs."[131]

With *Sciuscià* too began the long saga of De Sica's battle to make the
films he wanted. It marked the temporary end of his "commercial" film-
making and the beginning of his adventures with producers and in 1955 he
claimed that from that moment he had "never found credit either with pro-

ducers or distributors, in any part of the world."[131] Paolo Tamburella had
confidence in De Sica and left him to make the film in his own way, but as
it transpired *Sciuscià* "was a disaster for the producer. It cost less than a
million lire but in Italy few people saw it as it was released at a time when
the first American films were reappearing."[55] Ironically the film did exceptionally well in the United States, where it won an Oscar, but only after
Tamburella had sold the foreign rights for a derisory sum. None of the
distributors in France and in England who had made money with *Sciuscià*
were willing to advance money to finance *Bicycle Thieves* two years later
and De Sica had to turn to personal friends to raise the necessary funds.
Bicycle Thieves earned enough money to pay off the debts of *Sciuscià*
but it did not resolve the basic contradiction at the root of neo-realist art,
namely that mass audiences are uninterested in films dealing with their
own urgent problems. De Sica wrote in his memoirs: "The evening of the
premiere of *Bicycle Thieves* I hid myself from my friends; but after a while
I could not bear it any longer and I slowly approached the Roman cinema
where it was showing. I knew the manager and I asked with a throaty
voice, like a thief, how the audience was reacting. He was about to reply
when, suddenly, a working-class man with his wife and four children came
out of the cinema. They saw the manager and came up to him angrily, the
husband saying in broad Roman dialect: 'Give us our money back and put
up a notice to tell families like us that the film's a bloody horror!' "[55] *Miracle
in Milan* was made largely with De Sica's own money and five years later
he was, by his own account, still paying off the debts it incurred. The producer Angelo Rizzoli, who was also one of Italy's leading publishers, was
persuaded to finance *Umberto D* as the filmic equivalent of a limited classical edition but the film was commercially unsuccessful: "I very much hoped
that my good friend Rizzoli would have earned some profits with *Umberto
D*, but unfortunately he did not. This troubled me profoundly. Not only
did it flop financially in Italy but also abroad."[55] De Sica's personal solution
to the problem was to make money by acting in other people's films and
this allowed him to make the four films between 1946 and 1952. But his
interviews show how the financial problems came constantly to occupy his
mind and one can understand his later development as a commercial director. De Sica's films are among the most accessible in the neo-realist output
and when one considers their commercial failure one can only marvel at
the maintenance of the movement by Italian directors in the face of such
massive indifference on the part of the public.

15.   Bicycle Thieves

THE FILM *BICYCLE THIEVES* (*Ladri di biciclette*) is described in
the credit titles as being based on the novel by Luigi Bartolini but De
Sica is more exact in his memoirs when he records that Zavattini brought

him the novel with the words: "I think we could find an idea and a title for a film from it."[55] In fact the relationship of novel and film is so tenuous that one is not at all surprised to learn that as soon as he saw the film Bartolini protested violently about the treatment of his material, but the contrast of the two does show clearly the particular preoccupations of the film-makers and the direction in which their desire for realism was taking them. Bartolini's novel[9] is a rather trite little story told in first person narrative by an unattractive protagonist and containing very little of use to Zavattini apart from a Roman setting, the idea of a stolen bicycle, a long and difficult search and an eventual confrontation with the thief. Bartolini set his story in September 1944 when both crime and the black-market were at their height and chose as his hero a bourgeois artist, painter and writer, who has an anti-Fascist record but very little sympathy for the poor. The theft of the cycle is no more than an inconvenience for he uses it only to get away from town to "the far away fields" and in any case he owns another, also in perfect running order.

Whereas Visconti could derive most of his film *La terra trema* from Verga's novel *I Malavoglia* although this had been written some eighty years before, De Sica and Zavattini had to change the whole ethos of the story they found in Bartolini's little book. The novel's hero, for instance, is a man of enormous egotism who continually talks of his "sense of poetry" and his "unconquerable feeling for celestial anarchy," compares his own "elevated taste" to that of Baudelaire and of course takes care to assure us that he is "as a matter of fact extremely virile." None of this is echoed in the film whose hero Antonio is a simple workman concerned only with the pressing economic necessities of his existence. Bartolini's view of the cinema too is hardly one which would commend itself to De Sica: "I look upon cinematography as a vulgar art which, because of its very nature, will never be able to detach itself from the commonplace.", It is ironic indeed that a book in which such an opinion is expressed should have inspired a film that in the Forties did perhaps more than any other to raise the study of the everyday and commonplace to the level of art. One appreciates too the sympathy shown by the film-makers for the poor when one compares their treatment of their characters with the views of the novel's narrator, to whom the market of the Porta Portese "shows that the poor are poor despite their extreme cunning or a quickness of wit that is equal to ours if not superior to it." When Bartolini's narrator thinks of the poor it is from a comfortably superior bourgeois position and typically he recalls a scene of destruction: "That's what the poor do. They break up everything. They destroy everything within reach when they are hungry. They would destroy entire forests in order to heat a can of water and cook a fistful of corn meal." For such a man, "finding things again can become an entertaining pastime," but for De Sica and Zavattini the unavailing search for a lost bicycle can become a symbol of the tragic necessities of human existence.

The plot of the film *Bicycle Thieves* is simple and straightforward. Antonio Ricci is a workman who, after two years of unemployment, is offered a job as bill-poster. Before he can accept it he and his wife have to pawn the sheets from their bed to redeem the bicycle he must have. They do it willingly, for the job seems to be the answer to all their problems, but Antonio's sense of triumph is shattered on his very first morning when his precious cycle is stolen. The police can offer no assistance and for Antonio a long search for the bicycle and the thief begins. Accompanied by his young son Bruno and with the help of a few friends he scours the markets of the Piazza Vittorio and the Porta Portese where he is overwhelmed by the mass of cycles and accessories and by the thronging crowds of dealers and prospective customers. Discouraged and soaked to the skin by a sudden downpour, Antonio suddenly sees the thief but is unable to catch him. Pursuing an old man who talked to the thief, Antonio finds himself in church at a service in honour of the poor but his efforts to extract information meet with a sullen refusal. All seems lost when quite unexpectedly he comes face to face with the thief on an empty street. He chases him into a brothel and then drags him home, demanding the return of the cycle. But the thief, a young epileptic, is vigorously defended by his neighbours who turn on Antonio in hostile fashion. A policeman fetched by Bruno can give no help, for Antonio has neither evidence nor witnesses and so is forced to beat a retreat amid the curses and insults of the crowd. There seems now only one solution to his problem: sending Bruno to catch a tram, he tries to steal a bicycle himself. But his attempt is clumsy and ill-timed and he has the humiliation of being caught and treated as a thief in front of his young son. A gesture of affection from Bruno is his only comfort as he vanishes into the crowd.

When Antonio is at the police station reporting the theft of his bicycle, a journalist comes up to inquire what the case is. Nothing, replies the inspector, only a stolen cycle, and the journalist, no doubt disappointed, turns away. Yet out of this apparently small happening—too trivial to interest a newspaper reporter—Zavattini has built an engrossing ninety minute film. Despite its surface appearance, *Bicycle Thieves* is not a sociological inquiry or a mere slice of life. The extremely careful and skilful construction is brought out quite clearly by scenes like those involving the clairvoyant, Madame Sartona, from which a great deal of dramatic irony is extracted. Early in the film Antonio mocks his wife for her superstition but when things seem hopeless, it is to Madame Sartona that he too turns. Her reply— "Your bicycle? . . . Either you will find it straight away or you will never find it again"—seems to indicate that the woman is a mere charlatan, battening on the hopes and fears of the poor. For this reason Antonio's sudden confrontation with the thief, which follows immediately, has an added impact, since it seems to bear out her prophecy. De Sica has pointed out that six months were needed for the mere elaboration of the script and continually the dramatic contrasts are cunningly exploited: the opulent glamour of Rita Hayworth on a street poster is set against the grim poverty of Antonio, his anguished search for help is played against the background of the rehearsal of a cheerful, if drab, musical show, and the cheering crowds at the football match form a striking counterpoint for Antonio's desperate surrender to temptation. In terms of emotional impact, Alessandro Cicognini's music, though used fairly conventionally to underline the feelings of the characters, makes a most important contribution.

Six writers in all worked on the script of *Bicycle Thieves* but clearly the collaboration of De Sica and Zavattini was growing closer and the latter's decisive influence can be felt throughout the film. Zavattini has given a clear account of the nature of his contribution: "De Sica needs a perfectly elaborated and clearly defined material to begin his work. For *Bicycle Thieves* I did not establish a shot by shot shooting script as you do in France, but we discussed with De Sica the content of every scene and established the meaning of every image. And I was certain that De Sica would be able to show things as simply and directly as possible. I always try to simplify a problem to extremes. I mean my narration to be elementary, I want to attain a simple A.B.C., perfectly bare and comprehensible. And I want to have this simplicity even in the photographic style. In my view a director of photography does not have the right to enter upon the subject. If he makes himself noticed in a neo-realist film it is always at the expense of what must be said. And finally I attach the greatest importance to the editing. I worked for two months with De Sica on the editing of *Bicycle Thieves*."[45] The effect of this intensive preparation is seen most clearly in the delineation of the relationship of father and son which forms the emotional core of the film. When he sets off to his new job Antonio clearly has the total admiration of his son who models himself on him and busily cleans his bicycle for him. But already at his first appearance the little boy's argumentativeness is apparent in his reaction to the dented pedal. When the cycle is stolen, it is Antonio who dare not go in to face Maria and during the long scenes of searching Bruno is neglected: he is accosted by an elderly man, falls in the mud and almost gets run over, all without his father even noticing. It is therefore doubly unjust that when he makes a remark about what *he* would have done to prevent the thief's friend escaping, he should receive the full force of his father's pent-up fury. Antonio obviously feels this, for when he hears shouts from the bridge to which he has sent Bruno, he immediately fears that the boy has jumped into the river. He recovers the boy's affection by treating him to an expensive meal, but then suffers two humiliations before his son's eyes, firstly when the thief's neighbours insult him and secondly when he is apprehended as a thief himself. There can be no ending to Antonio's social problems—he is left without the cycle he needs to continue his work—but the emotional pattern at least is completed when Bruno slips his hand into his father's as they walk off at the end of the film.

If Zavattini's influence can be strongly felt in the structure of the film, De Sica's handling of the actors is equally decisive in the creation of the film's impact. Soon after completing *Bicycle Thieves* the director told an interviewer that for him working with actors was "the most exciting part" of his work, adding: "Before beginning the shooting—a month or two before

—I live as long as possible beside the characters I have chosen. In the beginning, knowing that they have to act, they stiffen, grow awkward and absurd. They would be incapable of sitting down without knocking over their chair. Time passes, we get to know each other better, we come closer together and I end by making them participate in the story they are supposed to bring to life. In the end they abandon themselves. We can begin shooting."[127] In all his work with non-professional actors, in *Bicycle Thieves* and elsewhere, De Sica found his own experience as an actor of immense value in achieving a satisfactory performance. *Bicycle Thieves* is an excellent example of the results that can be obtained with carefully chosen actors. Lamberto Maggiorani, who played Antonio, was a worker in the Breda factory whom De Sica first met when he brought his son to audition for the part of Bruno. De Sica immediately realised that Maggiorani was the man he was looking for and a film test confirmed this: "The way he moved, the way he sat down, his gestures with those hands of a working man and not of an actor . . . everything about him was perfect."[55] Excellent support was given by Lianella Carell who played the part of the wife with an admirable force and a total lack of glamour: her movements as she learns of the need for a bicycle and resolves to pawn the family sheets speak of a whole lifetime of poverty and drudgery. As in *I bambini ci guardano* and *Sciuscià* the casting of the child is a key to the film's success and De Sica has said that the discovery of Enzo Staiola on the first day of shooting made that one of the most satisfying days of his life. The qualities he found in his young player are very much like those possessed by Luciano De Ambrosis and Franco Interlenghi and his description of the boy shows clearly the warm heart that lies at the root of the De Sica conception of realism: "Enzo Staiola is the most lovable child in the world. He is good, sensitive, intelligent. I don't think it is possible to create a character like that of Bruno without having the qualities that Enzo possesses."[38] But important as these non-professionals are to the success of the film, the main actor remains the city of Rome itself, seen in all its diversity with its squares and markets, churches and brothels, slums and riverside cafés, alive with men going to work, shoppers, idlers, thieves and football supporters.

Like *Sciuscià*, *Bicycle Thieves* was inspired by De Sica's own experience. It was, he tells us, "born of a great desire I had to tell a simple and human story. I was not impelled by any literary idea. I have simply told the story of the workman Antonio, his wife Maria and their son Bruno. To see is very useful to an artist. Most men do not want to see, because often the pain of others troubles them. We, on the contrary, want to see. How many times the workman Antonio passed close to me: I met him in the street, at church, at the door of the cinema while he read the programme outside. I saw him several times with his son. In Italy men often go out with their sons. Children converse and argue with their father, become confidants, and very often become no longer children but 'little men.' "[38] Throughout his work of preparing the film De Sica was concerned to avoid treating Antonio's story as a mere "case book" history and conscious of the need to add emotional depth and resonance to the bare bones of the plot. As he told an interviewer: "I had no intention of presenting Antonio as a kind of 'Everyman' or a personification of what is called today 'the under privileged.' To me he was an individual, with his individual joys and worries, with his individual story. In presenting the one tragic Sunday of his long and varied life, I attempted to transpose reality into the poetical plane. This indeed seems to me one of the most important features of my work, because without such an attempt a film of this kind would simply become a newsreel. I don't see any future in neo-realism if it does not surmount the barrier separating the documentary from drama and poetry."[127] In this connection Vernon Jarratt has assembled some very interesting facts that totally destroy the superficial, but widely held notion that *Bicycle Thieves* was a cheap little film improvised on the streets. Far from being inexpensive, "the total cost of the finished picture came to almost exactly 100,000,000 lire; that was almost £50,000 at the then rate of exchange, and though this is a small budget by British standards, it is high by Italian standards; very few films indeed cost more, most cost less, and many much less."[80] The crowd scenes were all reconstructed by the director: for the market scenes at the Porta Portese, for example, he had to hire forty stall holders, pay extras to play the German seminarists and organise everything days in advance, so that on the first cloudy day these people could be brought together and the Roman fire brigade summoned to douse them all with water so as to produce the illusion of a sudden rainstorm disrupting a busy market. Some shots were taken amid the actual crowds on the busy Roman streets but here again everything was planned in advance down to the smallest detail. The theft of Antonio's bicycle for instance was minutely timed and choreographed so that the thief would be able to make his escape while the traffic lights were green and the whole sequence recorded by six cameras, "some concealed inside cars, some in windows high up, one on top of a car, and one most important one concealed behind a man who stood lounging up against a shop reading a newspaper while behind him stood a cameraman with an Arriflex."[80]

Bicycle Thieves, like all De Sica's neo-realist work, reveals a deep sympathy with the poor and an awareness of the way in which officialdom impinges on their lives. Though the official in the pawnshop does show sympathy with the needs of Antonio and his wife, the police are indifferent and unhelpful. Far from assisting Antonio, the police inspector to whom he reports the theft turns him away brusquely and prepares to go off with the riot squad to deal with some demonstration (no doubt one like that organised by the old-age pensioners at the beginning of *Umberto D*). In such a society as this there can be little hope of conditions being improved by action from the administration. Though made only a year or so later than *Caccia tragica*, De Sica's film reflects a situation in which the solidarity of the masses is a myth or at least an unattainable ideal (1947, it will be recalled, was the crucial year in which the unity of the left was shattered by the break-up of the Socialist party). Whereas in De Santis's film the whole collective had set off in pursuit of the bandits and the individual had been able to draw strength from his participation in a mass movement, in *Bicycle Thieves* the individual is isolated and Antonio in his search for the thief is aided by only a child, Bruno, and three ill-assorted dustmen: the fat Baiocco, the tall Maniconi and the elderly little Bagongli. It is at a party meeting that Antonio enlists Baiocco's help, but the speaker there cannot offer much hope: "Don't expect miracles from us, we always keep our eyes open . . . and when there is a possibility of getting you incorporated in this system, we'll certainly not neglect it. I know, and you are right, that the essential is to find work because when people work, the world begins to function." In this kind of atmosphere it is significant that the only group activity we see is the rehearsal of what seems a singularly inept musical show. With the possibilities of state intervention and political action denied in this way, the individual's actions cannot be viewed in a wider context and thus it is appropriate that Antonio's deeds are evaluated on a personal, family level. The child Bruno becomes not only one of the principal victims of the tragedy, but also to a large extent the touchstone by which his father's actions are judged. His gesture of renewed affection for his father at the end of the film acquires therefore an added significance in that it expresses our own judgement on Antonio: that despite his lapse in succumbing to temptation, he is a man worthy of love and respect.

16. Umberto D.

U*MBERTO D,* with which the neo-realist movement proper inaugurated by *Rome Open City* may be said to close, was scripted by Cesare Zavattini, who on this occasion worked for the first time without the customary bevy of script collaborators. For Zavattini therefore it was a most important film, representing his most successful attempt to escape from conventional narrative restrictions, though later he came to criticise it for being still too theatrical and to insist that it was merely a starting point for a new kind of cinema, not a summit and summation of neo-realist achievement. For De Sica too *Umberto D* was a crucial film and he has often described it as his own personal favourite among his films and a work made without compromise and with the aim of achieving absolute authenticity. He clearly developed a deep involvement with Zavattini's characters and he has recorded that on reading the original script he "thought again of that category of people who find themselves, at a certain moment, excluded from a world which they nevertheless helped to build; a tragedy which is most often hidden by resignation and silence but which sometimes explodes in resounding manifestations, driving men to horrifying premeditated suicides each of which has a touching detail."[38] The extent of De Sica's involvement is typified by his dedication of the film to his own father, Umberto De Sica, who, as we know from De Sica's memoirs, "was a bank clerk and later worked for an insurance company; he was also a journalist. The result, however, was poverty, extreme poverty for all of us, which we bore with dignity for a great many years."[55] The role of Umberto D was obviously suitable for interpretation by a non-professional actor for, as De Sica has said, "the man in the street especially if he is in the hands of a director who is at the same time an actor represents a malleable material which one can fashion as one wishes."[56] The man chosen to play the role was Carlo Battisti, a professor from the University of Florence, from whom De Sica obtained a moving portrayal without ever calling upon him to perform any really sustained feat of acting.

De Sica's use of non-professionals is aided by the construction of *Umberto D* as a collection of small scenes, fragmentary views of a life endured on the very brink of degrading poverty. Essentially the film records a succession of failures. It begins with Umberto's only attempt at collective action when he takes part in a demonstration of old-age pensioners in favour of increased allowances. The lack of weight behind this protest is clear even from the credit sequence when the line of old men moving at a seemingly awkward jog-trot is broken by a bus, and it comes as no surprise that the Italian riot police in their extremely mobile jeeps have little trouble in speedily dispersing the crowd. An attempt by Umberto to sell his watch merely leads to a snub from an equally proud but hard-up old gentleman, and when he does find a buyer it is for only just over half the money he needs. Later he meets with the same discouraging response when he tries to sell his few remaining books and so never acquires enough money to pay his arrears of rent. When he returns to his room he has the humiliation of finding out that it is being loaned out by the hour to adulterous couples by his rapacious landlady who is eager to get rid of him so as to use the room for her own purposes. A slight attack of tonsilitis allows him to go into hospital for a few days and so economise on his living expenses, but he is too diffident and honest to exploit the situation as readily as does his neighbour in the next bed. Even the burst of happiness he feels as he returns home is shattered by the double discovery that the wallpaper is being stripped off the walls of his room and that his beloved dog Flike is missing. He is at least able to recover it from the dogs' home when, after an agonising search, he finds it again, but his economic plight is unaltered. His efforts to borrow from former colleagues at the ministry meet with embarrassed indifference and for a brief moment he is even tempted to try begging, as he sees the ease with which the beggars on the street corners make money, but his sense of personal dignity prevents him. The last straw comes when he finds a hole knocked in one wall of his room—a part of the landlady's decorating scheme. Umberto has the sympathy of the maid Maria who tries to help him despite her own urgent problems resulting from an unwanted pregnancy but by now he knows that he is beaten. As he looks out of the window a zoom close-up of the tramlines in the street below gives a clear indication of which way out of his troubles he has decided on. But even when he has given up his room and abandoned hope he is still plagued with failure, this time in his attempts to find a home for Flike. The dog-minders in the Via Leccosa prove to be mean and grasping and his offer of the dog to a friendly little girl in the park is rejected out of hand by the child's governess. Even trying to simply abandon the dog proves futile and so he takes it in his arms as he goes to throw himself under a train. The dog, wriggling in his arms, causes him to bungle his suicide attempt but the film does end with a tiny victory—his recovery of the dog's trust and affection—even if his pressing financial problems are as insoluble as ever.

The basic pattern of the film as a succession of short scenes that are a kind of tragic variation on the comic "gag" (in that each encounter ends with the defeat, not the triumph, of the hero) is typified by the visit to his old ministry. He meets a former colleague who promptly leaps on a tram, calling out greetings to a common acquaintance who is in fact, as Umberto tells him, now dead. Seeing the beggars at work Umberto hesitantly tries to emulate them: he holds out his hand to a passerby but when the man stops his nerve fails and he turns over his hand, pretending to see if it is raining. He tries to make his dog beg for him, giving it his hat to hold, but immediately his old chief walks by. The initial smiles of greeting give way to embarrassment when the two find they have nothing to say to each other and only the departure of the *commendatore*'s tram relieves the situation. This collection of tiny, trivial incidents has no obvious dramatic build-up in a conventional sense and nothing is exaggerated or over-emphasised but in fact the meeting constitutes one of the turning points of the film— Umberto's last attempt to raise the necessary money to save his room. With the minimum of "drama" it movingly conveys the hopelessness of his position and the depths to which he has sunk with the destruction of his self-respect. One rather more developed sequence is that in which Umberto, slightly feverish and upset by the failure of the demonstration, tries to go to sleep. There is a succession of distractions and interruptions—the room has to be aired after its use by the lovers, Umberto has to go out to sell his books, the maid comes to and fro to examine his throat, collect the thermometer and signal to her lover from the window. Above all he is pestered by noises—the singing of the landlady's friends, the trumpet from the barracks, the sounds from a nearby cinema, the alarm clock he clumsily fumbles with—used with great sensitivity here as throughout the film. The whole pattern is extremely fragmentary but even such extended sequences are rare in *Umberto D* and this omission emphasises the authors' ability to convey their meaning without dialogued scenes and their deliberate concentration on the least obviously dramatic aspects of life.

The scene depicting the maid getting up in the morning after being woken by Umberto's telephone call is generally regarded as the classic example of Zavattini's concept of neo-realism. He described it in his script in the following words:

"Her eyes look at the glass roof up above her head.

On this roof a cat passes slowly.

With an acrobatic leap the servant jumps out of bed.

Then she sits down again on the edge of the bed, nodding her head as if going back to sleep again.

But she makes an effort and gets up. With her eyes half closed and her feet bare she goes into the kitchen.

The light is gradually getting better.

The servant, her eyes half-closed, comes in and goes towards the gas oven, takes a match from the holder and vainly tries to strike it; then she takes another one without managing to strike that either, so weary are her movements.

Finally she succeeds and holds the lighted match over the gas, but the gas does not light because she has not turned on the tap.

She realises what is happening, turns it on and the gas lights with a little bang while . . .

The servant looks at the courtyard (the window is just beside the oven). She looks at the yard dreamily, one hand pressed against her cheek.

The yard is empty. All the windows are shut. Not a single sound is to be heard.

She is motionless. Everything is motionless.

In the window-pane a light appears gradually: it is the sun rising.

The servant shrugs, goes to the sink, takes a kettle, fills it with water; then she puts the rubber hose on the tap to her mouth and drinks a mouthful of water, but the water squirts inside her night-dress; so she jumps back and shakes her night-dress to remove the water that has flowed onto her chest.

From the marble table she picks up an inkpot, a pen and a sheet of paper on which she has begun to write a letter and puts them on the sideboard.

Then she puts the kettle on the gas, sits down and stays there, dreaming and watching the gas flame.

Gradually her eyes fill with tears.

She looks at her belly. She stands up and looks at her belly to find out whether you can see that it's fat. Yes, you can see. The tears continue to flow slowly from her eyes. Then, with a sigh, she shrugs, takes the coffee-grinder, glances at the ants which have made a new path for themselves on the wall. She is about to put down the coffee-grinder (while still continuing to watch the ants) in order to make an attack on them, but she thinks better of it and sits down to begin grinding the coffee.

The dull sound of the coffee-grinder gives her the idea of shutting the door. She wants to do it without getting up. So she tries to reach it with the tip of her toe without stopping grinding. To do that she has to stretch as far as possible towards the door, at the risk of falling off the chair. But she doesn't want to get up, it has become a question of honour; finally she succeeds.

Suddenly the door bell is heard.

With a start the maid gets up, almost frightened. She puts down the coffee-grinder and runs into the corridor."[147]

This extract from the published script does not correspond exactly with the actual film in which several of the details are changed: she sees the cat in the yard, she doesn't watch the gas, our discovery of her tears comes at a different moment and so on. But the whole tone and atmosphere of the scene is here in Zavattini's concentration on trivial gestures and the under-playing of emotional crises. Such a passage also gives a clear idea of the extent of Zavattini's contribution to the film and the reason why it is fair to regard him as co-author. The systematic use of *temps morts* as a basis of construction is fundamental to Zavattini's conception of neo-realism but *Umberto D* is still a long way from his theoretical ideal of ninety minutes of a man's life in which nothing happens. Holding *Umberto D* together is the kind of emotional crisis which one can imagine a conventional film treating (if with other stylistic methods), namely a few days during which a man is driven to the verge of suicide.

In *Umberto D* there is no attempt of the kind made in *Sciuscià* to en-noble the characters. Umberto, as De Sica rightly notes, "is an old man with all the faults of old age. It would have been easy to make him a con-ventional and pathetic sentimental old man so as to make him closer to the spectator and more agreeable. But he is an old bourgeois. We know nothing of his past life: perhaps he is a widower or a bachelor. His past does not concern us. What counts is Umberto such as he is today, more than seventy years old, facing the approach of death alone, with a whole weight of bitterness and past battles which make him irritating and almost disagree-able. In his behaviour he is good only towards those who are good to him and extremely disagreeable only with those who are not friendly to him."[48] De Sica has toned down the script by omitting—either on his own account or for censorship reasons—a number of mordant scenes in Zavattini's script: a protest demonstration in the hospital, a meeting with a prostitute and an incident before Umberto's departure when he writes "merda" on the walls. But De Sica has by no means undermined the authenticity of the basic tragedy by the note of warmth he adds. One recalls his veneration for Charlie Chaplin in the surprising amount of humorous detail in the film which is, in a very real sense, a Chaplinesque story of a little man in a hostile world. The portions relating to the beggars give comic effects as well as revealing Umberto's degradation: he sells his watch for three thou-sand lire to a man who turns out to be a beggar, he sees another beggar imperiously recalling a passer-by who had ignored him, and his own at-tempt at begging is both comic and tragic. Umberto's relationship with his landlady is treated in much the same fashion: the two of them snort at each other from opposite sides of the door and Umberto, after recovering Flike, leaps out from a doorway to startle her. Comedy of a harsher kind is to be found in the treatment of the landlady's circle of friends, where the authors display a tone of biting irony and a keen eye for pretension and hypocrisy, castigated in the grotesque farewell kisses of the landlady and her cinema manager *fiancé* and her parting remark to the adulterous wife when they meet a second time: "Kiss the baby for me." As in Chaplin there is a degree of sentimentality in *Umberto D,* most noticeable in Alessandro Cicognini's musical score which obtrusively anticipates and underlines the emotional response, but also found in the scene at the dog-minder's when Flike is shown as frightened of a big ferocious dog. But generally speaking the core of the film is as hard and unsentimental as one can imagine in a film whose chief emotional charge is an old man's affection for his dog.

Umberto D is not primarily a social document, as is shown by the fact that it was originally conceived not as an analysis of Italian society but as a London story to star Barry Fitzgerald. Nevertheless, as De Sica pointed out in his open letter to Zavattini, it upset critics who were displeased that Umberto and Totò (the hero of *Miracle in Milan*) "came to disturb the quiet existence of a community that had already forgotten the war."[21] The film does not examine the root causes of poverty and inequality but accepts them as unavoidable realities and proceeds to treat with sympathy and understanding a single, perhaps untypical case. De Sica has opposed the contention that neo-realism is in essence a proletarian cinema and justly claimed that the one problem which spreads through all his films is that of the bourgeoisie: "Criticism of and satire on the bourgeoisie. Of course it is to be understood immediately that beneath the criticism is hidden love for this humanity so full of defects but still remaining human."[131] The analysis of middle-class life was an obvious subject largely ignored by neo-realists despite their predominantly middle-class background, so that *Umberto D* is virtually unique in its material as well as in its stylistic restraint. It is clearly closely linked to De Sica's own background in the impoverished middle-class and he has explained that he dedicated the film to his father "because he himself was an old bourgeois who fought against poverty and had his dignity to maintain. The dignity of a whole social class."[131] Much of the power of the film comes from its sense of life experienced at first hand and De Sica's own identification with his protagonist is evident: "Umberto D is each one of us, members of the middle classes who have a sense of dignity. All the film is a single word pronounced in defence of the bourgeoisie, in defence of the individual. All the problem is contained in the drama of the lack of communication between men, in the desire for greater comprehension and truer solidarity."[131]

Each of the three major characters of *Umberto D*—the old man, the landlady and the maid—can be seen as factors in an unequal social equation. Umberto himself represents the old bourgeoisie in retreat. His active life being over, society disregards him and the pension he is given does not allow him to live with any kind of security. His position no doubt aggravated by his lack of a family to help and support him, he has to sell even his last few possessions, but is still unable to avoid the humiliation. Eating in soup kitchens, going into hospital and scrounging money from acquaintances would preserve some sort of existence, but the humiliations he endures crush his self-respect and his will to live. As an outsider with no strong ties he meets the official face of society and without exception the policemen and waitresses, doctors, dog-catchers and stall-holders, tram conductors and governesses turn a blind eye to his needs and consistently show greater respect for rules than for human necessity. Another face of the bourgeoisie is represented by Umberto's landlady who embodies all the faults of a society hostile to the old man: hypocrisy, pretension, stupidity and callousness. Though hiring out Umberto's room for prostitution and adultery, she persecutes him for failure to pay his rent and is almost certain to dismiss the maid when she learns of her pregnancy. De Sica satirises cruelly the grotesque and pretentious musical evenings of her entourage and the foolish coyness with which she behaves with her fat and unappealing lover. She is indifferent to the fate of a man who has lodged with her for ten years and for whose help she was grateful in the past and regards her own convenience (she needs the whole flat for herself and her future husband) as sufficient reason for disrupting Umberto's entire existence. Her true character is revealed in the contrast between her normal immaculate appearance and the aged, haggard early morning face she reveals as Umberto is taken to hospital, between the elaborate furnishing of the sitting room in which she receives her guests and the ant-infested kitchen where the maid, Maria, works. The latter is a second victim of the landlady and of society, and an example perhaps of the sub-proletariat. A country girl who has come to Rome to work, she is desperately in need of guidance. Left on her own she has become pregnant by one of her two soldier lovers (she does not know which) and faces the prospect of an illegitimate child, unemployment and rejection by her family.

Important as these social aspects are, the root of the film lies elsewhere, in its study of the possibilities and difficulties of human relationships. To quote De Sica once more: "What is the meaning of the film? To show on the screen the drama of the impossibility experienced by man of communicating with his neighbour. It is not Umberto's economic condition that interests us, it is his moral and human relationships with society. What concerns us is the solitude of an old man."[48] To compensate for his lack of human contact Umberto has his dog Flike, and the relationship of the pair of them parallels those of Antonio Ricci and his son in *Bicycle Thieves* and Pasquale and Giuseppe in *Sciuscià*. Flike is Umberto's indispensable companion, his one remaining responsibility and the sole comfort of his life. Indeed it is concern for the dog that keeps Umberto alive at the end of the film and the relationship carries so strong an emotional charge that the film ends with a real sense of achievement when, after the attempted suicide, he regains the dog's trust. But Flike adds to the old man's vulnerability to society which often directs its hostility at him by way of the dog and above all blinds him to the needs of Maria. She acts as Umberto's ally against the landlady, is the only one he can trust to look after the dog and the only person concerned enough to visit him in hospital. But her un-

Top: Vittorio De Sica directing UMBERTO D (1951)
Bottom: Umberto (Carlo Battisti) sells his watch to a beggar

While Umberto is reduced to begging and trying to give away his dog, his landlady celebrates with her friends:

Carlo Battisti and Lina Gennari in Vittorio De Sica's UMBERTO D (1951)

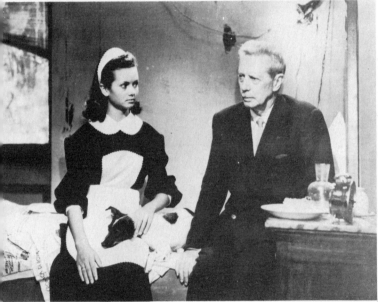

The innocents who cannot
cope in Vittorio De Sica's
world:

Above and left: Carlo Battisti
and Maria Pia Casilio in two
scenes from UMBERTO D

Left: Francesco Golisano and
Brunella Bovo in MIRACLE
IN MILAN (1950)

*The essential childlike good-
ness of Totò and Edwige:
Top: Totò as a child, middle:
Francesco Golisano as Totò
meeting the down-and-outs,
and left: Brunella Bovo as
Edwige in Vittorio De Sica's
MIRACLE IN MILAN (1950)*

*Scenes from Vittorio De Sica's
MIRACLE IN MILAN
(1950):
Above: The incongruous
wishes of the poor, and right:
the final fairy tale escape*

The confrontation of rich and poor in Vittorio De Sica's MIRACLE IN MILAN (1950)

The attempt to revive neo-realism in the mid Fifties:

Gabriella Pallotta and Giorgio Listuzzi in Vittorio De Sica's IL TETTO (1956)

Top: Cesare Zavattini, writer
of almost all of De Sica's films
Middle: Caterina Rigoglioso and her child in the episode of AMORE IN CITTÀ
(1953) directed by Franco Maselli and Cesare Zavattini
Bottom: Alberto Lattuada's episode in AMORE IN CITTÀ (1953)

bourgeois ways shock him and make him withdraw and he never feels any responsibility for having offered her lessons in grammar instead of affection. He does give her sporadic advice on how to plan her future and when she visits him in hospital he half claims her as his daughter, but immediately any thought or worry about Flike occurs he promptly forgets her problems which are in many ways so much more pressing than his own (as when he shouts at her on the street for not having prevented the landlady from throwing Flike out at the very moment when Maria is explaining her condition to her lover). De Sica himself has expressed the view that together the old man and the maid could have defended themselves against society and significantly one of the few lines added to Zavattini's script occur at their parting meeting when, in the film, Maria asks if she may visit him in his new lodgings. But whether or not one feels that the film itself really reflects this sense of missed opportunities it is clearly a highly complex work operating on a number of levels: as social study and meditation on solitude, as a critique of bourgeois rapacity and a defence of bourgeois dignity, as stark tragedy and warmly human story.

17. Miracle in Milan or the Lure of Imagination

MIRACLE IN MILAN (*Miracolo a Milano*), the film which De Sica and Zavattini made between *Bicycle Thieves* and *Umberto D*, is not strictly speaking a neo-realist film, but its roots lie so deep in the consciousness of its scriptwriter that it demands to be treated here. All Zavattini's film work oscillates between two poles: the purely imaginative approach to the world and to art that finds its most striking expression in this film of 1950 and the uncompromising struggle for absolute realism that underlies virtually all his theoretical essays and articles of the early Fifties. The trilogy of studies of urban poverty—*Sciuscià, Bicycle Thieves, Umberto D* —thus represents a kind of inner compromise between warring tendencies within the writer himself, as well as a more obvious external compromise between writer and director. *Miracle in Milan* on the other hand, though directed by De Sica, is an example—the purest he has given us in the cinema—of Zavattini's creative imagination, treating a theme that had preoccupied him since his very earliest days in the cinema: the contrast and conflict of rich and poor. Zavattini records that *Darò un milione*, his first script assignment in 1935, had for him "a well-determined subject: the relationship between rich and poor, seen in a satirical perspective"[131] and he tells us that from the first all his sympathies went out to the poor, although he was only too conscious of being himself one of the "rich."

The original idea for *Miracle in Milan* dates from 1938 when Zavattini wrote a short synopsis called *Diamo a tutti un cavallo a dondolo* (*Let's give everyone a rocking horse*) about the adventures of two families, a rich one by the name of Bot and a poor one called Gec. This idea interested De Sica and in 1940 a second scenario—entitled *Totò il buono* after the great Italian comic actor—was elaborated in collaboration with the director but again the project came to nothing. Zavattini's attachment to his material was such, however, that in 1943 he published it in the form of a novel, but even then he was not satisfied that he had given his ideas adequate expression. In 1948 he resumed his efforts to make a film from this same material and this time he was successful and 1950 saw the final completion of the film after twelve years of struggle. Some of the gags from the very first synopsis find their echo in this film of 1950 but naturally the basic structure and meaning of the work has undergone considerable modification in the course of its lengthy gestation. Whereas the 1940 synopsis was set in a totally imaginary country and the novel in a fictitious if more precisely defined town, the film itself is set, as its title suggests, in Milan and, for all its magical ingredients, paints an authentic picture of the shanty type slums (*borgate*) that disfigured several of Italy's major cities. Likewise De Sica's casting of actors shows a striking concern for authenticity. Though he chose professional actors for many of the leading parts, Emma Grammatica playing Loletta and Paolo Stoppa the treacherous Rappi for instance, he turned to real down-and-outs for the minor roles: "All those wretched people, so perfectly expressive, who are seen performing in *Miracle in Milan* and who so marvellously bear witness to their bitterness or their joy—it was in the district itself, in the suburbs of Milan, that I found them."

Despite these realistic elements *Miracle in Milan* remains a fairy tale, full of magic and impossible happenings, which begins in the most genuine "once upon a time" manner with the birth of the hero Totò, found in a cabbage patch by an old woman, Loletta. The latter teaches Totò to be good and happy and her influence persists after her death when he is sent to an orphanage. The film proper begins with Totò's re-entry into the world at the age of twenty. He is amazed when people react suspiciously to his cheerful attempts to help them, and is distressed and shocked when someone steals his suitcase. He follows the thief, strikes up a friendship with him and goes to live in the shanty settlement on the outskirts of Milan where all the poor and unemployed eke out a precarious existence. Such is their poverty, that they are unable to afford heating and can only get warm by standing in the sunshine, rushing from place to place around the camp when the sun vanishes momentarily from view. But Totò organises them, encourages them to improve their homes and makes friends with Edwige, a girl as naïve and innocent as himself. The whole community shares his joy when suddenly and unexpectedly they strike oil. The poor gather to sing their song (to a catchy tune by Alessandro Cicognini, whose music is excellent throughout):

"We only need a hut
Where we may live and sleep,
Some land we only need,
Where we may live and die.
Give us shoes, socks and bread,
We'll then be very happy
Today and days ahead."

But the oil arouses the greed of the rich landowner Mobbi who sends the police to evict the poor from their homes and to recover the land. Only a magic dove, stolen by Loletta from heaven, can save the poor by granting all Totò wishes. With its help the poor are able to perform miracles, like blowing away the tear-gas which the police use against them, and Totò is able to give them whatever they desire. But though Totò does all they ask, they are still hardly any happier, so confused are their immediate wishes. Unwittingly Totò loses the dove, allowing it to be recaptured by two angels sent down from heaven, and the poor have no defence when the police move in a second time. But happily Loletta contrives to steal the dove once more, enabling Totò to free his friends and ride off with them on broomsticks to a heaven where they can at last be out of the clutches of the rich and where the greeting "good-day," really does mean "good day."

No account of the plot of *Miracle in Milan* can do justice to the richness of its comic detail. There is the double-talk that characterises the sly Mobbi, who saves himself from the crowd's anger with specious logic—"A nose is a nose. A hand is a hand. We all have five fingers. We are all equal"—and then proceeds to cheat his all too trusting victims. There is a brilliantly surrealistic effect in the ballet-like chase of the frozen inhabitants of the slum as they pursue elusive rays of sun around the field, crowding together in the smallest patch of warmth. The magic powers of the dove too are employed to great effect. The wishes of the poor are incongruous and inconsequential: they clamour for fur coats to keep them warm, but also for top hats that will allow them to outdo the evil Rappi who has betrayed them to their enemy. A white girl in love with a Negro has herself turned black, not knowing that her lover too has had Totò change the colour of his skin. Alfredo the thief wants only a big new suitcase, while the ugly Arturo who has spent much of his time gazing longingly at a statue of a beautiful girl has her brought to life, only to find that she promptly scorns him. This profusion of humorous incident and the film's splendid freedom from the dull laws of probability, make one recall that De Sica's great idol is Chaplin and that the "gag" was the basis of Zavattini's early conception of the cinema. His description of this latter is worth recording: "The 'gag' was to me like a flower made to open in an artificial garden: that came from the store of imagination I had possessed since childhood. If I had been locked in a room, without being able to add new elements to my experience, I should still have found a way of making a certain type of film."[131]

Zavattini himself has pointed out that the film has another layer of meaning beneath this entertaining surface: "The fundamental emotion of *Miracle in Milan* is not one of escape (the flight at the end), but of indignation, a desire for solidarity with certain people, a refusal of it with others. The film's structure is intended to suggest that there is a great gathering of the humble ones against the others. But the humble ones have no tanks or they would have been ready to defend their land and their huts."[94] De Sica echoes this view by explicitly linking the film with *Sciuscià* and *Bicycle Thieves*, and describing it as "the burlesque development of the theme of man against solitude,"[45] but it would be wrong to overstress the element of "commitment" it contains. Totò, who never makes aggressive use of his magical powers against his adversaries, is a perfect innocent, not a political leader, and to talk of him (as Borde and Bouissy do) "crossing the threshold that separates Gandhi from Lenin"[17] is absurd. Totò has no social message or answer to the problems of poverty but instead, like the children in *I bambini ci guardano*, *Sciuscià* and *Bicycle Thieves*, serves to give an outsider's partial judgement on a situation whose complexities he is unable to comprehend, in this case those of social organisation and human motivation. De Sica gives a fairer evaluation of *Mircle in Milan* when he says that it "is not a political film but a fable, and my only intention was a Twentieth century fairy tale. As for the meaning of the film, it is for me the triumph of goodness: Let men be good to one another. This is the only political message of my film."[45]

De Sica's use of the word "fable" not only gives an excellent description of *Miracle in Milan*, it also pin-points an essential contradiction between Zavattini's theory and his practice, for only a year or so later he was to write that "the true function of the cinema is not to tell fables, and to a true function we must recall it."[94] His own feelings about the film are markedly ambivalent, for though, on the one hand, he was treating a theme about which he had felt deeply for a dozen years or more, on the other he was actually making the film at a time when his thoughts were turning more and more exclusively to realism and he was making statements such as "Finally we will have on the screen only real people with their own Christian names and surnames. We must indeed fear increasingly the imagination which continues to corrupt our duty towards reality, our link with mankind." This fundamental contradiction stands out distinctly in the defence of the film which he felt constrained to make in 1960: "*Miracle in Milan*, though made after the war, was born long before. It forms part of my intentions of the years 1935–40. Why then this flashback? Well, my present life is that of a man who seeks with all his strength not to do the things which he finds very agreeable. Sometimes I was even almost ashamed of going to the "store room" where I had shut up my reserve of imagination and charm, as if this had been too richly furnished to contain what I was looking for: a piece of dry bread earned with the sweat of my brow by daily work. And yet I often asked myself: Are you doing the right thing? Don't you have to be in life what you really are?"[131] His fear was that he had sacrificed a part of himself—a part of his reserve of imagination—to remain faithful to his ideal of the artist's duty, and his thoughts on *Miracle in Milan* conclude almost plaintively with the notion that "perhaps certain ideas which are apparently old and useless nevertheless miraculously bear the marks of a richer, deeper and more human experience."[131]

The abandonment of imagination, despite its attraction, in favour of close adhesion to reality comes only slowly in Zavattini. In 1952 he is concerned chiefly to separate the two approaches: "The former realism did not express the real. What I should like to know is the essence, which is really real. The inner reality as well as the exterior one. There is a narrow path between reality and imagination and it is this path which we have at first followed."[48] But by the following year imagination has already been given a sharply defined and limited role: "Of imagination in the traditional sense I have enough and to spare, but neo-realism demands of us that our imaginations be exercised *in loco*, on the actual, for facts only reveal their natural imaginative force when they are studied and examined in depth."[21] By imposing limits and qualifications—"imagination, but only on condition that it is exercised on reality and not in limbo"[21]—Zavattini devalues the whole notion of the free imagination found most vividly in *Miracle in Milan* but present too in all his work with De Sica. He returns again and again to this theme and the very reiteration makes one aware of the underlying but temporarily stifled lure of the imagination. But in his theories at least Zavattini has no doubts: his preoccupation is "to reconstruct news items in the most faithful manner"[21] and so he can use "only that little imagination which can come from the perfect knowledge of the fact itself."[21] The logical outcome of this kind of reasoning is a denial of the cinema as a reconstruction of reality and a substitution of the idea of a direct recording of reality, with the artist's freedom reduced to a mere choice of subject or angle—a conclusion that takes us outside neo-realism to the whole vexed question of *cinéma-vérité*. When some ten years later, Zavattini looked back on his work and thought in the early Fifties, he sought to redress the balance and give a more comprehensive evaluation of the complex relationship of imagination and reality: "I have never said—or, at any rate, I have never meant to say—that you should not 'invent,' that the artist's imagination—his *raison d'être*—should be bridled. But I have always maintained that the artist ought not to invent anything before really knowing his subject and having observed it closely. That ought, in my opinion, to become the new moral code of creation for a film-maker, whereas the traditional film— with a few notable exceptions—sets out from the conception of a pre-fabricated invention, that is to say a fiction. Invention is needed, but invention which rests on observation and knowledge of reality."[48]

18. Zavattini's Hunger for Reality

CESARE ZAVATTINI IS OFTEN SEEN as the theorist whose views underlie and indeed shape the whole neo-realist movement, but in fact this is something of a misrepresentation of his role. Though his contribution to neo-realist practice was as significant as that of anyone else, his most important theoretical writings and speeches date from 1951–53 and thus post-date the last generally recognised masterpiece of neo-realism, *Umberto D*. Moreover Zavattini does not analyse the past achievements and qualities of the moribund neo-realist movement but, in accordance with his total belief in contemporaneity, merely uses it as a starting point for the idea of a radically new cinema. The fact that his views were never put into practice does not detract from the interest of the mosaic of beliefs and opinions that can be put together from two interviews published in *L'Ecran Français* in 1951–52, he article "Some Ideas on the Cinema" which appeared initially in *La revista del cinema italiano* in December 1952, an article in the magazine *Emilia* in November 1953, the Parma conference speech of December 1953, his prefaces to various studies of the Italian cinema and his long account of how he did not make *Italia mia*, published first in March and April 1953. The very mass of material shows how eager Zavattini was to influence the Italian cinema despite his break with De Sica which, it eventually transpired, was decisive, and taken together these articles indicate one of the possibilities opened to the cinema by neo-realism.

The basis of Zavattini's theory of the cinema is his own moral impulse. He has described his discovery of realism in the early Forties as "a moral discovery"[94] and in 1951 characterised his progress since *Sciuscià* in terms of a mission: "I feel I must deepen my analysis of modern man, the life of man in the society of today: beyond myself, beyond what may be or may appear to me to be sentimentally dear or practically necessary, what may sometimes attract me or distract me better."[45] It is easy to see how this impulse arose during the war when Italians were faced with "the necessity of knowing, of seeing how these terrible events could have taken place"[21] and how it led him subsequently to deal with the issue of poverty. The latter is a necessary subject for any cinema with its roots in morality as Zavattini has explained: "We have begun with poverty for the simple reason that it is one of the most vital realities of our time, and I challenge anyone to prove the contrary."[94] It was during the war that Zavattini had felt the superiority of the cinema for the kind of investigation he wanted: "The cinema was the most direct and immediate means for this kind of enquiry, better than the other cultural media. The language of these latter had not been ready to express our reactions against the lies of the old general ideas with which we had been clad at the moment of the war and which had prevented us from attempting even the slightest revolt."[21] The strength of the cinema lies in its basic potential, its "original and innate capacity for showing things that we believe worth showing, as they happen day by day—in what we might call their 'dailiness,' their longest and truest duration."[94] But this unique quality precludes "turning imaginary situations into 'reality' and trying to make them look true" but instead brings with it the obligation to "make things as they are, almost by themselves, create their own special significance. Life is not what is invented in 'stories,' life is another matter."[94]

The view of the cinema of a moral force, which links Zavattini with Roberto Rossellini, finds expression in his case too in Christian terms, as an answer to the injunction to love one's neighbour as oneself. Zavattini has written: "Time has proved more and more that we do not love each other because we do not know each other well enough. This lack of solidarity stems from lack of knowledge: that is why I am determined more than ever not to spread that fictitious world born of the author's imagination, but rather to increase knowledge of the real world."[21] His statement of aims is a moving confession of faith: "There are the others . . . the others . . . the others are important . . . that is the most important thing . . . The men who live around us, what do they do, how do they live, are they well, do they suffer, and why are they ill, why do they suffer? . . . Everything that happens around us, often even the most banal things seen on the street, besides the most serious events whether they be far or near, has a significance, a human, social and dramatic meaning and raises great problems. Problems which are ours too, since nothing which happens around us is foreign to us, to the extent that we are men, a part of humanity. Here are my fascinating, inexhaustible fundamental sources—sources of inspiration, meditation and creative action, and they ought to be so for everyone in the cinema too."[45]

In view of this faith in reality Zavattini naturally opposes everything that comes between the film and life. In connection with *Miracle in Milan* we have already seen the ambiguity of his approach to imagination which, after *Umberto D*, grew to pronounced distrust. Of the projected *Italia mia* he wrote that it "would not be merely the product of the author's imagination, which is always, to some extent, isolated from reality," adding that he hoped that "the things-in-themselves could become a story, because only in that way could a film writer really listen to the 'cry of reality.'"[21] But imagination is only one of the hindrances which confront the would-be realist. Another is the economic structure of the film industry which Zavattini also attacked: "The cinema has not yet found its morality, its necessity, its quality, precisely because it costs too much; being so conditioned, it is much less an art than it could be."[94] The customary employment of specialised technicians and large numbers of collaborators is also to be abolished, for the new cinema "implies too the elimination of technical-professional apparatus, screen-writer included."[94] This rendering of himself —a professional scriptwriter *par excellence*—redundant is perhaps the most remarkable and ironical aspect of Zavattini's theorising, but he is very close

to modern critical thinking when he suggests that "we should arrive at
the sole author of the film"[94] and implies—though nowhere expressly states—
that this author should and indeed must be the director.

We have seen that for neo-realist directors the use of non-professional
actors was never a crucial issue. Zavattini, on the other hand, makes this
a basic requirement in his theoretical writings: "It is evident that, with
neo-realism, the actor—as a person fictitiously lending his own flesh to
another—has no more right to exist than the 'story.' In neo-realism as I
intend it, everyone must be his own actor. To want one person to play
another implies a calculated plot, the fable, not 'things happening.' "[94] The
implications of this thinking move far beyond the actual practice of neo-
realism where real fishermen embody characters derived from Giovanni
Verga and Lamberto Maggiorani, though not a professional, undoubtedly
"lends his flesh" to the invented character Antonio Ricci. After making
Bicycle Thieves Zavattini had dreamed of using Maggiorani again, this time
to tell his own story, that of a factory worker chosen to play in a film who
then finds it very difficult to reassume a normal role in society. By the
early Fifties this kind of approach had become generalised for Zavattini,
so that the new realist cinema "does not ask the men in which it is interested
to have the gifts of professional actors: their professional aptitudes derive
from their profession as men, of which they must be given a deepened
awareness."[21] In his view the impact of a film increases in proportion to
the authenticity of the characters: "If I use living, real characters with
which to sound reality, people in whose life I can directly participate, my
emotion becomes more effective, morally stronger, more useful. Art must
be expressed through a true name and surname, not a false one."[94] Such a
use of real people is a function of the kind of subject Zavattini thought
appropriate to the cinema. He was not surprised that "the cinema has
always felt the natural, unavoidable necessity to insert a 'story' in the
reality to make it exciting and 'spectacular,' " but he did question the
resulting assumption that reality "cannot be portrayed without the intervention of fantasy or artifice."[94] In his view the great discovery of neo-
realism—which had not been fully exploited even in *Umberto D*—was "to
have realised that the 'story' was only an unconscious way of disguising
a human defeat, and that the kind of imagination it involved was simply a
technique of superimposing dead formulas over living social facts."[94]

Though in this way Zavattini's formulation of the new cinema does
imply a rejection of many standard practices, including those of neo-realism
itself, it is not at all a negative conception of the cinema. When the in-
trusions of producers and scriptwriters, technicians, actors and stories have
been put aside, the film-maker comes face to face with reality: "Any hour
of the day, any place, any person is a subject for narrative if the narrator
is capable of observing and illuminating all these collective elements by
exploring their interior value," for reality "is richly huge . . . to be able to
look directly at it is enough."[94] The whole problem of the film artist becomes
that of "how to give human life its historical importance at every minute,"

of how to make reality "become spectacular not through its exceptional but through its normal qualities," so that "it will astonish us by showing so many things that happen every day under our eyes, things we have never noticed before."[94] If this is done the "missionary" aspect of Zavattini's approach to art becomes feasible, art conceived less as the creation of beauty than as the giving of a moral lesson: "I should like to teach men to see everyday life, everyday events with the same passion that they bring to the reading of a book. That seems to me the secret of happiness and love . . . And all this without the aid of the anecdote. What we must do with the anecdote is to pick it up with tweezers and throw it out of the window. That is the only way to give the unfolding of time its sacred importance."[45]

In one of his interviews Zavattini expressed a distrust of the Russian concept of montage on the grounds that it "falsifies time. It juggles with duration, operates a new synthesis with the event," whereas Zavattini's ideal ninety minute film would "of necessity be of one stretch, without editing."[3] In his view a respect for reality implies a respect too for real duration: "We must always deepen, analyse more the content of the present moment. There is a whole universe in a real minute of a man's suffering."[3] In this way the cinema can achieve its destiny which is "to follow time step by step by recounting what happens, or rather what is actually happening, and not what has happened."[3] This denial of an autonomous time scheme to a film which must always follow the chronology of our clocks and watches is paralleled by Zavattini's attempt to equate the spectators with the characters of the film and, by involving them, break down yet another barrier between film and reality. He explained this idea with reference to *Umberto D* in which, he said, there is no solution because for him "the solution has to be given by the audience. The spectacle continues in the auditorium, the spectators are the authors of the *dénouement* of the drama."[45] Elsewhere he elaborated this notion by saying that the characters in the film "require the solidarity of the public more than that of the other characters in the film. That is why they do not find a solution to their problems within the plot. The public must feel its responsibility and duty to find a concrete solution to the problem."

This respect for reality and real duration, combined with an intention to involve the audience directly in the action, naturally leads to a new concept of film narrative: "While the cinema used to make one situation produce another situation, and another, and another, again and again, and each scene was thought out and immediately related to the next (the natural result of a mistrust of reality), today, when we have thought out a scene, we feel the need to 'remain' in it, because the single scene itself can contain so many reverberations, can even contain all the situations we may need."[94] Equally, if a single situation—Zavattini's example is a woman going to buy a pair of shoes—is to bear the whole weight of a feature film it becomes imperative that it should be a real situation for those participating in it. In this way Zavattini is brought inexorably to an idea of the cinema as a record, not a reconstruction of reality and "the most irreplaceable experience" that the cinema can offer "comes from things happening under our eyes from natural necessity."[94] Thus one formulation at least of Zavattini's ideal cinema is a strikingly accurate anticipation of *cinéma-vérité*: "I have been saying up to now that the ideal film would be ninety minutes of the life of a man to whom nothing happens. Now I say: sit Peter or Paul on a chair and find the way to make them tell the truth about themselves and you will have the best film in the world."[3]

Zavattini's views in the early Fifties make a coherent whole, but it must be stressed again that these ideas are in no way a formulation of the attitudes underlying Italian neo-realism or even the writer's own work from *Sciuscià* to *Umberto D.* Rather, they represent an attempt to go beyond neo-realism equivalent to that of Visconti in *Senso*, Rossellini in *Viaggio in Italia* or Lattuada in *The Overcoat.* Where Zavattini differs from his contemporaries is that whereas they chose to enrich and diversify their stylistic methods in order to treat fresh subject matter, he tried to purify and refine neo-realism still more. Zavattini's basic concern with everyday reality constitutes a natural and unexceptional participation in the general realist tendency of Italian culture from around 1942 onwards, and we can place his 1952 view that "up to now, the film story was interested in life as represented by exceptional cases . . . (today) the old formula no longer serves us and we must focus our attention on the obvious, that which is everyday,"[98] alongside Cesare Pavese's terser formulation of 1943: "Narrating incredible things as though they were real—the old system; narrating realities as though they were incredible—the new."[113] But Zavattini's own distinctive belief in the superiority of the photographic reproduction over the acted, structured and reconstructed work of fiction is a reversion to Nineteenth century values and one is inevitably reminded of Emile Zola, who wrote in *The Contemporary Novel*: "Our contemporaneous novel becomes more simple every day from its hatred of complicated and false plots. One page of human life and you have enough to excite interest, to stir up deep and lasting emotions . . . We shall end by giving simple studies without adventures or climax, the analysis of a year of existence, the story of a passion, the biography of a character, notes taken from life and logically classified."[47] Zavattini's theories are thus open to the accusation that can justly be raised against all extreme formulations of naturalism, namely that despite their sincerity and impeccable normality they reduce art to the level of mere journalism.

This is a charge that Zavattini would probably have accepted with equanimity for he has on occasion defended his theories in journalistic terms and maintained that "the cinema approaches journalism to escape from the limits of 'translation'" (i.e. the application to the cinema of stylistic methods appropriate to other media).[16] It would have been interesting to see how far Zavattini's practice would have stayed within the limits propounded above but unfortunately this is impossible, since the films that were to embody the theories were never made. The immediate project with which he and De Sica hoped to follow *Umberto D*–a film taken from three sketches by Zavattini–came to nothing and neither *Stazione Termini* nor *L'oro di Napoli* can be said to incorporate the new ideas on narrative. The film which might have vindicated the theories was *Italia mia*. The basic idea of a series of episodes in the daily life of the Italian people went through various mutations: firstly a chronicle ranging from 1900 to 1950, then a study of Italy from the end of the war to the present, and finally the record of a three month trip across the country. But all had in common the notion he described in a letter to De Sica as "a film with no script but created immediately through our ears and eyes from direct contact with reality (the true destiny of neo-realism in my opinion). The facts are there; we must pick and choose them as they happen. Sometimes, though, we must stage them but always in relation to the theme being developed."[21] But as first De Sica and then Rossellini abandoned the project Zavattini saw the prospects of success vanish, for he never considered taking the obvious step, implicit in his theories, of becoming the director himself. Even when the producer Carlo Ponti offered him the chance to co-direct he answered that he "would not even consider it in view of a talent like Rossellini's."[21] Zavattini was technically so-director of *La storia di Caterina* with Francesco Maselli but he has admitted that the latter was "the real director of this episode which forms part of *Amore in città*."[32] This was the closest Zavattini came to realising his ideals but though Caterina Rigoglioso acted out her own story at the places where the various events really happened, critics found little to distinguish the episode from a conventional neo-realist piece of film-making. In the early Fifties Zavattini's diaries are full of ideas for films that were never made. An entry of June 1952 records an idea that did eventually find realisation as *Il tetto* in 1956, but in the four year interval between conception and completion the work was subjected to all the pressures of the technical apparatus of commercial film-making and emerged not as a new and revolutionary advance for the reunited De Sica-Zavattini team but as a tired reiteration of the techniques of ten years before.

19. Neo-Realism and Comedy: Zampa, Emmer and Castellani

THE QUESTION OF COMEDY is clearly a crucial one for an appreciation and definition of the neo-realist movement. Does one consider as neo-realist the vein of warm-hearted humour which, from Luigi Zampa's *Vivere in pace* of 1946 to Renato Castellani's *Due soldi di speranza* in 1951, runs parallel to the more seriously intended productions of Rossellini, De Sica and Visconti? Just as the years 1940–42 may be defined in terms of a balance between calligraphism and the realist impulse, so the late Forties are characterised by a split in approach and attitude between commitment and comedy. Like calligraphism, the Forties comedy style is part of a wider cultural tendency and Dominique Fernandez has convincingly linked it to certain works of the writers Pratolini and Calvino, Moravia, Vittorini and Vitaliano Brancati, the latter being, significantly enough, Zampa's script-writer on a number of films. In Fernandez's view some of the novels and stories by these men display a marked "niceness," made up of "the absence of any too conspicuous quality or of any too pronounced defect," and have as their aim to draw "sympathy and friendship, but not love or passion." He notes that "malice, humour, obligingness, devotion and solidarity regularly enter into the composition," for the authors have been "drawn to rehabilitate those aspects of human feeling which were previously not considered worthy of literary treatment: these resources, these good intentions latent in the hearts of the majority of men, these same sentiments that true heroes and heroic writers despise."[50] If Fernandez's definitions are accepted the cinema's parallel with literature is clearly a close one but the comedy can be seen as something quite distinct from neo-realism.

The all-too-easy optimism of both writers and film-makers may also be related to what Luigi Barzini, in another context, has aptly named the fatal charm of Italy, the infatuation suffered by people who "relish what they believe are the simple and genuine emotions of the Italians who are apparently unashamed of them and seldom try to hide them." Barzini is at pains to explain that far from being simple and genuine, these emotions are an almost consciously fabricated show designed to render a meaningless and frightening life acceptable, a public display that "can be so engrossing that many people spend most of their lives just looking at it." To strengthen the Italians' defences against a hostile world "dull and insignificant moments in life must be made decorous and agreeable with suitable decorations and rituals. Ugly things must be hidden, unpleasant and tragic facts swept under the carpet whenever possible." The Italians involved in these practices, believing that "man's ills cannot be cured but only assuaged, catastrophies cannot be averted but only mitigated," naturally prefer "to glide elegantly over the surface of life and leave the depths unplumbed."[10] While there may be much that can be said of such an approach when applied to the grim realities of life, it is open to serious criticisms as an attitude to art, and seen in this perspective the comedy of Zampa, Emmer and Castellani is the very reverse of true neo-realism: recording an illusion where the neo-realist cinema searches for reality, offering reassurance and comfort where neo-realism propounds attack and confrontation.

The basic drawbacks of this kind of comedy approach are graphically illustrated by the work of Luigi Zampa, best known for the widely successful *Vivere in pace*. Zampa, who had already had three plays staged in Rome before he went to the Centro sperimentale in 1935 at the age of thirty-one, became a director in 1941 after a conventional training as writer and assistant but made no impact on audiences or critics with his first six films.

His work in the late Forties was more ambitious but still represents a compromise between neo-realist and commercial values. Zampa takes a basically serious problem—the German occupation in *Vivere in pace* (1946), postwar poverty and the status of women in *L'onorevole Angelina* (1947), the ordinary man's complicity in Fascism in *Anni difficili* (1948)— and then proceeds to skim lightly over the surface, mixing warm-hearted humour, easy farce and just a touch of tragedy (the death of Uncle Tigna in the first of these films and the shooting of Piscitello's son in the third). The whole concoction is carefully and skilfully mixed according to the taste of the public with plenty of "typically Italian" passages and incidents of a kind likely to please foreign audiences. Zampa tends to rely for impact on star performances played with enormous gusto: in *Vivere in pace* Aldo Fabrizi as Uncle Tigna has scope for humour and genuine concern, rustic philosophising and a spectacular death scene, while in *L'onorevole Angelina* Anna Magnani mixes fiery tirades and bursts of violence with softer, senti- mental moments of womanly longing for male dominance. To fill in the background Zampa uses a host of noisy, ebullient extras and solid character actors like Ave Ninchi, Ernesto Almirante, Nando Bruno and Aldo Silvani.

There is no real widening of the neo-realist approach here, for Zampa uses location shooting and wretched dwellings as another director might use studio sets and "white telephones." There is no bite to the satire and *L'onorevole Angelina*—a crucial example—raises the problems of women's rights only to conclude that the woman's place, whatever her talents, is in the home. The film begins with a genuine social problem and includes, in its early scenes, a few moments of mass protest seemingly shot with the conviction of a De Santis. Then Zampa remembers he is supposed to be making a comedy. Political attitudes in general are mocked, and the proposi- tion advanced that going hungry is somehow better than struggling to change the social set-up. More troubling than the obvious contrivances of the plot with which the writers manipulate Angelina's relationship with the women she leads purely for effect, is the lack of any positive commitment or even involvement. The villainy of the profiteers is glossed over in *L'onorevole Angelina*, in much the way that the realities of Nazism vanished beneath the peasant farce of *Vivere in pace,* and the film's basic dishonesty about social conditions is evident if it is compared with *Miracle in Milan* which uses elements of fable and magic but still contrives to tell the truth. Although it was with such would-be neo-realist comedies that Zampa made his reputation, his own preference among his abundant *oeuvre* is for *Processo alla città,* made in 1952. This beautifully reconstructed portrait of a Nineteenth century scandal has the kind of force and convic- tion that Zampa's works of the Forties lack, but in the last analysis it remains no more than a solid piece of craftsmanship conforming comfortably to commercial requirements.

Luciano Emmer's most notable contribution to Italian comedy and his only feature film of real note, *Domenica d'agosto* (1949), is more satisfying than Zampa's work if only because it lacks any pretence of examining serious social issues. Emmer belongs to the same generation as Lattuada, Castellani and De Santis but whereas they all turned immediately to the fiction film, he devoted himself to the documentary. Between 1941 and 1949, working largely in collaboration with Enrico Gras, Emmer revolutionised the art film and prepared the way for films like Alain Resnais's *Guernica*. Then, in 1949, came an unexpected chance to direct a feature film and in a mere fortnight Emmer, Sergio Amidei, Cesare Zavattini and a few others devised a script. The director's aim was not to make an "omnibus" film composed of different episodes nor a documentary on a summer Sunday in Rome but, in his own words, "a dramatic story of that particular day and those people whose lives suddenly became entangled by fate or coincidence, whatever you like to call it."[127] Abandoning any literary pretensions in order to be "as sincere and unpretentious as possible," Emmer began *Domenica d'agosto* with "a minimal scenario which was later enriched as the work progressed by the inclusion of facts or characters that gradually presented themselves."[17] The film takes the fragmentary approach to extremes, for it deals, according to Emmer, with no less than 102 characters, all played by non-professionals or young unknown actors. This method naturally precludes any attempt at depth of analysis and in any case the director's interest is in achieving spontaneity and expressing his notion of potentiality: "I had never realised as I do today how important it is for the cinema to interest itself in things that may happen. Reality is in becoming. Truth lies not in prefabricated schemas but in perpetual change. This is the unique path open today for a cinema which wishes to be authentic, to respond to the demands of our time."[17]

Somewhat similar ideas are expressed in the films of Renato Castellani whose early works, particularly *Un colpo di pistola,* had been among the most notable products of the calligraphist style. His subsequent films show a clear response to the need for realism while maintaining a distinctive approach characterised by a basic optimism about human beings. As he told an interviewer: "I have always been full of ingenuousness and convinced that our fellows are better than they might have been, given the conditions in which they live."[131] Castellani is also the least committed, in a political sense, of all the Forties directors: "Why accuse and condemn then? It is much more just to understand and to love. It is there that the function of neo-realism lies."[131] His new realist intent was already apparent in his first two postwar projects, neither of which came to fruition. The first of these was a film that was to deal specifically with contemporary events, the story of a criminal who escapes from the Regina Coeli prison on September 8, 1943 (the time of the armistice with the allies) and is forced to hide from the Nazis. The other project, though adapted from a comedy by Luigi Capuana (who died in 1915), "was to have been shot completely on location, without actors and with characters drawn at random from everyday life."[131] The film Castellani actually made in 1946 to re-establish himself with producers—the comedy *Mio figlio professore*—was an agreeable work but reflected few of these concerns. Tracing a simple school porter's twenty-seven-year devotion to his only son, it included a few excellent gags and provided a fine role for Aldo Fabrizi, but one senses that Castellani was not deeply involved with his material. Far more significant were his next three films, all of them comedies made on the lines of the Capuana project.

With the first of this "trilogy," *Sotto il sole di Roma* (1947), Castellani pursued his avowed aim of "advancing on the path to a direct knowledge of man, without preconceived ideas, without social messages, with the unique preoccupation of not betraying the things which I saw, of telling the truth such as it offered itself to my eyes."[131] He based his film, a story of juvenile escapades leading to the brink of serious crime, on an extensive documentation of the lives of the young people from the working class districts of Rome collected by Fausto Tozzi, with whom he carried out long and minute enquiries, "mixing with the young people, following them in their adventures, their amusements, their follies."[131] The distinctive quality of the film is undeniable and, as Borde and Bouissy record, "it is always an agreeable spectacle, not lacking in irony. The detail is always of a high quality."[17] But the question remains: is *Sotto il sole di Roma* in its recording of the minutiae of life without comment really a neo-realist work? Castellani's next film, *E primavera* (1949), does little to give an answer to this query. Like *Domenica d'agosto* it numbered Cesare Zavattini among its scriptwriters, and his influence can be felt in a number of scenes. *E primavera* is a straightforward comedy about a friendly, extraverted delivery boy Beppe who, because of his national service, meets two women in towns far apart—one in Sicily and the other in Milan—and marries them both in order to make them happy. The early scenes are played with great verve and the characters, particularly Beppe (Mario Angelotti) and the Sicilian wife Maria (Elena Varzi) come splendidly to life. Later the film flirts with more serious issues, as when it deals with Maria's reaction to the truth—an attempt at manslaughter—but the comic tone is restored with the trial scenes towards the end of the film, when all the problems are neatly resolved. If the plot is perhaps excessively schematised and creaks rather badly in places, the humour rises naturally and spontaneously from the personalities of the characters and a general atmosphere of warm good nature prevails.

Due soldi di speranza (1951), which followed, is also built around the adventures of a young man after his national service. The hero, Antonio, returns from the army to his village near Naples to find his life complicated by his mother, his family, his need for a job and most of all by Carmela, the girl he eventually marries. More important than this plot is the concern with simple emotions and humorous detail shown by Castellani and his writers who spent about a year preparing the film. Great care was taken with the dialogue, which Castellani wrote with Titina De Filippo and which cunningly mixes local dialect and standard Italian, the material having been shaped and reshaped until a satisfactory tone was captured. Guido Aristarco, praising this aspect of the film, notes that the dialogue is "a sort of translation of Neapolitan, preserving a great number of the original words, dialect expressions, constructions, cast-offs, repetitions of subjects and replies, grammatical errors, frequent use of adverbs, proverbs and sayings."[21] He concludes that in *Due soldi di speranza* "the dialect expressions really carry with them the force and blood of popular language without any literary restriction."[21] Castellani has devoted much care to the surface authenticity of his actors, settings and language, but the film never becomes a realist work in the truest and deepest sense because of the limitations of approach and his conception of neo-realism as "a practical but also spontaneous fact" which "did not appear in order to discuss problems but to concern itself with men's lives such as they are."[131]

In this connection Castellani's account of the genesis of *Due soldi di speranza* is of great interest. The idea for the film came to him when he was in Pompei where he was preparing a film version of *Othello* which was in fact never produced. The setting provoked a direct response in him: "I walked for hours in those dead, empty streets beaten by the sun. It was one of the most extraordinary sensations I have ever had. It was here that the idea of the landscape which was to serve as a framework for the film came to me."[131] Only later came the human element, crystallised by a meeting with a peasant of whom Castellani has said: "One of his replies struck me. I had asked him how he was getting on. He replied with the words, 'Ce mantenimme' (we get by, we live . . .). The thought that there could exist in the world a human being whose sole ideal in life was not to improve things but simply to get by, provoked a violent reaction in me."[131] In the elaboration of the film from this point on Castellani's preoccupation was to re-create this "Ce mantenimme" as it were from the inside. To quote his own statement further: "The remarkable thing is that that did not make me create problems for myself, nor to superimpose on the reality I had discovered some preconceived idea. It would have been absurd to take tragically the experience of this peasant who became the inspiration of *Due soldi di speranza*. If I had not narrated this film with the kind of ease and lightness with which the young peasant had pronounced his 'Ce mantenimme' I would have lost the essential of the film. It seemed to me more attractive to adhere to the human condition of this simple man and to become myself someone who can say 'Ce mantenimme.' "[131] Castellani's deep love and sympathy for his characters are the chief driving forces of *Due soldi di speranza* and the principal reasons for its success but they cannot wholly compensate for the lack of any critical perspective. This latter is explicitly attacked: "If I had wanted to make a condemnation, I would have written a pamphlet."[131] But by rejecting in this way the need to see the experience in a social, political or economic context and deliberately limiting himself to a subjective viewpoint, Castellani, though able to fashion a distinctive, individual and satisfying comedy style, could not create a work of true realist import.

Castellani's best work is linked to the general mood of the postwar period even if it is essentially distinct from neo-realism proper. Like Vittorio

Neo-realist comedy:

The impact of the arrival of the Americans in Luigi Zampa's VIVERE IN PACE (1946)

Above: Luigi Zampa with his photographer Carlo Montuori
Left: Anna Magnani as a woman of the people in Zampa's L'ONOREVOLE ANGELINA (1947)
Below: A family portrait from Zampa's ANNI DIFFICILI (1948)

Left: *Luciano Emmer directing*

Below: *The holiday atmosphere captured in Emmer's* DOMENICA D'AGOSTO (1949)

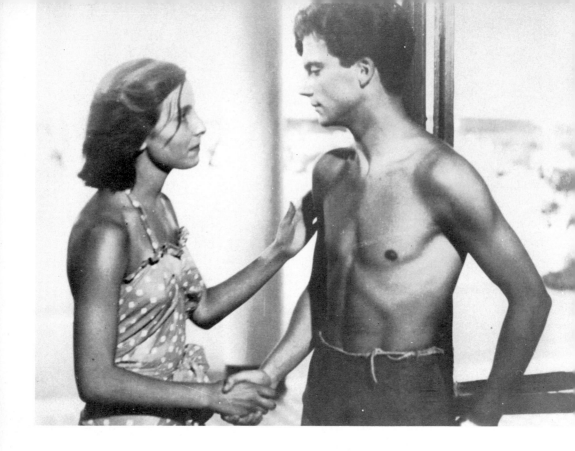

Anna Baldini with Franco Interlenghi and Anna Di Leo in Luciano Emmer's comedy DOMENICA D'AGOSTO (1949)

Above: The youthful heroes of Renato Castellani's SOTTO IL SOLE DI ROMA (1947)
Below: Elena Varzi as the Southern wife in Milan in Castellani's E PRIMAVERA (1949)

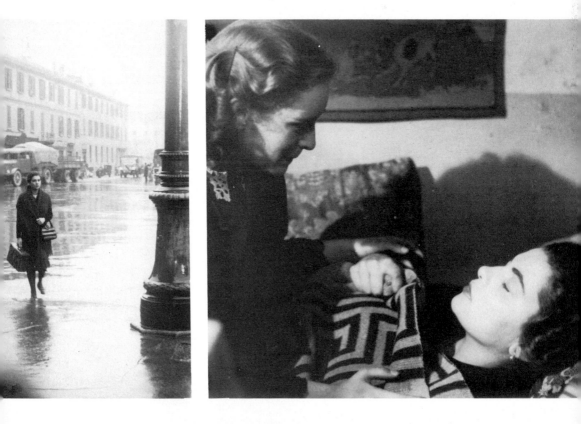

Left: Renato Castellani

Below: Maria Fiore and Vincenzo Musolino as the couple in search of happiness in Renato Castellani's comedy DUE SOLDI DI SPERANZA (1951)

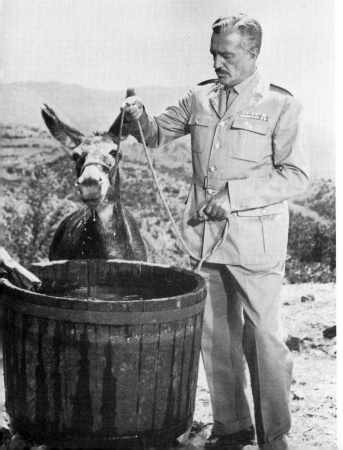

The Fifties comedy style:

Gina Lollobrigida and Vittorio De Sica in Luigi Comencini's BREAD, LOVE AND DREAMS (1953)

The move away from neo-
realism to a richer style:

Top: Renato Rascel and
Yvonne Sanson in Alberto
Lattuada's IL CAPPOTTO
(1951)

Middle: Amedeo Nazzari
(left) in Luigi Zampa's PRO-
CESSO ALLA CITTÀ (1952)

Right: Alida Valli and Farley
Granger in Luchino Visconti's
SENSO (1954)

De Sica, Castellani pursued an erratic and inconsistent course after 1951, following *Due soldi di speranza* with a decorative colourful version of Shakespeare's *Romeo and Juliet* and subsequently alternating between attempts to recreate the Forties style (*I sogni nel cassetto* and *Il brigante*) and films relying in Zampa fashion on star performance (*Nella città l'inferno* and *Mare matto*). The potential weakness of this comedy style becomes all too apparent in the films written by Ettore M. Margadonna, co-author of *Due soldi di speranza,* for Luigi Comencini and Dino Risi. The films of the *Bread and Love* series—*Pane, amore e fantasia* (1953), *Pane, amore e gelosia* (1954), *Pane, amore e . . .* (1955)—reduce the authenticity of Castellani to a glossy formula of "rosy realism." Poverty becomes a decorative back-drop for the talents of attractive stars like Vittorio De Sica and Gina Lollobrigida, any pretence of social concern is abandoned in favour of amorous intrigue and a product evolved that echoes less neo-realism than the "white telephone" era of the late Thirties. With *Poveri ma belli* (1956) and *Belle ma povere* (1957)—the titles are indicative of the routine that had been evolved—Dino Risi, who had directed the third *Bread and Love* film, gave a new twist to the formula by using personable unknowns and pretty starlets in place of world-renowned stars while retaining the basic pattern of cheery good-humour and light-hearted farce. These films are acceptable commercial products, designed for a large public and achieving great success at the box-office, but they represent a trivialisation of neo-realism, the fundamental tenets of which had already been largely disregarded by Castellani. The failure of the neo-realists to achieve a breakthrough in comedy akin to that in drama is emphasised by the achievements of Jacques Tati in France. Drawing inspiration from life encountered on the street and dialogue overheard in public, Tati shows a constant concern with reality in the widest sense, whether he is shooting on location for *Jour de Fête* or working with his scrupulously reconstructed sets in *Playtime.* Like Emmer and Castellani, Tati builds his films out of tiny fragments of life, successions of gags, but he adds a new dimension of realism. He probes and observes while the Italian film-makers slip happily from one slightly contrived situation to another, intent on no more than producing an amusing surface of comedy.

Part Four

EVALUATION

They have baptised
"neo-realism" films
where our Italian
friends display an
imagination analagous
with that of the
Arab story tellers.

JEAN COCTEAU

1. Anatomy of a Style

ONE OF THE MAIN PURPOSES of this study has been to show the presence, beneath the collective label of "neo-realism," of a wealth and diversity of stylistic approaches that together make the Italian postwar cinema rank, not alongside the British documentary movement of the Thirties as an interesting episode in an otherwise undistinguished national *oeuvre*, but as one of the major advances made by the cinema in its brief history. But even to begin to draw general conclusions from the works of the film-makers we have considered is extremely difficult, for as Roberto Rossellini has rightly said: "Everyone possesses his own realism and everyone thinks that his own is best."[137] As an example of this basic disagreement of neo-realists among themselves we need only confront two basic definitions: one by Visconti: "Neo-realism is above all a question of content"[21]—and one by Fellini: "Neo-realism is not a question of what you show, its real spirit is how you show it."[76] Perhaps the best way of tackling the problem is to take a totally hostile judgement, like that of the producer Battista in Alberto Moravia's novel *A Ghost at Noon*. Battista makes out the following case: "The neo-realist film is depressing, pessimistic and gloomy. . . . Apart from the fact that it represents Italy as a country of ragamuffins—to the great joy of foreigners who have every sort of interest in believing that our country really *is* a country of ragamuffins—apart from this fact, which, after all, is of some considerable importance, it insists too much on the negative sides of life, on all that is ugliest, dirtiest, most abnormal in human existence. . . . It is, in short, a pessimistic, unhealthy type of film, a film which reminds people of their difficulties instead of helping them to overcome them."[105]

This is a forceful statement of what one might call the "official" line, revealing the primitive mode of thinking behind, say, Andreotti's campaign against *Umberto D*. On the basic level of subject matter neo-realism is about such things as suffering, poverty and unemployment—subjects that governments would prefer left untouched—but the object is not to denigrate Italy but to reveal current circumstances honestly. Neo-realism is very much a contemporary cinema and, with the notable exceptions of *La terra trema* (the modernisation of a Nineteenth century novel) and *Il mulino del Po* (the adaptation of a historical novel published in 1935), it draws its inspiration exclusively from the years 1943–51. Even the two films quoted as exceptions reflect the situation of the years they were made, the one mirroring the left-wing hopes of 1947, the other the agricultural unrest of 1949. Given this contemporary approach, neo-realism must be closely linked to the war and its direct aftermath and deal with the violence of Liberation and Resistance (Rossellini, Vergano) or postwar crime and banditry (Lattuada, De Santis). To some extent the stylistic methods of neo-realist film-making demand striking and powerful subject matter of this kind and only De Sica and Zavattini were wholly successful in adapting a style born out of the war to the peaceful exigencies of Italy in the Fifties. All other major neo-realist film-makers adopted a different and richer style when they moved away from subjects with a strictly social contemporary interest: Visconti in *Senso*, Rossellini in *Viaggio in Italia*, Lattuada in *The Overcoat*, or Zampa in *Processo alla città*, for example.

There are limitations in the neo-realist range of subject matter, even if these are not of a kind that a character like Battista would appreciate. The neo-realist slogan was "Take your camera into the streets" and this was a revolutionary call in terms of the normal film-making of the time. But while it is true, as Lattuada has said, that the street is "rich in life . . . indicative in every country of the character of a people,"[53] the level of life it reveals is purely a social one. The street tells us comparatively little about history and neo-realist film-makers did not venture into the past to analyse the origins and growth of Fascism—though censorship problems may be partly responsible for this particular omission. Nor is it possible in terms of out-of-doors activity to offer any thorough analysis of the structure of society: the real power struggle in the capitalist system goes on behind closed doors and neo-realism deals only with the public face of authority: the bureaucrats and minor officials. The outcast or outsider—the man in search of a job, the criminal or prostitute—for whom the street is a centre of life constitutes the typical protagonist of a neo-realist film and the emphasis is always placed not on the particular psychological problems or obsessions of the individual but on his interaction with his environment: the bill-poster Antonio and the people he meets in the streets of Rome, the Valastro family and their neighbours or enemies, the American soldiers and the Italians they meet in the course of the Liberation.

Clearly there is a political element involved in this return to the ordinary man. In part it reflects a conscious rejection of the Mussolini cult of personality and a reaction against the "positive" hero of so many Fascist films and stories. Instead of glorifying the heroics of cheaply won victories, the neo-realist film takes the side of the victims. In part too it constitutes a genuine alignment with the parties of the Left, particularly the Communist Party. The electoral fortunes of the latter: 19 per cent of the votes in the first postwar elections, a falling away in 1948 when the Christian Democrats won an overall majority and then a steady increase to 25 per cent of the poll in 1963, find reflection in the Italian cinema. The great prestige of the Communist Party in the postwar years derived from various sources: the intransigence of Italian Communists during the Fascist era when they avoided any kind of compromising involvement with the authorities, the impression created by the Communist groups in the partisan struggle against the Germans, and the authority of Antonio Gramsci, the founder of the Party. Gramsci, whom John Cammett has described as "the first Italian to seriously apply the Marxist interpretation to all aspects of Italian history and culture,"[24] died in 1937, but his collected works, published during the late Forties, exercised an enormous influence that is neatly symbolised by the award of the Viareggio Prize in 1947 to his *Letters from Prison* and in 1957 to Pasolini's verse tribute "Le ceneri di Gramsci." The list of Marxist achievement in postwar Italian culture is striking—among novelists Vittorini, Pavese, Pratolini and Calvino, among film-makers Visconti, De Santis, Antonioni, Lizzani and Pasolini. But the Marxism by which these men were inspired was not a rigid, petrified orthodoxy for, as Dominique Fernandez has pointed out "the Communism of Italian intellectuals is more the expression of a disorientation, a moral and spiritual despair than an adhesion to precise dogmas."[50] Indeed the term "Communist" is perhaps best understood as defined by Cesare Pavese: "There are only two attitudes to life, the Christian's and the Stoic's. Probably the Communist's is a fusion of both. He has charity and a sense of stern reality; he knows the world is hard, yet he does good."[113]

Out of this commitment to the poor and underprivileged comes the forcefulness of all the best neo-realism which is an art of attack, not one of acceptance or reassurance. If the problems treated are insoluble in terms of existing society, then it is society that must be changed. This is recognised even by a man like Fellini who is far from being a Marxist: "The chief characteristic of neo-realism is that it doesn't just want to contemplate the world but also to transform it. . . . Neo-realism is a movement that has been actively inserted into the process of transformation of a society and, born for battle, cannot invoke the pacific life of other art forms."[55] Fortunately the climate of opinion in Italy drew a firm line between politics and art. In one of his prison notebooks Gramsci had made the essential distinction: "For a politician to demand that the art of his time express a determined cultural world constitutes political activity not art criticism: if the cultural world for which we are fighting is a living and necessary fact, its expansivity will be irresistible, it will find its artists."[24] This view was supported by Elio Vittorini, a distinguished novelist and editor of the Communist review *Politecnico*, and his remarks on the value of culture in a political struggle apply particularly to the neo-realist cinema: "The influence which culture can exercise as a means placed at the service of politics will always be very restricted. . . . On the other hand it can be all the more service to politics by fulfilling its own role and continuing to pose new problems and discover new objectives from which politics can draw stimulus for new developments in its own sphere."[50]

Seen in this context, the independence from stifling political orthodoxy displayed by neo-realist film-makers becomes easily comprehensible and one can understand the perplexity and exasperation of doctrinaire Marxist critics who are unwilling or unable to see this crucial distinction. Raymond Borde and André Bouissy, for instance, when they come to evaluate the achievements of the movement, have to look largely outside neo-realism proper to find films which fit their categories. The major neo-realist achievements: *Bicycle Thieves, Umberto D, La terra trema* and a work like *I vitelloni*, come for them only into the second category, that of "sober and honest statements . . . which had the defect of not being conclusive."[17] From an artistic viewpoint, however, much of the strength of neo-realism derives from the fact that its deep involvement with the problems of the poor does not lead to the imposition of a rigid party line. Typical in this respect is the use of the figure of a child instead of a party orthodoxy as the touchstone of truth, which one finds particularly in De Sica's films (the title of his 1942 film *The Children Are Watching Us* is symptomatic) but also in those of Visconti and Lattuada. With regard to their own personal political opinions all the major neo-realists conform to Lukács's demand that a realist be ruthless towards his own subjective world-picture: Visconti does not pretend that the Marxist vision is easily realisable or even to be appreciated by the Sicilian poor, De Sica does not try to hide the social evils that flourish under a Christian Democratic government, and while the Catholic Rossellini sympathetically portrays a Communist leader, the Communist Vergano gives a moving picture of a Catholic priest. To judge by their films of this period at least most neo-realists would sympathise with the non-conformist attitude of Lattuada: "In *Il mulino del Po* the Communists thought that the strike was not used to the maximum and the Right said that I had attacked the order of the middle-classes by showing a strike and showing peasants affirming their rights before the authorities. Personally I was proud of being attacked from both sides."[77]

Beyond these political concerns there are wider implications inherent in the neo-realists' return to the ordinary man as he lives in the shadow of poverty and war. Deep concern with humanity is common to them all but there is no attempt to probe beneath the surface into the mind of the individual, so that concepts like *Angst* or absurdity have no place in neo-realist art, and alienation is defined purely in social terms. In place of the traditional cinematic concern with the complexities of the individual psyche (a preoccupation inherited from the Nineteenth century bourgeois novel) comes a desire to probe the basically human, to undertake an investigation into man within his social and economic context but without bourgeois cultural accretions. The neo-realist film-makers, like their novelist counterparts, are for the most part highly educated and civilised individuals from a middle-class background but there is no trace of condescension in their treatment of the poor and semi-articulate. On the contrary, we find a distrust of the basic values of civilised life and cultured society which proved so little of a bulwark against Fascism (the handling of the figure of the landlady in *Umberto D* is a typical and striking example of this). Having grown to maturity under Mussolini's régime the neo-realists experienced an understandable need to purge themselves of the errors of the past and re-examine their own basic values. Their method was to concern themselves with individuals who experience the full impact of economic and social pressures in the context of their everyday life and are helpless to resist it, for it is in such confrontations of man and environment that humanity defines itself. In these preoccupations film-makers offer a parallel to the

novelists of postwar Italy whose approach Dominique Fernandez characterises as follows: "The misery of peasants or workers is not in itself the
object of neo-realist art: it is what new light this misery sheds on man that
interests writers. The characters of their novels are poor because poverty,
beyond the sociological truth about the poor man, reveals a pure, naked
quality of the human being."[50] It is on this simple and uncorrupted human
reality that the neo-realist writer or film-maker bases his inquiry into life.
Neo-realists found in the cinema an ideal medium for such an examination
of existence in terms of environment and social relationship and, by using
the camera to bring out the expressiveness of gesture and human environment in the quotidian context, they expanded the language of cinema and
brought about a revolution in our aesthetic awareness.

The neo-realist film's link with reality is a close one, implying, as Rossellini claimed, "an act of humility to life,"[137] in that the basic material is
experienced at first hand by the film-maker before the film is elaborated:
De Sica studied the shoeshine boys before making *Sciuscià* and Rossellini
went to Berlin before beginning work on *Germania anno zero*. The structure
of a neo-realist film thus grows out of the subject instead of being an external
scheme imposed upon it, and the planning is never so rigid as to deny the
possibility of settings and actors exercising a considerable influence at the
time of shooting: even Visconti maintains that there must be an "impression
of improvisation" in a film.[52] But the methods of neo-realism are never those
of the simple recording of reality that lies at the root of much documentary
work and characterises Zavattini's theories. As François Debrenczeni points
out the basic principle of neo-realist film-making is the reconstruction of
reality.[48] The movement began with a film (*Rome Open City*) that sought
to recapture the atmosphere of the recent past, and subsequently those
dealing with current postwar problems added a distinctive flavour to the
element of documentary: a touch of poetry (*Sciuscià*), of literature (*La
terra trema*), of melodrama (*Il bandito*). There is no attempt to film the
story with the people who inspired it—De Sica was never tempted to make
Sciuscià with the real Scimietta and Capellone—and it is not until the virtual
end of neo-realism, in *Amore in città*, that we find a person acting out his
or her own story in front of the cameras. Equally the involvement of the
film-maker is limited: he remains a (comparatively) prosperous, literate
bourgeois filming other people's social problems, not his own. Both *Germania anno zero* and *Umberto D* are "personal" in the sense of being dedicated, respectively, to Rossellini's son and De Sica's father. But the material
is distanced: Edmund is a German child corrupted by a Nazi education and
Umberto D is not a family portrait but a picture of a man without family
ties. Hence the neo-realist film remains a conscious artefact, never a simple
transcription of reality, and one can easily understand the readiness with
which neo-realist directors later turned to historical subjects in, for example,
Processo alla città, Francesco, giullare di Dio and *Senso*.

Because it is in essence a reconstruction and depends on an illusion of
reality, neo-realism entails the maintenance of the whole technical ap-

paratus of commercial film-making, with the possible exception of the set designer. The roles of these various collaborators and technicians are, however, redefined by neo-realism. The construction of an artefact implies the existence of someone who interprets reality and it is the director who, by filling this role, reasserts his supremacy. All the basic methods employed by neo-realism contribute, as we shall see, to this pre-eminence of the director, who emerges unrivalled as the creative force in neo-realism. In this connection the status of Zavattini perhaps needs closer definition as he seems, at first glance, to contradict this notion. Zavattini is often seen as the creator of neo-realism but this is a distortion of the truth. In the Forties he participated in the neo-realist movement, but only when it was already developing independently of him and he was in fact a late convert to realism (the impetus behind *Sciuscià* comes from De Sica, not from him). Moreover he has never claimed to have originated either the term neo-realism or the movement. His own account of his feelings during the crucial years 1942–43 is worth quoting: "At that moment I was the man who is astonished at everything which happens in the world, who wonders why he has allowed it and why he has wasted so much time. . . . And so I can understand why I was so enthusiastic about the movement in the Italian cinema which was developing at that time around the unanimously accepted definition: neo-realism."[131] In his long and varied career his collaboration as an equal with the director De Sica is virtually unique and only on *Umberto D* was he sole writer: elsewhere he has been merely part of a team of writers (one of seven in the case of *Bicycle Thieves* or *Caccia tragica* for instance) all producing material for the director. Even his theoretical writings do not imply the primacy of the writer: in effect, as we have seen, he eliminates his own role as professional scenarist in favour of the idea of a sole creator who is both writer and director. It was because of his own personal inability to fill both roles (despite the experiment of *Amore in città*) that Zavattini's theories could not be put into practice.

The neo-realist movement drew heavily on the French cinema of the Thirties but it did not take over that movement's high regard for writers. There are various reasons for this, some of which are inherent in the cinematic medium (though sometimes, as in France, disguised) while others are peculiar to Italian film-making methods. Among the former are some touched upon by Alberto Moravia in his novel *A Ghost at Noon*. This is a fictionalised account of the scriptwriter's function but many of the reflections put into the mouth of the hero, Riccardo Molteni, have the ring of Moravia's own experience as a film-writer. The paradox of the situation is well brought out: on the one hand the richness of a script which is "drama, mime, cinematographic technique, *mise en scène* and direction, all at the same time"; and on the other a basic subordination of the writer to the director. The writer "can be nothing more than a provider of suggestions and inventions, of technical, psychological and literary ideas; it is then the director's task to make use of this material according to his own genius and, in fact, to express himself."[105] The day eventually comes, for many writers, when they must make the transition to directing. The experience of Fellini is not untypical: "Nevertheless, as time passed, I noticed that for a man who has faith in the cinema, work on the shooting script means absolutely nothing. It is an ambiguous situation."[131] These sentiments are echoed by Zavattini writing in 1952 that since he is trying to say certain things and saying them in his own way, he cannot be satisfied "to offer a simple technical contribution" and therefore finds the role of the screen-writer "very equivocal."[21]

Among the specific ways in which the Italian postwar cinema differed from that of France in the Thirties, an obvious one is the lack of anyone of the literary stature of Prévert deeply involved in film-making. When, in Italy, writers like Moravia or Pasolini have worked as scriptwriters they have almost invariably been mere adaptors, usually of their own work, not men involved as Prévert was with the whole nature of a film (Pasolini's films as a director come into a different category). Again, it has been normal in Italy for directors to serve an apprenticeship as scriptwriters on other people's films (Visconti is one of the few exceptions) and so they lack the kind of awe for the mystique of writing such as one finds, in France, in the case of Carné or Resnais. Thirdly, the whole conception of neo-realism as a spontaneous cinema in which an element of improvisation is essential tends to work against the influence of the writer, whose work is normally finished before shooting begins. But perhaps the crucial factor in the subordination of the writer is the Italian method of collaboration in the writing of the script that denies the writer any possibility of genuine personal expression. Moravia's hero laments that this method means "the marriage and fusion of one's intelligence, one's own sensibility, one's own spirit, with those of the other collaborators," and the whole picture of scriptwriting that emerges from *A Ghost at Noon* is one of drudgery and collective agony: "From early morning until night-time the scriptwriters do nothing but talk, keeping to the work in hand most of the time, but often talking from sheer volubility or fatigue, wandering away together on the most varied subjects. One will tell dirty stories, one will expound his political ideas, one will psychologize about some common acquaintance, another talk about actors and actresses, another relieve his feelings by telling of his own personal circumstances; and in the meantime, in the room where they are working, the air is filled with cigarette-smoke, the coffee-cups pile up on the tables amongst the pages of the script . . ."[105]

Sergio Amidei, who was one of the scriptwriters of both *Rome Open City* and *Paisà* once claimed that reality itself was the only thing that had influenced him and that his prime quality was never having lost contact with it.[48] This is true of all neo-realist writers for just as the directors took their cameras into the streets, so too the writers left the calm of their studies for the bustle of the market-place. Zavattini has given us a full account of his own working methods that may be taken as typical: "I take most of all from nature. I go out into the street, catch words, sentences, discussions. My great aids are memory and the shorthand writer. Afterwards, I do with the words what I do with the images. I choose, I cut the material I have gathered to give it the right rhythm, to capture the essence, the truth. However great a faith I might have in imagination, in solitude, I have a greater one in reality, in people. I am interested in the drama of things we happen to encounter, not those we plan."[94] Zavattini also deals with the issue of dialect which is crucial to any form of cinema which wishes to be truly realistic. In this respect Visconti's use of a great deal of dialogue, all of it in an incomprehensible dialect, in *La terra trema* is unique. Zavattini's method is quite different: "Others have observed that the best dialogue in films is always in dialect. Dialect is nearer to reality. In our literary and spoken language, the synthetic constructions and the words themselves are always a little false. When writing a dialogue, I always think of it in dialect, in that of Rome or my own village. Using dialect, I feel it to be more essential, truer. Then I translate it into Italian, thus maintaining the dialect's syntax. I don't, therefore, write dialogue in dialect, but I am interested in what dialects have in common: immediacy, freshness, verisimilitude."[94]

The choice of actors in neo-realist films, like the method of writing in collaboration, tends to give additional authority to the director. Neorealism is often seen as a cinema depending on non-professional actors drawn from life, but this is in fact an over-simplification. The movement began, after all, with *Rome Open City* in which Anna Magnani and Aldo Fabrizi (both complete professionals) appeared, and Borde and Bouissy in their study of neo-realism list an impressive number of actors who established or enhanced their reputations in films directed by neo-realists— Massimo Girotti, Aldo Fabrizi, Raf Vallone, Vittorio Gassman, Folco Lulli, Paolo Stoppa, Amedeo Nazzari and Alberto Sordi—as well as a succession of internationally known actresses from Magnani and Mangano to Lollobrigida and Loren. All neo-realist directors, without exception, turned to professional actors when their films contained roles beyond the abilities of the most talented amateur and it is no surprise to find Visconti, despite his use of fishermen in *La terra trema,* claiming that "employing non-professionals is not an indispensable condition of neo-realism,"[21] and De Sica saying that he has no particular prejudice in this matter: "There are some characters which demand professional actors, while there are others which can come to life only through a certain face, which is only to be found in real life."[55] Lattuada makes a distinction between "actors made by a director and the true actors, those who not only 'take' from the director, but also 'give,' thereby bringing to the film something creative of their own," but he does not rate the one kind above the other. While non-professionals are excellent if properly handled on location, "the same result can be obtained in a studio, so long as there is a real actor before the cameras."[55]

Castellani perhaps sums the matter up when he makes it clear that he uses non-professionals merely for convenience, not as a matter of principle: "When you are working with young and inexperienced talent—usually the heroes and heroines of my films have been 'taken from the streets'—it is easy.

You can tell them everything you want them to do, and each piece fits into the mosaic you have conceived in your mind."[131] It is important to remember that in any case the contribution of non-professionals to the films in which they appear is virtually limited to their physical presence. Visconti's fishermen in *La terra trema* are unique in actually influencing the dialogue of the film, since normally the Italian technique of post-synchronisation deprives the non-professional of his voice and substitutes that of a trained actor (this is the case with Lamberto Maggiorani in *Bicycle Thieves,* for example). Furthermore neo-realist actors are invariably chosen for their face and physique, never for their experience of the situations involved in the film: Maggiorani for instance was a factory worker not a bill-poster to whom a bicycle was vital. To quote Lattuada again: "I look, in reality, for the ideal face which I have in my head and which I could draw. I have a very clear physical—and moral—idea of my characters. Given that, when I have found the physical appearance, I half force the actor to assume the 'morality' of the character."[33] The distinction between professional and non-professional actors is not one of the crucial issues of neo-realist technique: what is important is that there are no star roles and all performances are strictly controlled by the director.

The neo-realists' use of real settings and their liberation of the cinema from the stranglehold of the studio has been far more influential than any theories of theirs about acting. It can hardly be doubted that this represents one of the most decisive advances in the cinema in the last thirty years and it would be hard to think of any director of note who learned his craft in the postwar era who could use shoddy back-projection with the same happy insouciance as a member of the pre-neo-realist Hitchcock generation. On this point at least the new French cinema of Godard and Resnais joins hands with the Italian cinema of the Forties and likewise gains enormous power from the use of real locations. Streets, crowds and railway-stations, the countryside and the sea all provide marvellously expressive backgrounds for the film to use and the sense of life going on beyond the limits of the frame is one of the great qualities of this new cinema. This in no way invalidates the non-naturalistic, hermetic cinema that has flourished from *Ivan the Terrible* to *L'Année Dernière à Marienbad*—the two forms can co-exist as do the realist novel and the symbolist lyric in modern literature —but since neo-realism we are perhaps more conscious of the unreality of all but the very finest studio settings. With regard to the neo-realist film itself it must be remembered that even the most authentic location must be "organised" for film-making purposes, but the responsibility for the selection of significant detail rests not on a set-designer but on the director and his cameraman. In connection with the element of reconstruction needed during filming in real settings it is worth quoting De Sica's comments on *Stazione Termini.* Although this film as a whole was a compromise between neo-realist and Hollywood methods, the use of the actual railway station was in accordance with the Italian tradition. But about this De Sica writes: "For some extraordinary reason, many people think that all the scenes shot

of the station life were authentic, 'stolen from reality.' It may seem strange
for a neo-realist director to say so, but it upsets me that nobody recognises
the vast work of reconstruction we had to do. We could only use the station
at night. The trains stopped running around half past twelve. Everything
had to be re-built: trains, travellers, shops, porters, mechanics and so on."[55]
    The camera style adopted by the neo-realists was fully in accordance
with their aesthetic beliefs and reflected their faith in simple means of
expression: the cameraman's duty was to reveal actors and settings as
directly as possible. Freedom from the studio and the ponderous conven-
tionality of studio lighting techniques encouraged a more adventurous approach to the film image and a greater belief in its efficacity. As Lattuada
points out: "Arc lamps and theatrical spotlights, so useful and so anonymous,
disappeared. Cameramen knocked nails in everywhere and hung their
lamps on them, bringing back with sidelights and the necessity of single
lighting the force of the real image."[55] Indeed lack of technical resources,
when compensated for by the stimulus of real settings, by a liberty from
inflexible shooting scripts and by the greater scope given by the technique
of post-synchronisation of dialogue, could have positively beneficial effects
on directors of photography. To quote Lattuada again: "The luxury of a
studio gives a poor cameraman the chance to use far too many lights. One
corrects and neutralises another, frequently resulting in an unexpressive
confusion. Shooting on location, however, imposes space limits and obliga-
tory angles on the cameraman which often give a precise character to the
photography."[55] The result was a photographic style virtually free from
chiaroscuro effects or expressionistic devices and which at times—as with
Rossellini—achieved an almost newsreel simplicity. Yet this basic austerity
in no way lessened the expressiveness of neo-realist camerawork. The films
were readily appreciated abroad because their meaning was so clearly
legible from the images and the example of *La terra trema* showed that
location shooting was in no way incompatible with composed *mise en
scène*. As befitted a cinema engaged in recording man in his social context,
neo-realism made great use of medium and long shots that captured the
settings as well as the characters. Close-ups were rare, for several reasons:
the obvious difficulties posed by the use of non-professional actors, the
comparative unimportance of dialogue (making reaction shots redundant)
and above all the neo-realists' lack of interest in probing the psychological
development of their characters. For all its functional simplicity, however,
the shooting of a neo-realist film remained the prime creative moment of
film-making, with editing reduced to little more than the unobtrusive
linking of material.
    The major advances brought about by neo-realism—those that have
proved most influential on the subsequent development of the film art—lie
in its presentation of physical reality and take the form of a stripping away
of such outmoded conventions as reliance on actors, contrived lighting
and studio-built *décor*. Yet, as we have seen, the elements of reality uncov-
ered by neo-realist methods were never regarded as ends in themselves but

invariably used for the purpose of story telling, and it is precisely in its narrative structure that the crucial limitation of the neo-realist aesthetic becomes apparent. The neo-realists share a sense of actuality and a conception of the cinema as an art of the present, summed up in Zavattini's words: "The cinema should never turn back. It should accept, unconditionally, what is contemporary. *Today, today, today.*"[94] The neo-realist story line therefore rejects all such devices as the flashback and is conceived as a way of unobtrusively capturing a sense of human existence slowly unfolding and being shaped by social and economic forces. Yet such an attempt to make the narrative "invisible" is doomed to failure simply because of the dramatic necessities of the film medium. A mere rejection of theatrical devices and contrivances is not enough: a story cannot be found in reality, it must be constructed and composed by writers and directors. In the methods of composition they choose neo-realist film-makers show little homogeneity. Visconti favours an ample story line of the kind familiar from the Nineteenth century novel, while De Santis and Lattuada prefer to give their films a drive that borders on the melodramatic. On the other hand, Rossellini gravitates towards a loose, episodic structure in which the individual sequence has more predominance than any narrative or dramatic link and the De Sica-Zavattini films are built up of small scenes—often almost "gags"— but arranged in a calculated dramatic sequence. Only the Zavattini of the later theoretical writings abandons narrative altogether, reaching a kind of *reductio ad absurdum* with the notion of a ninety minute film which follows a man walking and in which nothing happens.

The basic chronological sequence of events, allowing the emphasis to fall squarely on the presentation of man defined in social terms, is one of the strengths of neo-realism. But in the long run it constitutes also a limitation because its inability to cope with the complexities of human life above the mere subsistence level links it to an aesthetic of appearances and surface conflicts. Zavattini's analysis of the problems of neo-realist narrative stresses the generally negative approach: "The first endeavour was often to reduce the story to its most elementary, simple, and, I would rather say, banal form. It was the beginning of a speech that was later interrupted. *Bicycle Thieves* provides a typical example. The child follows his father along the street; at one moment the child is nearly run over, but the father does not even notice. This episode was "invented," but with the intention of communicating an everyday fact about these people's lives, a little fact—so little that the protagonists don't even care about it—but full of life."[94] To the purist eye of Zavattini, even in *Paisà, Rome Open City, Sciuscià, Bicycle Thieves* and *La terra trema* the sense "remains metaphorical, because there is still an invented story, not the documentary spirit" and even in *Umberto D*, where "reality as an analysed fact is much more evident," the presentation "is still traditional."[94]

The failure to achieve a decisive breakthrough in the handling of the story element is a weakness of neo-realism which in its straightforward narrative simplicity remains fundamentally old-fashioned, nearer to the Nineteenth century novel than to the modern art of our own age. As such it is incapable of offering adequate scope to the creative expressiveness of film-makers who have outlived the overwhelming initial impact of the war and its aftermath of poverty and hardship. All those who continued to develop their creative powers were bound to break with the restrictions set by simple, ordinary characters and clear-cut social problems and so to seek new forms of stylistic expression, but it was only ten years later that film-makers like Antonioni, Resnais and Godard brought the cinema more in line with other Twentieth century art forms by treating the problems of time and discontinuity left untouched by neo-realism. By so doing these directors carried out the second major advance in the history of postwar cinema, but these more recent achievements should not blind us to the great virtues of the neo-realist cinema in its presentation of spatial reality. This aspect of Arnold Hauser's definition of the potentiality of the film is fully realised by the neo-realists in whose films space "becomes dynamic; it comes into being as it were before our eyes. It is fluid, unlimited, unfin-ished, an element with its own history, its own scheme and process of development."[67]

2. The Heritage of Neo-Realism

NEO-REALISM PROPER, from *Rome Open City* to *Umberto D*, lasted a bare half-dozen years, petering out as Italy changed from a war-torn ruin to a prosperous member of the European community. Its demise is unsurprising, for none of the great movements of world cinema—the Swedish school, German expressionism, Soviet expressive realism, the pre-war French "poetic realism"—lasted appreciably longer. As André Bazin has wisely stated, the cinema "is too young, too inseparable from its evolu-tion to allow itself repetition for long: five years is the equivalent of a literary generation."[12] Within its brief span, however, neo-realism produced both a handful of authentic masterpieces and a wealth of sound, enterpris-ing and uncompromising films, leaving its mark on the whole subsequent development of the cinema, not merely in Italy, but throughout the world. As we have seen, neo-realism drew on a diversity of sources, united a number of very distinct personalities and never possessed either a declared manifesto of aims or a universally accepted aesthetic. It was a joint reaction to a specific set of circumstances brought about by war and the fall of Fascism and drew its strength from the sense of moral purpose shared by all its proponents, whatever their religious and political leanings. As such it naturally declined when the circumstances which had brought it into being ceased to be vital issues and when the moral commitment was re-placed by other—aesthetically equally valid—imperatives. The neo-realists' attitude to reality was, as I have endeavoured to show, a complex one,

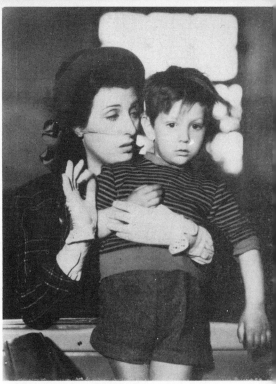

Neo-realist actors:
*Above: Lucia Bosé in Luciano Emmer's
RAGAZZE DI PIAZZA DI SPAGNA (1952)
Right: Anna Magnani (with Giorgio Nimmo) in
Mario Camerini's MOLTI SOGNI PER LE
STRADE (1948)*

*Above: Silvana Mangano in Alberto Lattuada's
ANNA (1951)
Right: Vittorio Gassmann in Alberto Lattuada's
ANNA (1951)*

Neo-realist actors:

Gino Cervi as the Communist mayor in Julien Duvivier's THE LITTLE WORLD OF DON CAMILLO (1951) (top left)
Aldo Fabrizi in Alessandro Blasetti's PRIMA COMMUNIONE (1950) (top right)
Raf Vallone in Curzio Malaparte's IL CRISTO PROIBITO (1950) (center)
Amedeo Nazzari in Federico Fellini's LE NOTTI DI CABIRIA (1957) (bottom)

Neo-realism and religion:

Roberto Rossellini's FRANCESCO GIULLARE DI DIO (1949)

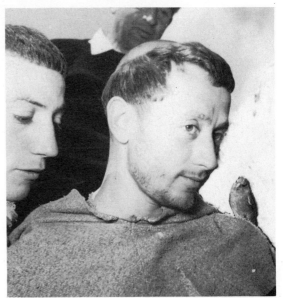

Neo-realism and religion:

Top: *Federico Fellini and Anna Magnani in
    Roberto Rossellini's* IL MIRACOLO (1948)
Middle: *Giulietta Masina in Federico Fellini's*
    LA STRADA (1954)
Right: *Mauro Matteucci in Augusto Genina's*
    CIELO SULLA PALUDE (1949)

The procession and the Christian imagery in Curzio Malaparte's IL CRISTO PROIBITO (1950)

Michelangelo Antonioni

The heritage of neo-realism:

*The study of social relation-
ships in Antonioni's LE
AMICHE (1955)*

*Federico Fellini directing
Anouk Aimée in LA DOLCE
VITA (1960)*

*The empty beaches of
Fellini's I VITELLONI (1953)*

Carlo Lizzani

Pier Paolo Pasolini directing
ACCATTONE (1961)

The Fifties and Sixties

*The urban world of Fascist
Italy in Lizzani's*
CRONACHE DI POVERI
AMANTI (1954)

Franco Citti in ACCATTONE

Francesco Rosi

Ermanno Olmi

The Sixties

The disaster in Rosi's LE MANI SULLA CITTÀ (1963)

Sandro Panzeri as the young clerk in Olmi's IL POSTO (1961)

varying in emphasis from individual to individual, but with all sharing the basic belief that the cinema is in essence an attempt to reconcile the contradictory demands of the documentary recording of reality (which is not art) and the fictional narrative (which is not real). In this respect neo-realism did not invalidate the conventional idea that the cinema is a reconstruction of reality: it merely showed new ways of making this reconstruction more convincing and more alive for the spectator, and the lesson that all the more important directors who fell under its sway drew from it was not simply that the cinema should record reality, but that the film artist's duty is to free himself from the shackles of outmoded convention and so capture not lifeless formulas and *idées reçues* but the throb of life around him.

Throughout this study, neo-realism has been referred to as a movement and from the perspective of the film historian this is precisely what it is. But the film-makers themselves involved in neo-realism lacked any sense of intense participation in a collective enterprise—they remained individuals with their own personal styles and concerns—and from their point of view neo-realism was in fact a discipline. It imposed on them an obligation to confront the immediate problems of postwar Italy and, while social reality does provide a rich terrain for the artist to explore, it can equally prove eventually to be something of a strait-jacket. The predilection of Marxist directors for treating the agrarian problems of the South in preference to the immediate industrial problems of their own urban environment may be seen, in part at least, as an attempt to escape this kind of limitation, but even given this effort to widen its scope it was inevitable that neo-realism should come to be seen by some directors—like the naturally eclectic Lattuada—as "to a certain extent narrow."[77] In Lattuada's view it "was necessary to explore other paths: satire, eroticism, the vision of the world of the future."[77] Moreover the stylistic means available were extremely limited and to remain within the neo-realist aesthetic film-makers had to maintain a surface of convincing realism while using the very minimum of contrivance. They were not free to indulge a taste for fantasy or a liking for flamboyant camerawork at the expense of social commitment, and in this respect the lack of theatricality in *La terra trema* and the tightly reined imagination apparent in *Umberto D* are examples of an iron self-discipline on the part of the film-makers concerned. With its richer style *Senso* is a far fuller expression of Visconti's total artistic personality than *La terra trema* but at the same time it represents a break with the ideals of neo-realist austerity. Similarly directors of the Fifties like Fellini and Atonioni felt a quite natural need to follow the promptings of their visual imagination even if this drove them away from direct and untrammelled reportage. Of the latter Fellini had a particularly low opinion, as his wry comment on neo-realism shows: "Why should people go to the movies, if films show reality only through a very cold and objective eye? It would be better just to walk around in the street."[76]

In so far as they remained true to neo-realism, the directors of this first generation had eventually to face up to the fact that, paradoxically enough, they were cutting themselves off from the very people whose lives and problems they were treating. Huaco has demonstrated conclusively that neo-realism, from *Rome Open City* onwards, depended for its continued existence on receipts from foreign, especially American, sources.[75] Great works like *La terra trema* and *Umberto D* were commercial flops and it is true to say that the mass of the Italian public was indifferent, if not hostile to the efforts of the neo-realist film-makers. Understandably, a man like De Sica came to feel the need of a mass audience and the kind of popular acclaim his talents deserved, even if this meant a lowering of his artistic standards. If a film-maker were to display total, monastic devotion to the cause of unremitting realism, it still remained unlikely that the neo-realist aesthetic—a cinema of poverty in both subject matter and means —would be valid for the treatment of an affluent society whose problems were less those of hunger and unemployment than the difficulties of achieving a full emotional and creative existence in an increasingly dehumanised environment. In this respect Lattuada's reaction—the feeling that "in the end neo-realism had become a sort of conformism, a sort of fashion"[77] —was a healthy one, vital to an artist who wished to make progress and maintain his creative powers. The comments of Francesco Rosi on neo-realism are of particular interest on this point since it was Rosi who, more than anyone else, produced in the early Sixties films displaying a social concern equal to that of any neo-realist work. Like Lattuada, he feels that neo-realism eventually became a formula: "After Visconti, Rossellini and De Sica people used the recipe: poverty, the people, poor people, people shouting in courtyards. That could make an audience laugh, so the neo-realist formula was doing well, like the Italian Western today . . . In the beginning audiences looked to neo-realist films for a deep emotion, they recognised their own problems, their own anguish; later all that no longer concerned them and they refused films of great depth, like De Sica's *Umberto D*, perhaps his best film."[77]

Whatever the precise causes of the decline of neo-realism, the film-makers themselves felt the year 1950 to represent some kind of a watershed. Zavattini himself, writing in the preface to a survey of the Italian cinema, said that "the year 1950 ought to be considered—and not only because it represents a round figure—as the year that closes a certain era of the cinema."[16] Looking back later on the movement De Santis recalled the pressures brought to bear on neo-realist film-makers: "At the end of the war there was an 'explosion' in which everyone was able to find the opportunity of expressing himself, but from 1950 onwards neo-realism was seen as a dangerous school."[32] Lattuada too sees the early Fifties as a time when the Italian cinema found a new direction, dating the change by means of one of his own films: "I believe that it was with *The Overcoat* that we began to leave realism, not only because of the story, but also by a certain way of seeing reality."[77] The tensions created in film-makers by the changed circumstances are vividly illustrated by the progress of Roberto Rossellini from *Rome Open City* to *Europa 51*. When Rossellini's first neo-realist film was shown in New York in 1946 James Agee wrote an enthusiastic review in which, however, he showed himself to be aware (in a way that most Italians of the time were clearly not) of the contradictions contained in an alignment of Communist and Catholic ideologies. "I see little," wrote Agee, "that is incompatible between the best that is in leftism and in religion—far too little to measure against the profound incompatibility between them and the rest of the world. But I cannot help doubting that the basic and ultimate practising motives of institutional Christianity and Leftism can be adequately represented by the most magnanimous individuals of each kind, and in that degree I am afraid that both the religious and the leftist audiences—and more particularly the religio-leftists, who must be the key mass in Italy—are being sold something of a bill of goods."[1] At the time of *Rome Open City* it was less evident to Italians than to outsiders like Agee that the incompatibility of the two ideologies was indeed fundamental, but six years later the realisation could be made by all and Rossellini's work reflects this new awareness. In *Europa 51* he analysed the predicament of Western civilization as he saw it and in doing so presented Catholicism and Communism as opposites that a saint may trancend but cannot reconcile.

One development of neo-realism that deserves more than a passing mention is the specifically Christian cinema in which religious belief replaced social concern as the mainspring of the action. As usual Rossellini was in the forefront and in 1949 made the film *Francesco, giullare di Dio* which illustrates eleven of the *Little Flowers* of Saint Francis. Like Zavattini's *Miracle in Milan*, it remains on the level of fable, setting the essential purity of its saintly hero against a caricatured personification of evil (in this case the tyrant Niccolo played with great gusto by Aldo Fabrizi). The film had little success in Italy but in France (where it was known as *Onze fioretti de François d'Assise*) it was rapturously greeted by critics. *Francesco, giullare di Dio* succeeds most impressively in capturing the genuine humility and childlike faith of St. Francis and his followers and in presenting religion as a reality. In many ways it is an elaboration of the monastery sequence of *Paisà*, using the same episodic structure and likewise employing real monks as actors. It conveys its Thirteenth century period setting with an air of great authenticity and with a camera style of the customary Rossellini newsreel simplicity. But though undoubtedly one of the director's major films, it lacks the social involvement and concern with contemporaneity that all true neo-realist works display. Like the episode in *Paisà* it no doubt owes something to the imagination of Federico Fellini who was one of its scriptwriters, but the roots of Fellini's own work—the most significant development of the religious branch of neo-realism—lie more in *Amore* which was made the previous year. There is a clear connection between the story *Il miracolo* written by Fellini for this film and *La strada* which he directed in 1954, but with the heroine of the latter—the character Gelsomina played by Giulietta Masina—we are in a world of

Chaplinesque pathos far removed from the disciplines of neo-realism.

This growth of a religious cinema in Italy reflects the increasing power and influence of the Church after the Christian Democratic party had won its absolute majority in the elections of 1948. Two films made in the following two years serve as examples of the religious tendencies of the Italian cinema during the closing years of the neo-realistic movement and present an uneasy amalgam of realism and religion. Augusto Genina's *Cielo sulla palude*, made in 1949, tells the life of a saint, Maria Goretti, using real settings and some non-professional actors but has little to offer beyond, in Borde and Bouissy's words, "some beautiful photographs in the Eisenstein manner, and some true details of the standards of living in under-developed country districts."[17] Curzio Malaparte's *Il cristo proibito*, made in 1950, is a more interesting work, a strange mixture of realism, theatricality and symbol. It is a tale of violence, confronting a man who seeks to avenge the betrayal of his brother to the Gestapo and meets a wall of silence in the village with a saintly carpenter who takes the burden of guilt upon his own shoulders. The carpenter dies but his example of selfless devotion keeps the man, Bruno, from further murder, even when he does finally come face to face with his true enemy. *Il cristo proibito* contains a number of startlingly effective scenes, particularly those featuring the passion play, and some authentic landscapes but in mood it is far removed from neo-realism. The reliance on dialogue is ultimately crippling, the music is lush and over-orchestrated and the artificiality of the central character of the saintly carpenter is typified by the casting of Alain Cuny, an actor more at home in Marcel Carné's *Les Visiteurs du Soir*. The incompatibility of this kind of film with neo-realism was ably expressed by Genina himself who admitted, when discussing *Cielo sulla palude*, that "the stories of saints and human beings whose life was worthy of sanctification, especially when told by minor writers, always fall short because of an almost total lack of reality. In the best cases we find ourselves in the presence of a fable."[17]

It would be wrong to imply that there was an abrupt break after *Umberto D*, for works obeying the basic rules of neo-realism were being made long after this date—De Sica's *Il tetto* in 1956 and even Mario Monicelli's *I compagni* in 1963—but from 1951 onwards the vital works of the Italian cinema are those made in other, more varied styles. The major directors of neo-realism themselves experienced a need to broaden their range and come to terms with the Hollywood system and so in the early Fifties we find films made with American stars: Rossellini's series of films with Ingrid Bergman, De Sica's *Stazione Termini* starring Jennifer Jones and Montgomery Clift and Visconti's *Senso* with Alida Valli and Farley Granger. There was also the need to express aspects of their artistic personality that could not find an adequate outlet within the context of neo-realism: the use of professional actors that attracted De Sica and became increasingly apparent in his films from *L'oro di Napoli* onwards, the taste for literature and opera evident in Visconti's *Senso* and *The*

Leopard, the concern to probe individual psychology as well as social issues that Rossellini displayed in *La paura* and Lattuada in *The Overcoat.* Even with these films the break is not absolute and there is often attempt to reconcile these interests with neo-realist practices (De Sica using his stars in an authentic station setting, for instance) but gradually the new predominates and the cinema of the Forties is left far behind.

Neo-realism did not die with this first generation, however, for it provided the training ground for the new directors of the Fifties, men like Carlo Lizzani, Federico Fellini and Michelangelo Antonioni. All these three were intimately connected with the movement: Lizzani and Antonioni had written criticism for the magazine *Cinema* in the early Forties, Lizzani and Fellini had worked extensively as writers on neo-realist films and Antonioni, though principally a documentarist, had contributed to a key film: *Caccia tragica.* Their sympathy with the ideals of neo-realism is obvious and when Antonioni spoke of his first documentary *Gente del Po,* he linked it explicitly with the origins of neo-realism: "At the same moment and almost in the same setting, Visconti was busy directing *Ossessione,* the first authentic film of Italian neo-realism. I can say without the slightest presumption that at that moment we were making the same discovery at the same time. We were anticipating what were to become the typical manner and forms of the postwar cinema: Visconti with a feature film, and I within the limits of the documentary."[131] In a similar way Fellini's work has one of its sources in his collaboration on *Paisà* when Rossellini taught him "humility to life" and "communicated his immense confidence in things, in men, in people's faces and in reality,"[131] thereby showing him that the role of the director was one that could fill his life. Fellini clearly felt himself to be a continuer of neo-realism, claiming that all his work "is definitely in the neo-realist style," which he defined as "a way of seeing reality without prejudice, without the interference of conventions—just parking yourself in front of reality without any preconceived ideas."[76]

There is a marked continuity of themes between the Forties and Fifties: Fellini prolongs and develops the autobiographical style of Rossellini, Lizzani shows the same political commitment to Marxism as Vergano and De Santis, while Antonioni's exploration of solitude can be related to the preoccupations of De Sica and Lattuada. But all three new directors are keen to define the differences between their own films and neo-realist works. For Fellini, the Fifties represent a widening of range: "Neo-realism means looking at reality with an honest eye—but any kind of reality: not just social reality, but also spiritual reality, anything man has inside him."[76] Antonioni sees greater interiority as a fundamental of the Fifties cinema: "Postwar neo-realism, when reality was so sharp and immediate, drew attention to the connection existing between the character and reality. It was just this connection which was important and which created a cinema of 'situations.' On the other hand, now that reality has been normalised after a fashion, it seems to me more interesting to examine what has been left inside the characters by their former experiences."[85] To illustrate his views Antonioni takes the example of *Bicycle Thieves,* pointing out that "it no longer seems important today to make a film about a man whose cycle is stolen . . . a character whose importance comes above all and exclusively from the fact that his bicycle has been stolen." In the Fifties "the problem of the bicycle has been eliminated" and the important thing is "to see what there is in the mind and heart of this man whose cycle has been stolen, how he has adapted himself, what has remained within him of all his past experiences of the war and the postwar period, and everything which has happened in our country."[85] Lizzani, looking back on the Marxist cinema with which he had been so closely associated, was forced to conclude that he and his colleagues "had never occupied a position of pure neo-realism."[18] *Il sole sorge ancora* to begin with "was a film in which we were not interested in the pure chronicle of the reality of that period. Perhaps we were wrong. Indeed *Rome Open City* was a greater film, even if *Il sole sorge ancora* has some very fine sequences." Similarly De Santis's films could be accused of being "constructed, romantic and polemical at a time when the most important path seemed to be that of absolute objectivity." In Lizzani's view there was a real need to examine closely "this desire to be epic at all costs, to place ourselves *a priori* in an epic romantic position, in a position reflecting an already mediated reality," which, he was forced to admit, has resulted in a certain coldness and schematisation. In contrast the new aim should be to create "a more human, living cinema, more integrated into everyday reality, containing all the implications and contradictions of contemporary reality."[18]

The films made by these directors in the early Fifties—works like Lizzani's *Cronache di poveri amanti,* Fellini's *I vitelloni* and Antonioni's *Le amiche*—show a desire to get beyond the confines of neo-realism and extend the scope of the Italian cinema. All three fragment the narrative line by dealing with a large number of characters as an initial step towards a more complex cinema and two show a strong literary influence, Lizzani's film being based on a Pratolini novel, while Antonioni drew inspiration from a story by Pavese. Of the three films Lizzani's *Cronache di poveri amanti* is the least satisfactory, being very obviously an adaptation of a novel of greater richness and strength. It has all the defects of an adapted work: an air of contrivance, a range of characters not defined quite precisely enough in visual terms, and a general superfluity of plot. To compensate for this Lizzani offers a fine technical command of the medium, political commitment and all the right anti-Fascist sentiments, but the result is not a work that constitutes a genuine advance. *I vitelloni* and *Le amiche* are more significant films because they—together with Rossellini's *Viaggio in Italia*—prepare the way for the introspective cinema of the mature Fellini and Antonioni. In both films the problems of the characters have ceased to be social ones for, as members of the middle-class, Fellini's youthful layabouts and Antonioni's bored socialites are faced not by monetary cares but by soul-searching endeavours to find a meaning for their existence. Their plight is symbolised by the use of landscape and settings to convey the essential isolation of their situation: the desolate autumnal beaches of *Le amiche* serving the same function as the windswept midnight squares of *I vitelloni*. In both films the camera style is rich and expressive, more clearly an anticipation of Fellini's mannered baroque and Antonioni's fastidious placing of figures in a landscape than a continuation of the sober austerities of neo-realist photography.

The influence of neo-realism is carried forward too into the work of the succeeding generation—film-makers like Francesco Rosi, Pier Paolo Pasolini, Ermanno Olmi, Elio Petri and Vittorio De Seta—whose work in the early Sixties is in a sense a return to the sources of the Forties cinema in contrast to the extravagance and poetic power of Fellini and Antonioni. Such is the force of the neo-realist heritage that virtually all of them have found the need to come to terms with the movement and their work preserves its stamp of social conscience and realistic intent. For them, as for their elders, the pure hermeticism of works like Jean Cocteau's *Orphée* or the Alain Resnais-Alain Robbe-Grillet film *L'Année Dernière à Marienbad* is inconceivable. They came to maturity at a time when the Italian realist cinema was at its height and inevitably, as Pasolini has pointed out, "the young artist growing up in that period chose to express himself through the medium which was then offering the most exiciting possibilities."[55] The prestige of the directors of the Rossellini generation has persisted, as Petri noted in 1962: "Many of the great neo-realists still have important ideas and points of view. If you think of the contribution that the artistic culture of the postwar period (right up to the present) has brought to the formation, for Italians, of a self-awareness, then their names are the first that spring to mind. And only later a few isolated names of writers and painters."[18] The neo-realist movement, with what Pasolini called its "rediscovery of every-day reality, in all its minute sociological details, in the Italy that was emerging from the war,"[55] has had a generally beneficial effect on young film-makers. A few talents have, however, been swamped by it. Vittorio De Seta, for example, proved to be perhaps too faithful a follower of the Forties tradition with his chosen subject-matter of "poverty in the South, the emigration of Southerners to the North and the alienation of the modern world" and his method of work which entailed an "indispensable basis of enquiry."[18] His first feature film was a sincere and efficiently made piece of work but Visconti's adverse comment was not altogether undeserved: "*Banditi a Orgosolo* is not enough for me, is no longer enough for me: we've already done all that."[52]

In this respect De Seta is unusual for the majority of the Sixties generation—like Antonioni and Lizzani—have been at pains to distinguish their own efforts from the neo-realism they admire so profoundly. To quote Petri once more: "The neo-realist tradition is always precious, as a window open onto people, feelings and reality," but "the neo-realist inquiry must be absorbed through the spirit which animated and no longer through the problems which it then revealed."[18] In his case the new subject matter—in films like *I giorni contati*—is the interior development of the characters:

"Today the workman of *Bicycle Thieves* must settle not only with the society in which he lives but also with his own conscience."[18] Olmi, in *Il posto* and *I fidanzati,* follows the neo-realists in "seeking poetry through truth . . . without figurative or literary mediation," but with films like these he makes a certain new range of subject-matter his own: "The world of work, people who work. I think I shall never grow tired of this extraordinary theme that epitomises so many others."[18] For directors like Pasolini and Rosi the difference in attitude and atmosphere between the Forties and Sixties is absolutely crucial. Looking at the problems of Fascism and Resistance, Pasolini was aware of the great deal of new thinking that had been done to change what, in the Forties, had been "an emotional outburst of protest" into a "more critical and objective process, with deeper roots."[55]

In Pasolini's view it is such a change that has given birth to what he calls "the new realism," but in point of fact this new thinking is by no means a prerogative of the young. From 1959 onwards the re-examination of Fascism was undertaken by directors of all generations from Rossellini (with *Il Generale della Rovere* and *Era notte a Roma*) and Lizzani (whose *Il processo di Verona* is a masterpiece of historical reconstruction) down to new-comers like Florestano Vancini (*La lunga notte del '43*) and Gianfranco De Bosio (*Il terrorista*). Francesco Rosi was at the very heart of the neo-realist movement, having served as Visconti's assistant on *La terra trema,* and his films *Salvatore Giuliano* and *Le mani sulla città* are powerful and authentic examples of the cinema of social examination and protest, but he too is aware of a gulf in attitude that makes mere imitation of the Forties style impossible: "The difference between my way of treating problems and that of the authors of the neo-realist period results essentially from the events themselves. In postwar Italy the unique preoccupation was reconstruction. As directors came to feel they had solved the more elementary problems, the way of treating these problems changed, they brought the characters out from the crowd that had been the only character in neo-realist films."[77]

To fit neo-realism fully into the context of world cinema would be an undertaking requiring a book of its own. In discussing the origins of neo-realism we have already traced many of the principal debts, like those of Visconti to Jean Renoir and De Sica to Charles Chaplin and there are other connections that could be made by, for example, confronting Flaherty's *Man of Aran* and Visconti's *La terra trema.* But this does not mean that we have done more than demonstrate the inevitable similarity of works born of the same kind of realistic impulse. Neo-realism takes its place in the mainstream of realist cinema and the efforts of the Italian film-makers should not be seen as isolated efforts. Elsewhere in the world, other directors were pursuing similar courses at precisely the same time. We know, for instance, that Akira Kurosawa had a great admiration for *Bicycle Thieves* which he mentioned in his Venice Film Festival speech on the occasion of the award of the Grand Prix to *Rashomon,* when he said: "If I'd made something reflecting more of present-day Japan, such a film as

Bicycle Thieves, and then received a prize, there would be more meaning to it and I'd probably be happier."[118] But to claim to detect an influence of neo-realism on Kurosawa's work would be rash, for the film of his that comes closest to *Bicycle Thieves* is *Stray Dog* which was made in 1948, the year of De Sica's masterpiece. Given this kind of coincidence of style and inspiration one can only echo the words of Sacha Ezratty: "It is clear that in identical circumstances what will in future be generally called neo-realism can manifest itself in versions as different as the two cities of Rome and Tokyo or the two personalities of De Sica and Kurosawa. For the one, dream and reality are indissolubly mingled with an ease that is truly Mediterranean, while for the other, the accent is on the contrast between the lyricism and the harshness of life."[49]

When we come to trace the actual influence of neo-realism on subsequent generations outside Italy, the cross-currents are more easily discernible if only because the younger film-makers are so critically aware of their sources. In France, for example, the admiration of Godard and Truffaut is well known and there are clearly affinities between Visconti and Resnais. But these influences—if such they be—are totally assimilated and counterbalanced by the strength of the French cinematic tradition. More striking perhaps has been the effect of neo-realism on film-makers in small or backward countries who, like Michael Cacoyannis in Greece, lacked a national film tradition on which they could base their work and were therefore compelled to turn to foreign sources. Spanish film-makers of the Bardem and Berlanga generation fall into this category for, as Marcel Oms has pointed out, "Franco's Spain has such a strong resemblance to Fascist Italy that the comparison imposes itself of its own accord. It is therefore from the theoreticians of neo-realism (Zavattini, Aristarco, De Santis, Lizzani etc.) and from the experience of the Italian postwar cinema that the young Spanish generation which dreams of finally creating an authentic cinema will draw its example and its encouragement."[109] One specific example of neo-realist influence that can stand for many is the case of the Indian director Satyajit Ray, who arrived in London for a five month stay in 1950. During this time Ray saw, by his own account, some ninety-five films, including Renoir's *La Règle du Jeu* and works by Flaherty and Donskoi, but the decisive influence was that of neo-realism and, more precisely, the film which he saw on his first evening in London, *Bicycle Thieves.* Of this latter Ray has said: "That film, about which one can think what one wants today, exercised a decisive influence on me. I was pleasantly surprised to discover that one could work exclusively in exterior settings, with non-professional actors, and I thought that what one could do in Italy, one could do in Bengal as well, in spite of the difficulties of sound recording. Then I saw *Miracle in Milan,* the beginning of which I liked very much, with its character of Totò, the stream of milk etc. It was much later, in Paris, after *Pather Panchali,* that I discovered Rossellini and *La terra trema* of Visconti."[104] Here at least the influence is clear and undeniable for we have Ray's own assurance that having seen *Bicycle Thieves* in London, he "decided to film *Pather Panchali* according to neo-realist methods,"[104] writing his first treatment immediately after his return to Calcutta in October 1950.

In more general terms it is fair to describe neo-realism as having transformed our cinematic awareness, as the Soviet cinema had done twenty years earlier and the French New Wave was to do ten years later. It was part of the complex of realist influences that, combined with economic forces, eventually broke the power of the studio-based Hollywood system and it now forms a part of our general film culture. Seen in its widest perspective, the true lesson of neo-realism may be said to lie not merely in its advocacy of location shooting, non-professional actors and improvisation but in the example it gives of the true application of the principles of realism to the cinema. Whatever their personal differences and divergences Visconti, Rossellini, De Sica and their fellows are true realists and as such their inspiration is of incalculable value. For the realist is not a man who simply uses a movie camera to record reality: he is, in Nathalie Sarraute's words, one who, above all, "however great his desire to amuse his contemporaries, to reform them, to instruct them, or to fight for their emancipation, applies himself, while making an effort to cheat as little as possible, and neither to trim nor smooth anything for the purpose of overcoming contradictions and complexities, to seizing with all the sincerity of which he is capable, to scrutinizing as far as his sharpness of vision will permit him to see, what appears to him to be reality."[125]

Part Five

DOCUMENTATION

*What is the cinema's
function? To bring men
face to face with things,
with realities such as
they are, and to make
known other men, other
problems.*

ROBERTO ROSSELLINI

Chronology

1932 GLI UOMINI, CHE MASCALZONI / MEN ARE SUCH RASCALS
      prod: Cines. *dir*: Mario Camerini. *sc*: Mario Camerini & Aldo De Bene-
      detti. *adapt*: Mario Soldati, Mario Camerini, Aldo De Benedetti. *ph*:
      Massimo Terzano, Domenico Scala. *des*: Gastone Medin. *mus*: Cesare
      Andrea Bixio, Armando Fragna. *cast*: Vittorio De Sica, Lya Franca,
      Cesare Zoppetti, Anna D'Adria, Pia Locchi, Giacomo Moschini, Tino
      Erler, Maria Montesano, Didaco Chellini.

1933 1860
      prod: Cines. *dir*: Alessandro Blasetti. *sc*: from a story by Gino Mazzucchi.
      adapt: Alessandro Blasetti, Gino Mazzucchi. *ph*: Anchise Brizzi, Giulio
      De Luca. *des*: Vittorio Cafiero, Angelo Canevari. *mus*: Nino Medin. *cast*:
      Alida Bellia, Gianfranco Giachetti, Otello Toso, Maria Denis, Giuseppe
      Gulino, Laura Nucci, Mario Ferrari, Totò Majorana, Cesare Zoppetti,
      Vasco Creti, Ugo Gracci, Umberto Sacripante.

1934 LA SIGNORA DI TUTTI
      prod: Novella Films (Emilio Rizzoli). *dir*: Max Ophuls. *sc*: from a novel
      by Salvator Gotta. *adapt*: Curt Alexander, Hans Wilhelm, Max Ophuls.
      ph: Ubaldo Arata. *des*: Giuseppe Capponi. *mus*: Daniele Amfitheatrof.
      cast: Isa Miranda, Nelly Corradi, Memo Benassi, Tatiana Pawlova, Fed-
      erico Benfer, Andrea Checchi, Lamberto Picasso, Franco Coop, Gildo
      Bicci.

1939 L'ASSEDIO DELL'ALCAZAR / THE SIEGE OF ALCAZAR
      prod: Bassoli. *dir*: Augusto Genina. *sc*: Alessandro De Stefani, Augusto
      Genina, Pietro Caporilli. *adapt*: Augusto Genina, Alessandro De Stefani.
      ph: Jan Stallich, Francesco Izzarelli, Vincenzo Seratrice. *des*: Gastone
      Medin. *mus*: Antonio Veretti. *cast*: Rafael Calvo, Maria Denis, Carlos
      Muñoz, Mireille Balin, Fosco Giachetti, Andrea Checchi, Aldo Fiorelli,
      Silvio Bagolini, Carlo Tamberlani, Guido Notari.

1940 LA CORONA DI FERRO / THE IRON CROWN
      prod: ENIC/Lux. *dir*: Alessandro Blasetti. *sc*: Alessandro Blasetti, Renato
      Castellani. *adapt*: Corrado Pavolini, Renato Castellani, Alessandro Bla-
      setti, Guglielmo Zorzi, Giuseppe Zucca. *ph*: Vaclav Vich, Mario Craveri.
      des: Virgilio Marchi. *mus*: Alessandro Cicognini. *cast*: Elisa Cegani,
      Luisa Ferida, Gino Cervi, Massimo Girotti, Osvaldo Valenti, Rina Morelli,
      Dina Perbellini, Paolo Stoppa, Ugo Sasso, Primo Carnera, Adele Gara-
      vaglia.

1940 PICCOLO MONDO ANTICO / LITTLE OLD-FASHIONED WORLD
     prod: ATA/ACI. *dir*: Mario Soldati. *sc*: from the novel by Antonio Fogaz-
     zaro. *adapt*: Mario Bonfantini, Emilio Cecchi, Alberto Lattuada, Mario
     Soldati. *ph*: Carlo Montuori, Arturo Gallea. *des*: Gastone Medin, Ascanio
     Coccè. *mus*: Enzo Masetti. *cast*: Alida Valli, Massimo Serato, Ada Don-
     dini, Annibale Betrone, Mariù Pascoli, Giacinto Molteni, Elvira
     Bonecchi, Enzo Biliotti, Renato Cialente.

1941 UN COLPO DI PISTOLA / THE PISTOL SHOT
     prod: Lux. *dir*: Renato Castellani. *sc*: from the story by Pushkin. *adapt*:
     Mario Bonfantini, Renato Castellani, Corrado Pavolini, Mario Soldati.
     ph: Massimo Terzano. *des*: Nicola Benois, Gastone Medin. *mus*: Vincenzo
     Tommasini. *cast*: Assia Noris, Fosco Giachetti, Antonio Centa, Rubi
     Dalma, Renato Cialente, Mimi Dugini.

1941 LA NAVE BIANCA
     prod: Scalera/Centro cinematografico del Ministero della Marina. *dir*:
     Roberto Rossellini. *supervision & sc*: Francesco De Robertis. *adapt*:
     Francesco De Robertis, Roberto Rossellini. *ph*: Giuseppe Caracciolo.
     des: Amleto Bonetti. *mus*: Renzo Rossellini. *cast*: non-professionals.

1941 TERESA VENERDÌ
     prod: ACI/Europa Film. *dir*: Vittorio De Sica. *sc*: from a novel by Rudolf
     Török. *adapt*: Gherardo Gherardi, Franco Riganti, Vittorio De Sica,
     Margherita Maglione, Aldo De Benedetti. *ph*: Vincenzo Seratrice. *des*:
     Ottavio Scotti. *mus*: Renzo Rossellini. *cast*: Adriana Benedetti, Vittorio
     De Sica, Irasema Dilian, Anna Magnani, Nico Pepe, Giuditta Rissone,
     Guglielmo Barnabo, Olga Vittoria Gentilli, Virgilio Riento, Arturo
     Bragaglia, Annibale Betrone, Giacomo Almirante.

1941 UOMINI SUL FONDO / S.O.S. SUBMARINE
     prod: Scalera/Centro cinematografico del Ministero della Marina. *dir &
     sc*: Francesco De Robertis. *ph*: Giuseppe Caracciolo. *des*: Amleto Bonetti.
     mus: Edgardo Carducci-Agustini. *cast*: non-professionals.

1942 GIACOMO L'IDEALISTA
     prod: ATA. *dir*: Alberto Lattuada. *sc*: from the novel by Emilio De
     Marchi. *adapt*: Emilio Cecchi, Aldo Buzzi, Alberto Lattuada. *ph*: Carlo
     Nebiolo. *des*: Ascanio Coccè. *mus*: Felice Lattuada. *cast*: Massimo
     Serato, Marina Berti, Andrea Checchi, Tina Lattanzi, Armando Migliari,
     Giacinto Molteni, Domenico Viglione Borghese, Roldano Lupi, Giulio
     Tempesti.

1942 I BAMBINI CI GUARDANO / THE CHILDREN ARE WATCHING US
     prod: Scalera/Invicta. *dir*: Vittorio De Sica. *sc*: from the novel *Prico* by
     Cesare Giulio Viola. *adapt*: Cesare Zavattini, Vittorio De Sica, Cesare
     Giulio Viola, Adolfo Franci, Gherardo Gherardi, Margherita Maglione.
     ph: Giuseppe Caracciolo. *des*: Vittorio Valentini. *mus*: Renzo Rossellini.
     cast: Isa Pola, Emilio Cigoli, Luciano De Ambrosis, Adriano Rimoldi,
     Ernesto Calindri, Tecla Scarano.

1942 MALOMBRA
      prod: Lux Film. *dir*: Mario Soldati. *sc*: from the novel by Antonio Fogaz-
      zaro. *adapt*: Mario Bonfantini, Renato Castellani, Ettore M. Margadonna,
      Tino Richelmy, Mario Soldati. *ph*: Massimo Terzano. *des*: Gastone Medin.
      mus: Giuseppe Rosati. *cast*: Isa Miranda, Irasema Dilian, Andrea Checchi,
      Gualtiero Tumiati, Nino Crisman, Enzo Biliotti, Giacinto Molteni, Ada
      Dondini, Nando Tarberlani.

1942 OSSESSIONE / OBSESSION
      prod: ICI. *dir*: Luchino Visconti. *sc*: from the novel *The Postman Always
      Rings Twice* by James M. Cain. *adapt*: Mario Alicata, Antonio Pietrangeli,
      Gianni Puccini, Giuseppe De Santis, Luchino Visconti. *ph*: Aldo Tonti,
      Domenico Scala. *mus*: Giuseppe Rosati. *cast*: Clara Calamai, Massimo
      Girotti, Juan De Landa, Elio Marcuzzo, Dhia Cristani, Vittorio Duse,
      Michele Riccardini, Michele Sakara.

1942 QUATTRO PASSI FRA LE NUVOLE / FOUR STEPS IN THE
      CLOUDS
      prod: Cines/Amato. *dir*: Alessandro Blasetti. *sc*: Cesare Zavattini, Piero
      Tellini. *adapt*: Cesare Zavattini, Piero Tellini, Giuseppe Amato. *ph*:
      Vaclav Vich. *des*: Virgilio Marchi. *mus*: Alessandro Cicognini. *cast*: Gino
      Cervi, Adriana Benedetti, Aldo Sivani, Giacinto Molteni, Guido Celano,
      Giuditta Rissone, Enrico Viarisio, Carlo Romano, Lauro Gazzolo, Silvio
      Bagolini.

1945 ROMA, CITTÀ APERTA / OPEN CITY / ROME OPEN CITY
      prod: Excelsa Film. *dir*: Roberto Rossellini. *sc*: Sergio Amidei, Alberto
      Consiglio. *adapt*: Sergio Amidei, Federico Fellini, Roberto Rossellini. *ph*:
      Ubaldo Arata. *mus*: Renzo Rossellini. *ed*: Eraldo da Roma. *cast*: Anna
      Magnani (*Pina*), Aldo Fabrizi (*Don Pietro*), Marcello Pagliero (*Man-
      fredi*), Harry Feist (*Major Bergmann*), Maria Michi (*Marina*), Francesco
      Grandjaquet (*Francesco*), Giovanna Galletti (*Ingrid*), Vito Annichiarico
      (*Marcello, Pina's son*), Carla Revere (*Lauretta*), Nando Bruno (*Agos-
      tino*), Carlo Sindici (*Roman police chief*), Joop van Hulzen (*Hartmann*),
      Akos Tolnay (*Austrian deserter*), Eduardo Passarelli (*Police officer*),
      and Amalia Pellegrini, Alberto Tavazzi, C. Giudici.

1946 IL BANDITO / THE BANDIT
      prod: Lux–R.D.L. (Dino De Laurentiis). *dir*: Alberto Lattuada. *sc*:
      Alberto Lattuada. *adapt*: Oreste Biancoli, Mino Caudana, Alberto Lat-
      tuada, Ettore M. Margadonna, Tullio Pinelli, Piero Tellini. *ph*: Aldo
      Tonti. *des*: Luigi Borzone. *mus*: Felice Lattuada. *cast*: Amedeo Nazzari
      (*Ernesto*), Anna Magnani (*Lydia*), Carla Del Poggio (*Maria*), Carlo
      Campanini (*Carlo*), Eliana Banducci (*Rosetta*), Mino Doro (*Mirko*),
      Folco Lulli (*Andrea*), Mario Perrone (*hunchback*), Gianni Appelius
      (*Signorina*), Thea Ajmaretti (*la padrona*), Amato Garbini (*il tenutario*),
      Ruggero Madrigali (*il negriero*).

1946   PAISÀ / PAISAN
prod: O.F.I., Foreign Film Prod. Inc. *dir*: Roberto Rossellini. *sc*: Sergio Amidei, Roberto Rossellini, Marcello Pagliero, Federico Fellini, Klauss Mann, Alfred Hayes. *adapt*: Federico Fellini, Roberto Rossellini. *Eng. dialogue*: Annalena Limentani. *ph*: Otello Martelli. *mus*: Renzo Rossellini. *ed*: Eraldo Da Roma. *cast*: SICILY: Carmela Sazio (*girl*), Robert van Loon (*Joe from Jersey*), Benjamin Emmanuel, Raymond Campbell, Albert Heinz, Harold Wagner, Merlin Berth, Leonard Penish, Mats Carlson. NAPLES: Dots M. Johnson (*Negro*), Alfonsino (*little boy*). ROME: Gar Moore (*Fred, the soldier*), Maria Michi (*Francesca*), FLORENCE: Harriet White (*Harriet, the nurse*), Renzo Avanzo (*Massimo*). FRANCISCAN CONVENT: Bill Tubbs (*Catholic chaplain*). PO DELTA: Dale Edmonds (*OSS man*), Cigolani (*partisan*), Allan, Dane, Van Loel.

1946   SCIUSCIÀ / SHOE SHINE
prod: Alfa Cinematografica (Paolo W. Tamburella). *dir*: Vittorio De Sica. *sc*: Cesare Giulio Viola, Cesare Zavattini. *adapt*: Sergio Amidei, Adolfo Franci, Cesare Giulio Viola, Cesare Zavattini, Vittorio De Sica, Marcello Pagliero, William Tamburella. *ph*: Anchise Brizzi. *des*: Ivo Battelli. *mus*: Alessandro Cicognini. *cast*: Rinaldo Smordoni (*Giuseppe*), Franco Interlenghi (*Pasquale*), Aniello Mele (*Raffaele*), Bruno Ortensi (*Arcangeli*), Pacifico Astrologo (*Vittorio*), Francesco De Nicola (*L'Abruzze*), Enrico Da Silva (*Giorgio*), Antonio Lo Nigro (*Righetto*), Angelo D'Amico (*Siciliano*), Emilio Cicogli (*Staffera*), Giuseppe Spadaro (*Avv. Bonavino*), Leo Caravaglia (*Commissario P.S.*), Luigi Saltamerenda (*Il Panza*), Maria Campi (*Fortune teller*), Irene Smordoni (*Giuseppe's mother*), Anna Pedoni (*Mannarella*).

1946   IL SOLE SORGE ANCORA
prod: A.N.P.I. (G. Giorgi Agliani). *dir*: Aldo Vergano. *sc*: Giuseppe Gorgerino (from an idea by Anton Giulio Majano). *adapt*: Guido Aristarco, Giuseppe De Santis, Carlo Lizzani, Carlo Alberto Felice, Aldo Vergano. *ph*: Aldo Tonti. *des*: Fausto Galli. *mus*: Giuseppe Rosati. *ed*: Gabriele Variale. *cast*: Vittorio Duse (*Cesare*), Elli Parvo (*Matilde*), Lea Padovani (*Laura*), Massimo Serato (*Major Heinrich*), Carlo Lizzani (*priest*), Marco Levi, Checco Rissone, Marco Sarri, Riccardo Passani, Gillo Pontecorvo, Mirkan Korcinsoi, Ruggerio Giacobbi.

1946   VIVERE IN PACE / TO LIVE IN PEACE
prod: Lux-Pao (Carlo Ponti). *dir*: Luigi Zampa. *sc*: Suso Cecchi D'Amico, Aldo Fabrizi, Piero Tellini, Luigi Zampa. *ph*: Carlo Montuori. *des*: Ivo Battelli. *mus*: Nino Rota. *cast*: Aldo Fabrizi (*Uncle Tigna*), Gar Moore (*Ronald*), Mirella Monti (*Silvia*), John Kitzmiller (*Joe*), Heinrich Bode (*Hans*), Ave Ninchi (*Corinna*), Ernesto Almirante (*grandfather*), Nando Bruno (*party secretary*), Aldo Silvani (*doctor*), Gino Cavalieri (*priest*), Piero Palermini (*Franco*), Franco Serpilli (*Citta*).

1947   CACCIA TRAGICA / PURSUIT
prod: A.N.P.I. (G. Giorgi Agliani). *dir*: Giuseppe De Santis. *sc*: Giuseppe

De Santis, Carlo Lizzani, Lamberto Rem Picci. *adapt*: Umberto Barbaro, Michelangelo Antonioni, Carlo Lizzani, Giuseppe De Santis, Cesare Zavattini, Corrado Alvaro, Ennio De Concini. *ph*: Otello Martelli. *des*: Carlo Egidi. *mus*: Giuseppe Rosati. *ed*: Mario Serandrei. *cast*: Vivi Gioi (*Daniela*), Andrea Checchi (*Alberto*), Carla Del Poggio (*Giovanna*), Vittorio Duse (*Giuseppe*), Massimo Girotti (*Michele*), Checco Rissone (*Mimi*), Guido Dalla Valle (*German*), Folco Lulli, Piero Lulli, Michele Riccardini, Ermano Randi, Eugenia Grandi.

1947 GERMANIA ANNO ZERO
prod: Teverfilm—Sadfi. *dir*: Roberto Rossellini. *sc*: Roberto Rossellini. *adapt*: Roberto Rossellini, Max Colpet, Carlo Lizzani. *ph*: Robert Juillard. *des*: Roberto Filippone. *mus*: Renzo Rossellini. *ed*: Eraldo Da Roma. *cast*: Edmund Moeschke (*Edmund*), Werner Pittschau (*Father*), Ingetraut Hinze (*Eva*), Franz Kruger (*Karl-Heinz*), Erich Gühne (*schoolmaster*), Barbara Hintz, Sandra Manys, Babsy Reckvell, Hans Sangen, Hedi Blankner, Count Treuberg, Karl Kauger.

1947 L'ONOREVOLE ANGELINA / ANGELINA
prod: Ora/Lux (Paolo Fasca). *dir*: Luigi Zampa. *sc*: Piero Tellini, Suso Cecchi D'Amico, Luigi Zampa. *ph*: Mario Craveri. *des*: Luigi Gervasi, Piero Filippone. *mus*: Enzo Masetti. *ed*: Eraldo Da Roma. *cast*: Anna Magnani (*Angelina*), Nando Bruno (*Pasquale*), Gianni Glori (*Libero*), Maria Grazia Francia (*Annetta*), Anita Angius (*Adriane*), Adalberto Tenaglia (*Giuseppe*), Ave Ninchi (*Carmela*), Agnese Dubbini (*Cesira*), Ugo Bertucci (*Benedetto*), Vittorio Mottini (*Roberto*), Armando Migliori (*Callisto*), Franco Zeffirelli (*Filippo*), Maria Donati (*Signora Garrone*), Ernesto Almirante (*Luigi*).

1947 SOTTO IL SOLE DI ROMA
prod: Universalcine (Sandro Ghenzi). *dir*: Renato Castellani. *sc*: Renato Castellani & Fausto Tozzi. *adapt*: Renato Castellani, Fausto Tozzi, Sergio Amidei, Emilio Cecchi, Ettore M. Margadonna. *ph*: Domenico Scala. *mus*: Nino Rota. *cast*: Oscar Blando, Giuseppe Golisano, Liliana Mancini.

1947 LA TERRA TREMA
prod: Universalia (Salvo D'Angelo). *dir & sc*: Luchino Visconti (inspired by Giovanni Verga's novel *I Malavoglia*). *ph*: G. R. Aldo. *mus*: Luchino Visconti, Willy Ferrero. *ed*: Mario Serandrei. *cast*: Sicilian workers and fishermen.

1948 ANNI DIFFICILI / DIFFICULT YEARS / THE LITTLE MAN
prod: Folco Laudati. *dir*: Luigi Zampa. *sc*: (from the novel *Il vecchio con gli stivali* by Vitaliano Brancati). *adapt*: Sergio Amidei, Vitaliano Brancati, Franco Evangelisti, Enrico Fulchignoni. *ph*: Carlo Montuori. *des*: Ivo Battelli. *mus*: Franco Casavola. *ed*: Eraldo Da Roma. *cast*: Umberto Spadaro (*Aldo Piscitello*), Ave Ninchi (*Rosina*), Massimo Girotti (*Giovanni, their son*), Odette Bedogni (*Elena, their daughter*), The Stefano Twins (*the twin sons*), Ernesto Almirante (*The Grand-

father), Enzo Biliotti (*Fascist Mayor*), Carletto Sposito (*Mayor's son*), Aldo Silvani (*chemist*), Milly Vitale (*Maria*), Giovanni Grasso, Olunto Cristina, Agostino Salvietti, Rainero De Cenzo, Giuseppe Nicolosi (*Malcontents*).

1948   IN NOME DELLA LEGGE / IN THE NAME OF THE LAW
prod: Lux Film (Luigi Rovere). *dir*: Pietro Germi. *sc*: Giuseppe Mangione (from the novel *Piccola pretura* by Giuseppe Loschiavo). *adapt*: Aldo Bizzarri, Federico Fellini, Pietro Germi, Giuseppe Mangione, Mario Monicelli, Tullio Pinelli. *ph*: Leonida Barboni. *des*: Gino Morici. *mus*: Carlo Rustichelli. *cast*: Massimo Girotti (*Guido Schiavi*), Jone Salinas (*Baroness*), Camillo Mastrocinque (*Baron*), Charles Vanel (*Passalacqua, the Mafia chief*), Turi Pandolfini (*Don Fifì*), Peppino Spadaro (*Lawyer*), Saro Urzi (*Police sergeant*), Ignazio Balsamo (*Ciccio Messana*), Saro Arcidiacono (*Clerk of the court*), Nanda De Santis (*Lorenzina*), Nadia Niver (*Vastianedda*), Bernardo Indelicato (*Paolino*).

1948   LADRI DI BICICLETTE / BICYCLE THIEVES / THE BICYCLE THIEF
prod: P.D.S. (Produziona De Sica). *dir*: Vittorio De Sica. *sc*: Cesare Zavattini (loosely based on a novel by Luigi Bartolini). *adapt*: Cesare Zavattini, Oreste Biancoli, Suso Cecchi D'Amico, Vittorio De Sica, Adolfo Franci, Gherardo Gherardi, Gerardo Guerrieri. *ph*: Carlo Montuori. *des*: Antonino Traverso. *mus*: Alessandro Cicognini. *ed*: Eraldo Da Roma. *cast*: Lamberto Maggiorani (*Antonio Ricci*), Enzo Staiola (*his son Bruno*), Lianella Carell (*Maria Ricci*), Gino Saltamerenda (*Baiocco*), Vittorio Antonucci (*thief*), Giulio Chiari (*old man*), Michele Sakara, Elena Altieri, Carlo Jachino, Nando Bruno, Fausto Guerzoni, Umberto Spadaro, Massimo Randisi.

1948   IL MULINO DEL PO / THE MILL ON THE RIVER
prod: Lux (Carlo Ponti). *dir*: Alberto Lattuada. *sc*: (from the novel by Riccardo Bacchelli). *adapt*: Federico Fellini, Tullio Pinelli, Riccardo Bacchelli, Alberto Lattuada, Mario Bonfantini, Carlo Musso, Sergio Romano. *ph*: Aldo Tonti. *des*: Aldo Buzzi. *mus*: Ildebrando Pizzetti. *ed*: Mario Bonotti. *cast*: Carla Del Poggio (*Berta*), Jacques Sernas (*Orbino*), Leda Gloria (*La Suiza*), Dina Sassoli (*Susanna*), Guilio Cali (*Smarazzacucco*), Anna Carena (*L'Argia*), Giacomo Giuradei (*Princivale*), Nino Pavese (*Raibolini*), Domenico Veglione Borghese (*Luca*), Isabella Riva (*Cecilia*), Pina Gallini.

1948   RISO AMARO / BITTER RICE
prod: Lux (Dino De Laurentiis). *dir*: Giuseppe De Santis. *sc*: Giuseppe De Santis, Carlo Lizzani, Gianni Puccini. *adapt*: Corrado Alvaro, Giuseppe De Santis, Carlo Lizzani, Carlo Musso, Ivo Perilli, Gianni Puccini. *ph*: Otello Martelli. *mus*: Goffredo Petrassi. *ed*: Gabriele Variale. *cast*: Raf Vallone (*Marco*), Silvana Mangano (*Silvana*), Vittorio Gassman (*Walter*), Doris Dowling (*Francesca*), Checco Rissone (*Aristide*), Nico Pepe (*Beppe*), Adriana Sivieri (*Celeste*), Lia Corelli (*Amelia*), Maria

Grazia Francia (*Gabriella*), Dedi Ristori (*Anna*), Anna Maestri (*Irene*), Mariemma Bardi (*Gianna*).

1948   SENZA PIETÀ / WITHOUT PITY
        prod: Lux. *dir*: Alberto Lattuada. *sc*: Federico Fellini, Tullio Pinelli
        (from an idea by Ettore M. Margadonna). *adapt*: Federico Fellini, Tullio
        Pinelli, Alberto Lattuada. *ph*: Aldo Tonti. *mus*: Nino Rota. *ed*: Mario
        Bonotti. *cast*: Carla Del Poggio (*Angela*), John Kitzmiller (*Jerry*), Pierre
        Claudé (*Pier Luigi*), Folco Lulli (*Giacomo*), Giuletta Masina (*Marcella*),
        Lando Muzio (*South American Captain*), Daniel Jones (Richard), Otello
        Fava (*dumb man*), Romano Villi (*bandit*), Mario Perrone (*Second
        bandit*), Enza Giovine (*Sister Gertrude*).

1949   CIELO SULLA PALUDE / HEAVEN OVER THE MARSHES
        prod: Arx Film (Renato & Carlo Bassoli). *dir*: Augusto Genina. *sc*: Augusto Genina, Suso Cecchi D'Amico, Fausto Tozzi. *ph*: G. R. Aldo.
        des: Virgilio Marchi. *mus*: Antonio Veretti. *ed*: Edmondo Lozzi. *cast*:
        Ines Orsini (*Maria Goretti*), Mauro Matteucci (*Alessandro Serenelli*),
        Giovanni Martella (*Luigi Goretti*), Assunta Radico (*Assunta Goretti*),
        Francesco Tomolillo (*Giovanni Serenelli*), Rubi Dalma (*La contessa*),
        Michele Malaspina (*il conte*), Domenico Viglione Borghese (*il dottore*).

1949   DOMENICA D'AGOSTO / SUNDAY IN AUGUST
        prod: Colonna Film (Sergio Amidei). *dir*: Luciano Emmer. *sc*: Sergio
        Amidei. *adapt*: Franco Brusati, Luciano Emmer, Giulio Macchi, Cesare
        Zavattini. *ph*: Domenico Scala, Leonida Barboni, Ubaldo Marelli. *mus*:
        Roman Vlad. *ed*: Jolanda Benvenuti. *cast*: Anna Baldini (*Marcella*),
        Franco Interlenghi (*Enrico*), Anna Di Leo (*Yolanda*), Massimo Serato
        (*Roberto*), Marcello Mastroianni (*Ercole*), Vera Carmi (*Adriana*),
        Elvy Lissiak (*Luciana*), Ave Ninchi (*Fernanda Meloni*), Andrea Campagnoni (*Cesare Meloni*), Fernando Milani (*Catone*), Emilio Cigoli
        (*Mantovani*), Pina Malgarini (*Ines*).

1949   E PRIMAVERA / SPRINGTIME IN ITALY
        prod: Universalcine (Sandro Ghenzi). *dir*: Renato Castellani. *sc*: Renato
        Castellani, Suso Cecchi D'Amico, Cesare Zavattini. *ph*: Tino Santini.
        mus: Nino Rota. *ed*: Jolanda Benvenuti. *cast*: Mario Angelotti (*Beppe*),
        Elena Varzi (*Maria Antonia*), Donato Donati (*Cavallucio*), Ettore
        Janetti (*Avvocato Di Salvo*), Grazia Idonea (*Signora Di Salvo*), Gianni
        Santi (*Albertino Di Salvo*), Irene Genna (*Lucia*), Adia Giannini (*Portinaia*).

1949   FRANCESCO GIULLARE DI DIO / FLOWERS OF ST. FRANCIS
        prod: Rizzoli (Angelo Rizzoli). *dir*: Roberto Rossellini. *sc*: (from the
        Little Flowers of St. Francis): Roberto Rossellini, Federico Fellini. *ph*:
        Otello Martelli. *des*: Virgilio Marchi. *mus*: Renzo Rossellini. *ed*: Jolanda
        Benvenuti. *cast:* Aldo Fabrizi (the tyrant), Arabella Lemaître and the
        monks of Nocere Inferiore Monastery.

1949   NON C'E PACE TRA GLI ULIVI / NO PEACE AMONG THE OLIVES
       prod: Lux Film (Domenico Forges Davanzati). *dir*: Giuseppe De Santis.
       sc: Giuseppe De Santis, Gianni Puccini. *adapt*: Libero De Libero,
       Giuseppe De Santis, Carlo Lizzani, Gianni Puccini. *ph*: Piero Portalupi.
       des: Carlo Egidi. *mus*: Goffredo Petrassi. *ed*: Gabriele Variale. *cast*:
       Lucia Bosè (*Laura*), Raf Vallone (*Francesco Dominici*), Folco Lulli
       (*Agostino Bonfiglio*), Maria Grazia Francia (*Maria Grazia*), Dante
       Maggio (*Salvatore*), Michele Riccardini (*Police Sergeant*), Vincenzo
       Talarico (*Lawyer*).

1950   IL CAMMINO DELLA SPERANZA / THE ROAD TO HOPE
       prod: Lux Film (Luigi Rovere). *dir:* Pietro Germi. *sc:* (from the novel
       Cuori sugli abissi by Nino Di Maria): Pietro Germi, Federico Fellini,
       Tullio Pinelli. *adapt*: Federico Fellini, Tullio Pinelli. *ph*: Leonida Bar-
       boni. *des*: Luigi Ricci. *mus*: Carlo Rustichelli. *ed*: Rolando Benedetti.
       cast: Raf Vallone (*Saro*), Elena Varzi (*Barbara*), Saro Urzi (*Ciccio*),
       Saro Arcidiacono (*il ragioniere*), Franco Navarra (*Vanni*), Liliana Lat-
       tanzi (*Rosa*), Mirella Ciotti (*Lorenza*), Cammela Trovato (*Cirmena*),
       Assunta Radico (*Beatificata*), Francesca Russella (*la Nonna*), Francesco
       Tomolillo (*Misciu*), Angelo Grasso (*Antonio*), Giuseppe Priolo (*Luca*),
       Paolo Reale (*Brasi*), Renato Terra (*Mommino*), Giuseppe Cibardo
       (*Turi*), Nicolò Gibilaro (*Nanno*), and the children: Ciccio Coluzzi
       (*Buda*), Luciana Coluzzi (*Luciana*), Angelina Scaldaferri (*Diodata*).

1950   IL CRISTO PROIBITO / THE FORBIDDEN CHRIST / STRANGE
       DECEPTION
       prod: Excelsa Film. *dir. & sc*: Curzio Malaparte. *ph*: Gabor Pogany. *des*:
       Leonida Maroulis. *mus*: Curzio Malaparte. *ed*: Giancarlo Cappelli. *cast*:
       Raf Vallone (*Bruno*), Elena Varzi (*Nella*), Alain Cuny (*Mastro An-
       tonio*), Rina Morelli (*Bruno's Mother*), Philippe Lemaire (*Pinin*), Anna
       Maria Ferrara (*Maria*), Gualtiero Tumiati (*Bruno's Father*), Luigi Tosi
       (*Andrea*), Ernesta Rosmino (*The Old Woman*), Gino Cervi (*The
       Hermit*).

1950   MIRACOLO A MILANO / MIRACLE IN MILAN
       prod: P.D.S. (Produziona De Sica)—E.N.I.C. *dir:* Vittorio De Sica. *sc*:
       Cesare Zavattini (from his novel *Totò il Buono*). *adapt*: Cesare Zavattini,
       Vittorio De Sica, Suso Cecchi D'Amico, Mario Chiari, Adolfo Franci. *ph*:
       G. R. Aldo (*special effects*: Ned Mann). *des*: Guido Fiorini. *mus*: Ales-
       sandro Cicognini. *ed*: Eraldo Da Roma. *cast*: Emma Grammatica (*Lo-
       lotta*), Francesco Golisano (*Totò*), Paolo Stoppa (*Rappi*), Brunella Bovo
       (*Edwige*), Gugliemo Barnabo (*Mobbi*), Anna Carena (*proud lady*),
       Alba Arnova (*statue*), Flora Cambi (*unhappy girl in love*), Virgilio
       Riente (*sergeant*), Erminio Spalla (*Gaetano*), Arturo Bragaglia (*Al-
       fredo*), Riccardo Bertazzolo (*athlete*), Angelo Prioli (*police chief*),
       Francesco Rissone (*second in command*).

1951   BELLISSIMA
       prod: Bellissima Films (Salvo d'Angelo). *dir*: Luchino Visconti. *sc*:

(from a story by Cesare Zavattini). *adapt*: Suso Cecchi d'Amico, Francesco Rosi, Luchino Visconti. *ph*: Piero Portalupa, Paul Roland. *des*: Gianni Polidori. *mus*: Franco Mannino. *ed*: Mario Serandrei. *cast*: Anna Magnani (*Maddalena Caccioni*), Walter Chiari (*Alberto Annovazzi*), Tina Apicella (*Maria Cecconi*), Gastone Renzelli (*Spartaco Cecconi*), Alessandro Blasetti (*himself*), Tecla Scarano (*acting teacher*), Lola Braccini (*photographer's wife*), Arturo Bragaglia (*photographer*), Linda Sini (*Mimmetta*).

1951   DUE SOLDI DI SPERANZA / TWO PENNYWORTH OF HOPE
       prod: Universalcine (Sandro Ghenzi). *dir*: Renato Castellani. *sc*: Renato Castellani, Ettore M. Margadonna. *adapt*: Renato Castellani, Titina De Filippo. *ph*: Arturo Gallea. *mus*: Alessandro Cicognini. *ed*: Jolanda Benvenuti. *cast*: Maria Fiore (*Carmela*), Vincenzo Musolino (*Antonio*), Filomena Russo (*his mother*), Gina Mascetti (*Signora Flora*), Luigi Astarita (*Carmela's father*), Luigi Barone (*priest*), Carmela Cirillo (*Giulia*), Felicia Lettieri (*Signora Artu*), Alfonso Del Sorbo (*Sacristan*), Tommaso Balzano (*Luigi Bellomo*), Anna Raida (*Signora Bellomo*).

1951   UMBERTO D
       prod: Rizzoli-Amato. *dir*: Vittorio De Sica. *sc*: Cesare Zavattini. *adapt*: Cesare Zavattini, Vittorio De Sica. *ph*: G. R. Aldo. *des*: Virgilio Marchi. *mus*: Alessandro Cicognini. *ed*: Eraldo Da Roma. *cast*: Carlo Battisti (*Umberto D*), Maria Pia Casilio (*maid*), Lina Gennari (*landlady*), Alberto Albani Barbieri (*the landlady's fiancé*), Ileana Simova, Elena Rea, Memmo Cartenuto.

1952   ROMA ORE UNDICI / ROME ELEVEN O'CLOCK
       prod: Transcontinental (Paul Graetz). *dir*: Giuseppe De Santis. *sc*: Cesare Zavattini, Giuseppe De Santis, Basilio Franchina, Renato Sonego, Gianni Puccini. *ph*: Otello Martelli. *des*: Leon Barsacq. *mus*: Mario Nascimbene. *cast*: Eva Vanicek (*Gianna*), Carla Del Poggio (*Lucinna*), Massimo Girotti (*Mando*), Lucia Bosè (*Simona*), Raf Vallone (*Carlo*), Elena Varzi (*Adriana*), Lea Padovani (*Caterina*), Delia Scala (*Angelina*), Irene Galter (*Clara*), Paolo Stoppa (*Clara's father*), Maria Grazia Francia (*Cornelia*), Naudio Di Claudio (*Mr Ferrari*), Armando Franciolo (*Romolo*).

1953   AMORE IN CITTÀ
       prod: Faro Film (Cesare Zavattini, Riccardo Ghione, Marco Ferreri). *dir*: Dino Risi (PARADISO PER TRE ORE), Michelangelo Antonioni TENTATO SUICIDIO), Federico Fellini (UNA AGENZIA MATRIMONIALE), Cesare Zavattini, Franco Maselli (STORIA DI CATERINA), Alberto Lattuada (GLI ITALIANI SI VOLTANO), Carlo Lizzani (L'AMORE CHE SI PAGA). *sc*: the directors and Aldo Buzzi, Luigi Chiarini, Luigi Malerba, Tullio Pinelli, Vittorio Veltroni. *ph*: Gianni Di Venanzo. *des*: Gianni Polidori. *mus*: Mario Nascimbene. *ed*: Eraldo Da Roma. *cast*: non-professionals recreating their own roles.

Bibliography

For reasons of space this bibliography is limited to books and pamphlets and to those magazines from which quotations are taken. Most of the monographs on directors cited include extensive lists of articles and reviews.

1. AGEE James: *Agee on Film—Reviews and Comments*. (Beacon Press. Boston, U.S.A. 1964).
2. AGEL Henri: *Vittorio De Sica*. (Club du Livre de Cinéma. Brussels. 1957).
3. ———: *Vittorio De Sica*. (Ed. Universitaires. Paris. 1955, 1964).
4. ARISTARCO Guido: *Miti e relatà nel cinema italiano*. (Il Saggiatore. Milan. 1961).
5. ARRIGHI Paul: *La Littérature Italienne*. (Presses Universitaires de France. Paris. 1966).
6. AUERBACH Erich: *Mimesis—The Representation of Reality in Western Literature* (trans. Willard R. Trask). (University of Princeton Press. 1953. Doubleday Anchor Books. New York. 1957).
7. BARBARO Umberto (ed): *Il cinema e l'uomo moderno*. (Ed. Soziali. Milan. 1950).
8. BARBARO Umberto: *Servitù e grandezza del cinema*. (Riuniti. Italy. 1962).
9. BARTOLINI Luigi: *Bicycle Thieves*. (Michael Joseph. London. 1952. Panther Books. London. 1964).
10. BARZINI Luigi: *The Italians*. (Hamish Hamilton. London. 1964. Penguin Books. Harmondsworth. 1968).
11. BAZIN André: *Vittorio De Sica*. (Guanda. Parma. 1953).
12. ———: *Une Esthétique de la Réalité—Le Néo-réalisme (Qu'est-ce que le Cinéma? Vol. IV)*. (Ed. Cerf. Paris. 1962).
13. BERTIERI Claudio: *30 anni di cinema italiano*. (Circolo Aziendale Cornigliano. Genoa. 1960).
14. BEYLIE Claude: *Max Ophuls*. (Ed. Seghers. Paris. 1963).
15. *Bianco e nero*. Oct 1947; Feb 1952 (Rossellini interview); Jan-Feb 1955; Apr, Nov 1955; Dec 1955 (Italian cinema); Jun 1961 (Lattuada interview); Jun 1963 (Zavattini interview).
16. BLASETTI Alessandro, and RONDI Gian Luigi: *Cinema italiano oggi*. (Bestetti. Rome. 1950).
    ———: Re-edited in French: *Cinéma Italien d'Aujourd'hui*. (ibid.)
17. BORDE Raymond, and BOUISSY André: *Le Néo-réalisme Italien—Une Expérience de Cinéma Social*. (Clairefontaine. Lausanne. 1960).
18. ———: *Nouveau Cinéma Italien*. (Serdoc. Lyon. 1963).
19. BREE Germaine, and GUITON Margaret: *An Age of Fiction*. (Chatto and Windus. London. 1958).
20. BUDGEN Suzanne: *Fellini*. (British Film Institute. London. 1966).
21. *Cahiers du Cinéma*. 7, 33, 98 (Zavattini articles); 28 (De Sica open letter); 37, 50, 52, 55, 94 (Rossellini interviews and articles); 84 (Fellini interview); 93, 106 (Visconti interviews); 131 (Situation du Cinéma Italien).
22. CAIN James M.: *The Postman Always Rings Twice*. (Jonathan Cape. London. 1934. Panther Books. London. 1960).

23. CALMAN John: *Western Europe—A Handbook*. (Anthony Blond. London. 1967).
24. CAMMETT John M.: *Antonio Gramsci and the Origins of Italian Communism*. (Stanford University Press. 1967).
25. CARPI Fabio: *Cinema italiano del dopoguerra*. (Schwarz. Milan. 1958).
26. CASTELLO Giulio Cesare: *Il cinema neorealistico italiano*. (Radio Italiana. Turin. 1956).
27. CASTELLO Giulio Cesare: *Luchino Visconti*. (Premier Plan 17. Serdoc. Lyon. 1956).
28. CERVONI Albert: *Marc Donskoi*. (Ed. Seghers. Paris. 1966).
29. CHAZAL Robert: *Marcel Carné*. (Ed. Seghers. Paris. 1965).
30. CHIARINI Luigi: *Il film nella battaglia delle idee*. (Fratelli Bocca. Milan and Rome. 1954).
31. *Cinema*. 116, 130 (De Santis); 119, 173–4 (Visconti); 151.
32. *Cinéma 55, 56* etc. 4, 5, 9 (Zavattini diary); 7 (De Sica interview); 23 (Vergano article); 35 (De Santis interview); 36, 46 (Lattuada interviews); 79 (Visconti interviews); 98 (Antonioni article).
33. *Cinémonde*. Feb 13, 1962 (Lattuada interview).
34. DEAKIN F. W.: *The Brutal Friendship—Mussolini, Hitler and the Fall of Fascism*. (Weidenfeld and Nicholson. London. 1962. Peuguin Books. Harmondsworth. 1966).
35. DEGO Giuliano: *Moravia*. (Oliver and Boyd. London, Edinburgh. 1966).
36. DE LA COLINA Jose: *El cine italiano*. (Cuadernos de Cine 3. UNAM. 1962).
37. DE SANCTIS Filippo Maria: *Alberto Lattuada*. (Guanda. Parma. 1961).
———: Re-edited in French: *Alberto Lattuada*. (Premier Plan 37. Serdoc. Lyon. 1965).
38. DE SICA Vittorio: Publicity material relating to *Umberto D*.
39. DE SICA Vittorio (and ZAVATTINI Cesare): *Il tetto* (script in Italian). (Cappelli. Bologna. 1956).
40. DE SICA Vittorio (and ZAVATTINI Cesare): *Le Voleur de Bicyclette* (script in French). (L'Avant-Scène du Cinéma 76. Paris. Dec 1967).
———: Re-edited in English: *Bicycle Thieves*. (Lorrimer. London. 1969).
41. DE SICA Vittorio (and ZAVATTINI Cesare): *Miracle in Milan* (script in English). (Orion Press. New York. 1968).
42. DI GIAMMATTEO Fernaldo (ed): *Essenza del film*. (Ed "Il Dramma" SET. Turin. 1947).
43. DOLCI Danilo: *Poverty in Sicily*. (MacGibbon and Kee. London. 1959. Penguin Books. Harmondsworth. 1966).
44. DURGNAT Raymond: *Films and Feelings*. (Faber and Faber. London. 1967).
45. *L'Ecran Français*. 60 (Italian cinema); 72 (Rossellini interview); 121, 199, 302, 332, 336 (De Sica interviews and articles); 242, 336 (Zavattini interviews and scenario); (De Santis interview).
46. ELIZONDO Salvador: *Luchino Visconti* (Cuadernos de Cine 11. UNAM. 1963).
47. ELLMAN Richard, and FEIDELSON Charles (ed): *The Modern Tradition*. (Oxford University Press. New York. 1965).
48. *Etudes Cinematographiques*. 26–27 (*Luchino Visconti—L'Histoire et l'Esthétique*); 32–35 (*Le Néo-réalisme Italien—Bilan de la Critique*).

49. EZRATTY Sacha: *Kurosawa.* (Ed. Universitaires. Paris. 1964).
50. FERNANDEZ Dominique: *Le Roman Italien et la Crise de la Conscience Moderne.* (Grasset. Paris. 1958).
51. FERRARA Giuseppe: *Il nuovo cinema italiano.* (Le Monnier. Florence. 1957).
52. ——: *Luchino Visconti.* (Ed. Seghers. Paris. 1963).
53. *Film d'oggi.* 1, 3 (De Sica articles); 4 (Lattuada article).
54. *Le Film Français.* Jun 1949 (De Sica interview).
55. *Films and Filming.* Dec 1955, Jan, Feb, Mar 1956 (De Sica memoirs); Apr 1959 (Lattuada articles); Jan 1961 (Pasolini article); Jan 1961 (Visconti article).
56. *Films et Documents.* 57 (*L'Ecole Néo-réaliste Italienne*).
57. FISCHER Ernst: *The Necessity of Art.* (Penguin Books. Harmondsworth. 1963).
58. FRANK Nino: *Cinema dell'arte.* (André Bonne. Paris. 1951).
59. FREDDI Luigi: *Il cinema—miti, esperienze e realtà di un regime totalitario.* (L'Arnia. Rome. 1949).
60. GAY François, and WAGRET Paul: *L'Economie de l'Italie.* (Presses Universitaires de France. Paris. 1964).
61. GERMI Pietro: Publicity material relating to *Il cammino della speranza.*
62. GORDIANI Fritz: *Italien—Ein Politischer Reiseführer.* (Fischer. Frankfurt. 1966).
63. GRINDROD Muriel: *Italy.* (Benn. London. 1968).
64. GROMO Mario: *Cinema italiano 1903–1953.* (Mondadori. Milan. 1954).
65. GUICHONNET Paul: *Mussolini et le Fascisme.* (Presses Universitaires de France. Paris. 1966).
66. GUILLAUME Yves: *Visconti.* (Ed. Universitaires. Paris. 1966).
67. HAUSER Arnold: *The Social History of Art.* (Routledge and Kegan Paul. London. 1951).
68. HEARDER H., and WALEY D. P. (ed): *A Short History of Italy.* (Cambridge University Press. 1963).
69. HEINEY Donald: *America in Modern Italian Literature.* (Rutgers University Press. New Brunswick. 1964).
70. HINTERHAUSER Hans: *Italien Zwischen Schwarz und Rot.* (Kohlhammer. Stuttgart. 1956).
71. HJORT Oystein: *Neorealismen in Italien.* (Danish Film Museum. Copenhagen. 1968).
72. HOVALD Patrice G.: *Roberto Rossellini.* (Club du Livre de Cinéma. Brussels. 1958).
73. ——: *Le néo-réalisme.* (Club du Livre de Cinéma. Brussels. 1958).
74. ——: *Le Néo-réalisme Italien et ses Créateurs.* (Ed. Cerf. Paris. 1959).
75. HUACO George A.: *The Sociology of Film Art.* (Basic Books. New York. 1965).
76. HUGHES Robert (ed): *Film: Book One.* (Grove Press. New York. 1959).
77. *Image et Son.* 195, 196 *Le Cinéma Italien.* (May–Jun 1966).
78. *Inquadrature.* 5–6 (Italian cinema); 11 (Lattuada interview).
79. JACKSON W. G. F.: *The Battle for Italy.* (Batsford. London. 1967).
80. JARRATT Vernon: *The Italian Cinema.* (Falcon Press. London. 1951).
81. *Jeune Cinéma.* 27–28 (Spécial Italien). (Jan–Feb 1968).

82. KOGAN Norman: *A Political History of Postwar Italy.* (Pall Mall Press. London. 1966).
83. KRACAUER Siegfried: *Theory of Film—The Redemption of Physical Reality.* (Oxford University Press. New York. 1965).
84. LAJOLO Davide: *Cesare Pavese—Le Vice Absurde.* (Gallimard. Paris. 1963).
85. LEPROHON Pierre: *Michelangelo Antonioni.* (Ed. Seghers. Paris. 1961).
86. ———: *Vittorio De Sica.* (Ed. Seghers. Paris. 1966).
87. ———: *Le Cinéma Italien.* (Ed. Seghers. Paris. 1966).
88. LEVI Carlo: *Christ Stopped at Eboli.* (Cassell. London. 1948).
89. ———: *Words are Stones—Impressions of Sicily.* (Gollancz. London. 1959).
90. LEWIS Norman: *The Honoured Society.* (Collins. London. 1964. Penguin Books. Harmondsworth. 1967).
91. LIZZANI Carlo: *Il cinema italiano.* (Parenti. Florence. 1953).
    ———: Re-edited in French: *Le Cinéma Italien.* (Editeurs Français Réunis. Paris. 1955).
92. ———: *Storia del cinema italiano (1895–1961).* (Parenti. Florence. 1961).
93. LUKÁCS Georg: *The Meaning of Contemporary Realism.* (Merlin Press. London. 1963).
94. MacCANN Richard Dyer (ed): *Film—A Montage of Theories.* (Dutton. New York. 1966).
95. MacGREGOR-HASTIE Roy: *The Day of the Lion.* (MacDonald. London. 1963).
96. MALAPARTE Curzio: *Kaputt.* (Alvin Redman. London. 1948. Panther Books. London. 1964).
97. ———: *The Skin.* (Alvin Redman. London. 1952. Panther Books. London. 1964).
98. MALHERBA Luigi (ed): *Cinema italiano 1945–51.* (Bestetti. Rome. 1951).
    ———: Re-edited in French: *Le Cinéma italien 1945–51.* (ibid).
    ———: Re-edited in English: *Italian cinema 1945–51.* (ibid).
99. MALHERBA Luigi, and SINISCALCO Carmine (ed): *Cinquanta anni di cinema italiano.* (Bestetti. Rome. 1953).
    ———: Re-edited in English: *Fifty years of Italian cinema.* (ibid).
100. MARINUCCI Vinicio: *Tendenze del cinema italiano.* (Unitalia Film. Rome. 1959).
    ———: Re-edited in French: *Tendances du Cinéma Italien.* (ibid).
    ———: Re-edited in English: *Tendencies of the Italian Cinema.* (ibid).
101. MECCOLI Domenico: *Luigi Zampa.* (Cinque Lune. Rome. 1956).
102. MIDA Massimo: *Roberto Rossellini.* (Guanda. Parma. 1953, 1961).
103. MISTRORIGO Luigi: *La Culture Italienne depuis la Guerre.* (La Renaissance du Livre. Paris. 1967).
104. *Montage.* 5/6. (July 1966). (Satjayit Ray interview).
105. MORAVIA Alberto: *A Ghost at Noon.* (Secker and Warburg. London. 1955. Penguin Books. Harmondsworth. 1964).
106. ———. *Two Women.* (Secker and Warburg. London. 1958. Penguin Books. Harmondsworth. 1961).
107. *Il neorealismo italiano.* (Quaderni della mostra internazionale d'arte cinematografica di Venezia. Rome. 1951).
108. NOWELL-SMITH Geoffrey: *Visconti.* (Secker and Warburg. London. 1967).

109. OMS Marcel: *Juan Bardem*. (Premier Plan 21. Serdoc. Lyon. 1962).
110. PACIFICI Sergio: *A Guide to Contemporary Italian Literature*. (Meridian Books. Cleveland, New York. 1962).
111. PALUMBO Mario: *La Sicilia nel cinema*. (Sicilia Domani. Palermo. 1963).
112. PAOLELLA Roberto: *Storia del cinema sonoro 1926–39*. (Giannini. Naples. 1966).
113. PAVESE Cesare: *This Business of Living—A Dairy 1935–50*. (Ed. and trans. A. E. Murch). (Peter Owen. London. 1961. Consul Books. London. 1964).
114. PELZER Helmut: *Vittorio De Sica*. (Henschel. Berlin. 1964).
115. *Positif*. 23 & 28 (Cinéma Italien); 30 (Antonioni article).
116. PRITCHETT V. S.: *The Living Novel*. (Chatto and Windus. London. 1946).
117. *La Revue du Cinéma*. 13 (Numéro Spécial sur le Cinéma Italien); 18 (Lattuada interview).
118. RICHIE Donald: *The Films of Akira Kurosawa*. (University of California Press. Los Angeles. 1965).
119. *Rivista del cinema italiano*. 3 (Italian cinema).
120. RONDI Brunello: *Il neorealismo italiano*. (Guanda. Parma. 1956).
121. ———: *Cinema e realtà*. (Cinque Lune. Rome. 1957).
122. RONDI Gian Luigi: *Cinema italiano oggi*. (Bestetti. Rome. 1966).
    ———: Re-edited in English: *Italian Cinema Today*. (Hill and Wang. New York; Dobson. London. 1966).
123. ROSSELLINI Roberto: *Rome Ville Ouverte* (script in French). (L'Avant-Scène du Cinéma 71. June 1967).
124. SADOUL Georges: *Histoire Générale du Cinéma* (Tome VI: Le Cinéma pendant la Guerre 1939–45). (Denoël. Paris. 1954).
125. SARRAUTE Nathalie: *Tropisms and the Age of Suspicion*. (Calder and Boyars. London. 1963).
126. SCHLAPPNER Martin: *Von Rossellini zu Fellini*. (Origo. Zurich. 1963).
127. *Sight and Sound*. Apr 1950 (De Sica interview); Feb 1951 (Rossellini interview); Jan 1951 (Summer interview).
128. SOLMI Angelo: *Storia di Federico Fellini*. (Rizzoli. Milan. 1962).
    ———: Re-edited in English: *Federico Fellini*. (Merlin Press. London. 1963).
129. STRAZZULA Gaetano: *Cinema italiano*. (Cenobio. Lugano. 1963).
130. SYMONDS John Addington: *Renaissance in Italy*. (Smith, Elder and Co. London. 1909).
131. *La Table Ronde*. 149 (Antonioni, Castellani, Fellini, Lattuada, Rossellini, De Sica, Visconti, and Zavattini interviews).
132. *Télérama*. 19 Feb 1961 (Lattuada interview).
133. TEXIER Jacques: *Gramsci*. (Ed. Seghers. Paris. 1966).
134. TOMASI DI LAMPEDUSA Giuseppe: *The Leopard*. (Collins. London. 1960. Fontana. London. 1963).
135. TREVELYAN Raleigh (ed): *Italian Writing Today*. (Penguin Books. Harmondsworth. 1967).
136. VERDONE Mario, and TINAZZI Giorgio: *Roberto Rossellini*. (University of Padua. 1960).
137. VERDONE Mario: *Roberto Rossellini*. (Ed. Seghers. Paris. 1963).
138. VERGA Giovanni: *Cavalleria Rusticana*. (Jonathan Cape. London. 1928. Four Square Books. London. 1962).

139. VERGA Giovanni: *The House by the Medlar Tree* (Weidenfeld and Nicholson. London. 1950).

140. VILLARI Luigi: *The Liberation of Italy*. (C. C. Nelson. Appelton. Wisconsin. 1959).

141. VISCONTI Luchino: *La terra trema* (script in Italian). (Bianco e nero. Rome. 1951).

142. VISCONTI Luchino: *Rocco e i suoi fratelli*. (Cappelli. Bologna. 1960).
———: Re-edited in French: *Rocco et ses Frères*. (Buchet/Chastel. Paris. 1961).

143. VISCONTI Luchino: *Senso*. (Cappelli. Bologna. 1955).

144. WALDEKRANZ Rune: *Italiensk film*. (Wahlström and Widstrand. Stockholm. 1953).

145. WEST Paul: *The Modern Novel*. (Hutchinson. London. 1963).

146. WHITFIELD J. H.: *A Short History of Italian Literature*. (Penguin Books. Harmondsworth. 1960).

147. ZAVATTINI Cesare: *Umberto D* (script in Italian). (Fratelli Bocca. Milan, Rome. 1954).

Index